A young John A. Macdonald, ca. 1856. (*LAC 014918*)

PRIVATE DEMONS

THE TRAGIC PERSONAL LIFE OF
JOHN A. MACDONALD

PATRICIA PHENIX

McCLELLAND & STEWART

Library and Archives Canada Cataloguing in Publication

Phenix, Patricia
    Private demons : the tragic personal life of John A.
Macdonald / Patricia Phenix.

ISBN-13: 978-0-7710-7044-0
ISBN-10: 0-7710-7044-6

1. Macdonald, John A. (John Alexander), 1815-1891. 2. Prime ministers – Canada – Biography. I. Title.
FC521.M3P44 2006   971.05'1'092   C2006-902164-3

We acknowledge the financial support of the Government of Canada through the Book Publishing Industry Development Program and that of the Government of Ontario through the Ontario Media Development Corporation's Ontario Book Initiative. We further acknowledge the support of the Canada Council for the Arts and the Ontario Arts Council for our publishing program.

The author has made every effort to properly credit the photos and will be happy to amend the credit lines as necessary in subsequent editions.

Typeset in Janson by M&S, Toronto
Printed and bound in Canada

This book is printed on acid-free paper that is 100% recycled, ancient-forest friendly (100% post-consumer recycled).

McClelland & Stewart Ltd.
75 Sherbourne Street
Toronto, Ontario
M5A 2P9
www.mcclelland.com

1 2 3 4 5   10 09 08 07 06

CONTENTS

AUTHOR'S NOTE

John A. Macdonald's life made perfect tabloid fodder. In public, he possessed unlimited charisma, in private he disappeared on drinking binges that latest for days. He could be tender, yet had an incendiary temper, once challenging a colleague to a duel. He was the first, and probably the only prime minister, to have once defended an assault charge against him in court. He regularly stared bankruptcy in the face. On September 1, 1867, a mere three months after Confederation, he received from Ottawa's Tax Collection office a notice informing him that if he did not pay taxes amounting to $65.84* on his law office property, a warrant would be issued for his arrest. Unfazed, he stalled a year before paying the bill. No one dared arrest him. At the lowest point in his administration, during the Pacific Scandal, newspapers reported that he had attempted suicide by jumping off a bridge near Rivière-du-Loup. Days later, John A. turned up in Parliament, emotionally bruised, yet not broken. He had summoned the inner strength to survive. And the public loved him for it, re-electing him as prime minister virtually continuously between 1867 and 1891.

---

*MG26A, vol. 549, LAC

He married twice. His first wife, Isabella, the mother of his only surviving son, Hugh John, spent most of their thirteen-year marriage confined to bed in an opium-induced haze. After her death, John A. remained a bachelor for ten years, enjoying the company of a variety of eligible women. Ironic as it seemed, the Father of Confederation wasn't very fatherly after all. He entrusted Hugh John's care to his sisters, Louisa and Margaret, as well as Margaret's husband, James Williamson, a mathematics professor at Queen's University. The Williamson papers at Queen's contain letters that cast new light on the extent of Williamson's affection for the boy.

John A.'s second wife, Agnes, was his intellectual equal, and their marriage in 1867 began on an optimistic note. Her diary includes descriptions of the couple's domestic habits as well as a behind-the-scenes view of the rigours of election campaigning. In 1868, Agnes documented the events that unfolded in the Macdonald home on the night D'Arcy McGee was murdered. Coupled with the official inquest notes, they present a harrowing account of the first few hours following McGee's death. In 1869, Agnes gave birth to a daughter, whom the couple named Mary. Weeks later, Mary was diagnosed with hydrocephalus. In this book, Dr. James Drake, a neurosurgeon at the Hospital for Sick Children in Toronto, who has examined photographs of Mary, provides fresh insights into the severity of Mary's illness, and speculates that she might also have suffered from cerebral palsy.

Throughout this book, I have tried to analyze how John A.'s personal life affected his public policies. In order to do so, I have used excerpts from letters John A. wrote to his family members and friends, as well as examined the literally hundreds of invoices, receipts, memos, and other minutia comprising the extensive John A. Macdonald fonds at Library and Archives Canada (LAC). My goal was not to reinvent the wheel when it comes to John A.'s life, but to re-interpret available material. Nevertheless, I discovered a few surprises. One was the presence of several death threats levelled against John A. shortly after he authorized Louis Riel's execution. I also uncovered a series of startlingly passionate love letters from Frank Muttart, the teenaged son of Dr. Ephraim Muttart, a Conservative member of Parliament from Nova Scotia, to an elderly John A. Also, Agnes Macdonald's watercolour paintings, stored at LAC, are reproduced in this book for the first time in any publication.

PRIVATE
DEMONS

ESCAPING THE PAST

In a melancholic mood one evening, an elderly Prime Minister John A. Macdonald revealed to his private secretary, Sir Joseph Pope, a shocking secret. At the age of seven he had witnessed the brutal murder of his five-year-old brother, James Shaw Macdonald, at the hands of a drunken childminder.

Years later, in his book, *Memoirs of the Right Honourable Sir John Alexander Macdonald*, Pope exposed in detail John A.'s recollection of the crime. The babysitter had dragged both of the children to a Kingston tavern where he forced gin down their throats. "Not liking the taste," the young John A. grabbed James Shaw's hand and "started for home." Angry, and by now thoroughly drunk, the childminder raced to catch up with the boys. When James Shaw tripped and fell, the babysitter struck him with his cane hard enough to force the boy into convulsions.

Hours later, Hugh and Helen Macdonald watched their youngest son's life ebb away in his own bed, where they had placed him after retrieving him from the street, the childminder having vanished into the night. Had John A. not exposed the circumstances of James Shaw's murder, his father might have blamed the childminder for administering no more than an overly enthusiastic round of corporal punishment. After all, even an anonymous

letter published in the *Toronto Globe* of March 12, 1822, speculated that it was "absurd to talk of the degrading influence of
corporal punishment. It was cheaper than sending children to jail."

Despite Hugh's outrage, however, he did not race to the
police station to file a report – though he had never been reticent
about filing reports in the past. In fact, months earlier, he had had
a boy and his sister arrested for stealing socks from his general-
goods store. More likely, he failed to report his son's murder
because the childminder, a man named "Kennedy," was not only
a friend, but an employee.

In the April 23, 1822, edition of the *British Whig* newspaper,
an individual offered a twelve-dollar reward for the return of a
parcel containing muslin "lost or mislaid near Mrs. Stephen's
Fairfield's Tavern." Another individual offered a "liberal reward"
for information leading to the discovery of a "small dark Bay
Horse about five feet high, a white stripe in his forehead and three
white feet," that had strayed away from its farm. There was no
reward offered for the apprehension of James Shaw's murderer.
Indeed, the murder – for certainly it could have been called this –
never made the papers at all.

In 1822, the law viewed children as chattel. The police were
unlikely to devote much time to investigating the murder of a
child, especially if his or her parents didn't compel them to do so.
Kingston did not yet have a penitentiary or an efficient court
system. Jails were cramped and small, merely holding pens for
drunks, prostitutes, and transients. The worst punishment Kennedy
might have faced was banishment to another country. Therefore,
James Shaw's murder ended up being a relatively easy crime to
ignore. Even nature could play her part, the spring rain quickly
washing away any traces of the crime.

No doubt on Hugh's instructions, from then on the family
treated the murder only as an unfortunate incident. The sole public
acknowledgement of James Shaw's death appeared in the May 3,
1822, issue of the *Kingston Chronicle*, buried amidst religious

poems and ads for the latest in men's and women's fashions. The cryptic obituary read: "On Monday the 22 ult., James, second son of Mr. Hugh MacDonald, Merchant of this town, aged five years and six months."

The father who meticulously maintained in his Memorandum Book the exact dates and precise times of his children's births (James Shaw was born on October 17, 1817, at 2:30 p.m.) curiously failed to record James Shaw's date and time of death. Years later, as if to rectify his father's omission, John A. entered in his father's same Memorandum Book: "James died on Monday 22 April at 20 minutes 6 o'clock p.m." What does this revelation suggest? Most compellingly that, while Hugh may have chosen not to remember the incident, John A. seems to have been unable to forget it.

Even more tragically, James Shaw's burial place remains a mystery. He is not officially listed among those buried in the Macdonald family plot in Cataraqui Cemetery in Kingston, which John A. purchased in 1850. Hugh and Helen may have buried James Shaw at the "Lower" Burial Ground, after a funeral at St. Andrew's Presbyterian Church; if so, the ceremony probably provoked a religious battle, since the Lower Burial Ground was reserved for the interment of members of the Church of England. If Hugh and Helen Macdonald were able to afford to purchase a tombstone for James Shaw in 1822, there is no sign of its existence in any cemetery in the Kingston area.

James Shaw Macdonald's murder reminded John A. that the more things changed, the more they stayed the same. In moving from Scotland to Canada, his family had found a new country to live in but had brought their old brutalities with them. "I never had a childhood," John A. confessed to a colleague later in life. He shared a sombre recollection of a day from his early childhood in Glasgow, when he was sitting in a police court, waiting for his father to pick him up. How he had got to the court, he couldn't remember. At one moment he had been "clinging by the hand to the hem of his nurse's dress, with his eyes fixed on the ground," while in the next he had awoken from his "reverie" to discover he was holding somebody else's dress, and his nurse was nowhere in sight. When his father arrived at the court, four-year-old John A. became tongue-tied and incapable of explaining what had happened to him. As punishment, Hugh took John A. home and whipped him.

Against this Dickensian backdrop of genteel poverty and violence, John A. plotted his political future. Ultimately, rather than embrace the demons of his past, he sacrificed friends and family members in his unquenchable quest for power. He soared to unparalleled political heights, yet descended into despairs so deep he couldn't leave his bed for days. He was charismatic and sociable, but built bolt-holes into his home to avoid visitors. He was gentle, still he settled more than one argument with his fists. Most of all, he used people, often ruthlessly. He acknowledged Thomas D'Arcy McGee's help in attracting Irish Catholic votes, but disparaged his "brutishness" behind his back. Shortly after McGee's murder, Reform Party member Dr. John Workman, who had worked with Macdonald to establish female insane asylums separate from men's, nevertheless summed up in a letter to a fellow Reform acquaintance, psychiatrist Dr. John Clarke, his opinion of John A.'s method of discarding those no longer useful to him. "Macdonald indeed kills off all he can," he wrote, "but whom he cannot kill with kicks, he kills with kindness. Die somehow, they must."

To understand John A.'s true nature, one must understand where he came from.

John A. Macdonald's family roots sprang up in spite of the most inhospitable soil, the jagged rocks of the Scottish Highlands. His mother, Helen Macdonald (née Shaw), was born near Dalnavert to a family whose military achievements stretched back several centuries. Her father, James Shaw, had fought for the Young Pretender at Culloden, and had taken service in the Hanoverian armies after the ruin of the Stuart cause.

Helen's mother, Margaret Grant, had married twice, the first time to William Shaw and the second time to James Shaw (no relation). Helen had two older stepsisters, fathered by William Shaw. One of those step-sisters, Anna, married Lt. Col. Donald Macpherson and moved to Kingston, Ontario. The Macphersons extended

Helen Macdonald, John A.'s mother. *(LAC 68632297)*

an open invitation for Helen and her family to join them at their home in Canada whenever they wished to do so.

Hugh Macdonald, nicknamed "Little Hughie" for his stubby, bantam-rooster-like stance, lived with his parents on Dornoch Firth by the North Sea, where his father, John, operated a general store. John was a calm and patient man. On the other hand, the young and restless Hugh yearned to leave a place he considered a primitive backwater. He soon received unsolicited help. Beginning in 1811, the Duke and Duchess of Sutherland expropriated vast acres of land in Sutherlandshire for raising sheep. Those sharecroppers who refused to raise sheep sought work in the already overcrowded cities, where factories equipped with power looms sprang up. Dubbed "The Clearances," these relocations enabled the Duke and Duchess to regain control over their property, as well as to break up the Scottish clan system that threatened to overtake the Sutherlands in power and influence.

Hugh was eager to earn his spurs as a businessman in Glasgow. Until this time, he had expended his energies only in his father's general store, entertaining customers with fantastical tales, his tongue usually loosened by liberal amounts of whisky or beer. He was particularly adept at ingratiating himself with those individuals he sensed could help him realize his dreams, though he was confused about what those dreams really were.

While his father remained in Dornoch, Hugh moved to the city of Laing, near Glasgow. There he met Helen Shaw, whose family had also moved there. The relationship seemed mismatched from the start. The two young people were exact opposites. Helen was thirty-four to Hugh's twenty-nine. She was a big-boned barrelhouse of a woman, with large, mirthful eyes and a warm smile, while Hugh was trim and boyishly handsome, with curly hair that resisted wax, large jug ears, and sad, puppy-dog eyes that peered out from beneath heavy eyelids. Helen was quiet by nature; Hugh was bombastic. She was industrious. He could be indolent. She liked to read; he liked to be read to. She outranked him socially and intellectually. Yet, somehow, they clicked. Possibly, she wanted children before it was too late to avoid the social stigma of spinsterhood, or perhaps his elfin charm simply melted her reserve.

Whatever the attraction, the two married on October 21, 1811, in Glasgow. Soon after, they moved into a tenement house near the ferry landing linking Laing to Glasgow. For the remainder of their years in Scotland, the Macdonalds lived in tenement houses, fighting rats in damp basements and bracing against the icy blasts of wind that blew through the cracks in the buildings' limestone-block exteriors. Despite her age and the austerity of her living conditions, Helen gave birth to five children in rapid succession. William, the first, who died of unknown causes in infancy, was born in 1812; Margaret, in 1813; John Alexander in 1815; James Shaw in 1816; and Louisa, in 1818.

Attempting to establish a life as a serious husband and father, Hugh hooked up with a man named McPhail and opened a cotton-manufacturing business. Hugh gleefully broke rules to bolster his professional reputation. For example, in 1817 he received a certificate confirming him as a Brother of the Burgh.

Hugh and Helen Macdonald's marriage certificate.
Glasgow, October 21, 1811. *(Queen's University Archives MF 1263)*

As a condition of his membership, he had to promise not to "brew or cause to be brewed any malt but such as is grinded at the Town's milnes." His solemn pledge lasted about as long as it took him to brew up his own homemade recipe, which filled barrels to each side of his house's doorway, into which friends could dip their mugs.

After his cotton-manufacturing business failed, he decided to manufacture bandanas. Business wasn't good, but it wasn't bad either. There was at least a limited market in Laing and Glasgow, to some extent due to Hugh's novel advertising practice of strapping billboards to the sides of sheep and herding them through the town's streets.

Ultimately, one of Hugh's strongest talents lay in persuading people to see past his faults. He knew how to stay on the good side of the right people. In fact, Hugh's likeability quotient was so high that, when his second business failed, friends and admirers bestowed on him a full library of books (which only the more literate Helen was inclined to read), as well as letters of reference.

Despite his efforts to maintain a sunny disposition, however, the same bad luck of almost biblical proportions that seemed to afflict many families at the time struck Hugh Macdonald's. In 1818, typhus swept through Glasgow and its suburbs, including Laing. Government officials fumigated five thousand apartments, the Macdonalds' among them. Unemployment figures rose astronomically. The following year, citizens out of work and out of patience marched through the streets, demanding government compensation. Social-welfare groups organized food and clothing drives. Citizens packed the churches to pray.

Staying in business in Scotland remained a constant struggle, so Hugh tried to decide which course of action would most benefit his family. Perhaps it was finally time to leave Scotland altogether, he thought. Luckily, he and Helen had an important ace up their sleeve in Kingston, Ontario: Helen's stepsister Anna and her husband, Lt. Col. Donald Macpherson. Hugh was also perceptive enough to recognize that, rather than being judged strictly by clan affiliations, as he would be in Scotland, he could attain status through the wealth he would acquire in North America. That sounded like freedom, so he decided to take his family west across the Atlantic, as so many other families before his had done.

On June 24, 1820, Hugh and Helen Macdonald, along with their four children, nervously gathered on the pier at Greenock, gazing back at a country the adults would never see again. To finance their trip, the couple had sold most of their belongings. What items they retained had already been locked up in the ship's hold along with the belongings of the 350 other passengers. Few of the total passengers were heading for cabins. The majority, like the Macdonalds, were heading for steerage. There was no confusing the two. For one thing, those passengers who travelled cabin class were referred to as "colonists"; steerage passengers, including the future prime minister of Canada, were merely "emigrants."

During his lifetime, the first Earl of Buckinghamshire's motto had been "We never go backwards," but the motto of the ship named after him might as well have been "We'll never move forward." For a good portion of the voyage, the ship bobbed like a cork in the ocean. Once the wind finally rose, those on board, especially in steerage, stumbled back and forth like drunkards, their feet soaked from the water sloshing around them.

The *Earl of Buckinghamshire*'s overcrowded steerage compartments reeked of stale sweat and rotted fruit. If one passenger coughed, his germs infected dozens of fellow passengers. Hugh, James Shaw, and John A. found privacy from the female members of the family only by suspending a lice-filled blanket from a rope. Toilet facilities were poorly maintained; their contents foul and malodorous. Helen had brought bread, cheese, and other foodstuffs on board to help protect her family from illness. This was sound thinking, since the main fare was meat stew ladled out of giant, unhygienic kettles. But finding amusements for the children was possibly the most difficult challenge of all. John A.'s favourite card game was Patience, but he rarely got the chance to enjoy this solitary pursuit, due to the tumult around him. Instead, he suffered the indignity of hearing through metal grates the cabin-class children enjoying billiards, cards, dominoes, and backgammon on the upper decks.

As it turned out, the Macdonalds had chosen the right year to sail on the *Earl of Buckinghamshire*. Just two years later, the ship drifted ashore at Galway Bay and broke into pieces.

The entire trip to Quebec City took forty-two days. Forty-two days of hell. And this was the easy part of the trip. Unfortunately for the Macdonald family, there were no trains, taxis, or steamers that could transport them from Quebec City to Kingston. Instead, they navigated the St. Lawrence River by Durham boats that were sailed, rowed, and drawn by horses or oxen through the swifter currents.

At times, the current subsided so dramatically that the flat-bottomed boats noisily scraped the rocks lying beneath the surface of the shallow water. At other times, the current surged so violently that it took two horses to draw the boats forward. All able-bodied men, Hugh among them, jumped into the river and hauled the boats through the pounding water, nearly drowning in the process. Many passengers died from exposure to the elements. Children faced the greatest danger of falling overboard, and it must haven taken all the strength in Helen's body for her to shield her toddlers from the water's force. Passengers cooked their food over open fires on the riverbank. As beds, they used their rolled-up clothes. Wild bears often shared the day's leftovers.

Docking still didn't end the travellers' struggles. Families had to line up for days waiting for waggoners to transport them and their belongings to their final destinations. This mode of travel at least allowed families to take shelter in the low-priced inns that lined the roadways.

On August 13, an exhausted Macdonald family arrived at Lt. Col. Donald Macpherson's spacious two-storey stone house at the corner of Bay and Montreal Streets in Kingston, which the army had granted to Macpherson upon his retirement. Hugh felt content. Rather than being driven out of somewhere, he was actually being welcomed with open arms into a world that promised a good living for an industrious man. It was a new concept for him and he was determined not to waste his best chance to make a fresh start. Macpherson had already promised to provide to Hugh his list of business contacts. For Hugh, this was as good as money in the bank.

Rather than being a cultural melting pot, in its early years Kingston was more like a military fort. In his book *The Rock and the Sword: A History of St. Andrew's Presbyterian Church, Kingston, Ontario*, Dr. Brian Osborne reveals that after the American Revolution more than six thousand "displaced American settlers and British military personnel" made Kingston and its surrounding area their home. Thereafter, according to Osborne, "together with Niagara and York [Toronto], Kingston became one of the centres of military, political, and social control administered by the Loyalist elite known as the 'Family Compact.'"

By 1812, Upper Canada's population had grown to ninety thousand, with Kingston's closing in on three thousand. Immigrants expecting Kingston to be a city of architectural and cultural sophistication were soon disappointed, however. Fort Henry had been built that year to defend the southern end of the St. Lawrence River. As a result, houses, some made from limestone, others from logs, resembled barracks more than elegant living quarters. Roads thick with mud mixed with horse manure sucked shoes from owners' feet. With seventy-eight taverns catering to the tastes of military personnel on the prowl for prostitutes, Kingston gained a reputation for moral laxity and debauchery. Osborne also notes that, while the number of ordained ministers in Upper Canada increased from "eight in 1790 to forty-four in 1812," each religious faction strove to dominate the other, including Church of England members, Presbyterians, Roman Catholics, Lutherans, Dutch Reformed Church members, and Mennonites. To keep pace, churches sprouted up like weeds.

A month prior to the Macdonalds' arrival, St. Andrew's Presbyterian Church had opened in Kingston. The *Kingston Gazette* invited the public to attend services at 11 a.m. and at 2 p.m. The title of Rev. Gerald Barclay's first sermon was "But the Gift of God Is Eternal Life through Jesus Christ Our Lord." The Macdonald family arrived too late to hear that particular sermon, but they arrived in plenty of time to lease some pews. Even better, thanks to his connection to Lieutenant Colonel Macpherson, Hugh was ordained as an elder of the church, a position that required him to dispense advice concerning both temporal and spiritual matters, and raised his social profile in the community. Fellow elders included John Mowat (whose son Oliver would soon become best friends and an eventual law partner of John A.), Sheriff John McLean, Dr. Anthony Marshall, and Samuel Shaw.

Through Macpherson's impressive social connections, Hugh managed to collect enough loans to open his first shop on King Street in Kingston a mere three months after his arrival. On October 11, 1820, he placed an ad in the *Kingston Chronicle* informing potential customers that, in addition to "his former stock of dry goods, he had received an assortment of NEW and FANCY GOODS suitable for the season," stressing that he always had in supply "groceries, wine, spirits, brandy, shrub, vinegar, powder and shot, English window glass, and putty etc."

The best feature of the shop, its second floor where the family lived, was spacious and, thanks to four sets of windows, surprisingly airy, especially to a family who had recently escaped the claustrophobia of the steerage compartment of a ship. The living quarters featured a place for family members to wash themselves, and individual rooms containing cots. The children were still too young to work full-time in the shop, so Hugh hired employees, among them the general worker and childminder named simply "Kennedy," who may or may not have lived with the family at various times.

Hugh's renowned charm, however, threatened to become his greatest liability. Customers came to chat, not shop, and soon Hugh was struggling to keep debt collectors, most of them Macpherson's friends, at bay. Together, Hugh and Helen hoped that relocating their shop might bring them better luck.

Within a year, Hugh placed an ad in the *Kingston Chronicle* informing the public that he had "moved his stand to Store Street." As a favour to Macpherson, Hugh welcomed Macpherson's seventeen-year-old son, Evan, as an official partner in the store. This was a risky tactic, since Evan's interests lay more in military service; he was already serving in the Frontenac militia. In the early months, the store flourished under Evan's management, so much so that Hugh felt confident enough to open a potash store on the side. In October 1821, however, Evan accepted the military position of cornet. Shortly afterwards, through his father's largesse, he purchased a commission in the Durham Light Infantry, a British regiment stationed in Kingston. Predictably, once Evan departed for military duty, Hugh's shop began to fail, as did his potash business.

Hugh's crumbling fortunes fuelled his desire to retreat to one of the multitudinous taverns throughout Kingston. He remained a man who liked to quench his thirst, long and often. Taverns continued to provide the perfect refuge from the constant demands and obligations of everyday life.

Possibly out of sympathy for his misfortunes, or as a result of his strong connections with Macpherson, on July 19, 1822, just three months after James Shaw's murder, a merchant's co-op bank appointed Hugh Macdonald as one of its directors. Soon afterwards, St. Andrew's Church, in tendering for a steeple, indicated that the plans were available for viewing at Hugh Macdonald's house.

With her acute intelligence and love of reading, Helen Macdonald instilled educational ambition in her children, especially in John A. Both Helen and Hugh felt John A., now their only son, was destined for greatness in the business world, or perhaps even in the law. After all, it would be nice to have a lawyer in the family to raise its status. "There goes the star of Canada," Hugh would brag to customers whenever a red-faced John A. hurried by. "Ye'll hear something from Johnny yet."

When Hugh's second general store failed, he concluded that his best chance of success was relocating to one of the adjoining counties. He chose Hay Bay, a sleepy hamlet twenty-five miles west of Kingston, along the craggy shoreline of Lake Ontario. He even snagged a second job. On November 5, 1824, the *Kingston Chronicle* announced that Hugh Macdonald would be its new agent in the Hay Bay area.

Soon after moving to Hay Bay, the family settled into a red clapboard house perched precariously on a high road eighty feet above the shoreline. The house's wood-shingled roof was barely visible above a field of overgrown pea vines, weeds, and grass. The cellar kitchen was filled with leaves, and a red willow had grown up in the middle of the basement. Hugh had prospered so well as an agent of the newspaper that he could afford to perform extensive renovations on the house, opening a general store in one half while moving his family into the other. Hugh also leased a store directly across the bay.

John A. was almost nine years old at the time. Helen Macdonald had big plans for her children, and so she arranged for all three – John A., Margaret, and Louisa – to attend school in Adolphustown, located less than three miles from Hay Bay. At least in the beginning, each day, rain or shine, the three Macdonald children walked to and from school together.

The school was a sixteen-foot-long log cabin built by the United Empire Loyalists in the middle of the woods. Inside, there were no individual desks. Instead, students sat on wooden benches that circled the wood-burning stove in the middle of the room. Boys sat on one side of the room and the girls on the other, as the teacher, Mr. Hughes, "Old Hughes" as students called him, presided over the room from behind a crudely constructed wooden desk at the front of the class. The tall and lean Hughes inspired fear in those students familiar with his special talent for simultaneously lifting a boy off his feet while whacking his backside with a willow switch. Even students who committed mild infractions, such as reciting poetry poorly, found themselves severely reprimanded. Boys were compelled to wear bonnets and sit on the girls' side of the room, while "deviant girls" wore suspenders and sat on the boys' side. Alama Allison, a classmate of John A. recalls that Mr. Hughes's teaching skills compensated for his temper. "He was considered the best teacher far and wide, and many persons came to this school from a distance on account of his superiority over other teachers," she said.

John A. made a favourable impression on the female members of the school such as Allison, because he was already a tall, slim, striking boy, with thick black hair that exploded into a glistening halo of matted curls if it was humid or raining. His skin was white, almost translucent, unless he laughed hard, or after a run, when bright red blotches appeared on each cheek. Extraordinarily sparkling blue eyes offset a large potato-shaped nose that earned him the nickname "ugly John Macdonald." Even as a pre-adolescent, he was something of a dandy, preferring silk vests and velvet jackets, although in summer he had a propensity to forsake shoes to walk barefoot into class. He loved to read verse, Byron being one of his favourites, but he established his academic excellence with his superior mathematical skills. Alama Allison recalls that he was looked upon by other students as funny, sociable, and "rather superior in ability" to themselves.

Yet another quality distinguished John A. from his schoolmates: his air of mystery. No one really knew what he thought about issues, because he so rarely blurted out his opinions. When bored, he was fond of doodling flowers of no particular species on the covers of his exercise books. Of those exercise books that remain, one shows an unflattering caricature John A. drew of himself, featuring a bulbous nose and no chin, accompanied by stream-of-consciousness jottings.

John A.'s daydreaming doodles. (Queen's University Archives, Macdonald Papers, Personal Correspondence MF1258-1262, vol. 549)

In spite of his veneer of imperturbability, John A. possessed a temper. He hated being manipulated or held up as superior to his fellow students. On one occasion, he refused to sit for an exam after Old Hughes informed him in advance that he was planning to use his exam as an example to other students. When the day of the exam arrived, Hughes was unable to budge John A. from his bed at home.

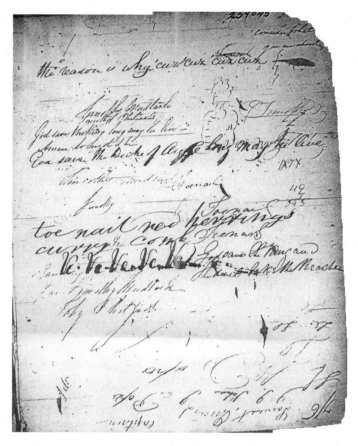

John A.'s caricature of self, upper right, with random thoughts.
(Queen's University Archives, Macdonald Papers,
Personal Correspondence MF 1258-1262, vol. 549)

John A. got into his share of scrapes while living in Hay Bay. While exploring the rocky cliffs and beaches around his home on a fine summer's morning, he came upon an elderly neighbour quietly casting his reel into the lake. The old man's previous catches, including perches, bass, and pickerel, lay on a nearby rock. Just as he was about to attach another worm to his hook, out of the corner of his eye the man spotted a "big-nosed Scotch kid" approaching him. With impressive precociousness, John A.

extended his hand and introduced himself, chatting amiably about his family as he watched the old man slowly rewind his reel, then recast it into the lake. As his fishhook sank into the water, the old man walked to the water's edge, with his back to John A. As he did so, John A. grabbed "the biggest black bass" the man had caught from off the rock and ran home as fast as he could. The louder the old man yelled after him, the faster John A. ran.

The conclusion to this story did not occur until late in 1837, at a political gathering that John A. was addressing in the Adolphustown Town Hall. During a lull in the proceedings, Mr. Gilbert "Guy" Casey rose and, with mock solemnity, shared his story of a young boy who thirteen years before had deliberately stolen a large bass from off a rock, then raced home with it, as Casey bellowed after him to stop. That boy, Casey made clear, was none other than the candidate on stage named John A. Macdonald. Casey issued a threat. Unless John A. acknowledged his crime, and asked Casey's pardon, Casey would use his influence against him. As Casey finished his fish tale and sat down, the audience of electors, breathlessly awaiting a contrite confession, turned their heads in unison toward John A.

John A. rose from his seat, bearing an expression of grave solemnity. He walked slowly to the centre of the stage, his head bowed. Hushed with anticipation, the crowd stared at him. Once he had found his mark, he raised his eyes from the floor and addressed the audience of his peers, his tone contrite, but his message filled with the wry wit for which he would soon become renowned. "Mr. Chairman, and yeomen of Adolphustown," he began. "What my old neighbour has told you about my theft of his beautiful fish is absolutely true. I can recall as though it were but yesterday how frightened I was at that unearthly yell of our good friend, which almost caused me to drop the fish so as to make better speed, but I managed to hold on to it when I saw he was not chasing me. I was clean out of breath when I burst into the house and fell headlong with it on the floor, and gasped for breath as I told my father where I found it, and that there were lots more where this came from. I humbly beg your pardon, Guy, and my only regret is that I can't steal another one like it here tonight and have it for breakfast in the morning. Mother said it was the best black bass she ever cooked."

With this, the audience members, including Guy Casey, erupted into sustained laughter. John A.'s charm had won the day.

The fact that John A. stole a fish could be easily dismissed as the misadventures of a mischievous boy, but he exhibited signs that he was also capable of extreme acts of cruelty, even toward family members.

As a childhood lark, John A. pushed his sister Louisa and a female friend out onto Lake Ontario in a boat without oars. The farther out the girls drifted, the louder they screamed, trying frantically to paddle back to shore by hand. His mother, who saw the events from her front window, rushed down to the shore and scolded her son. "You wicked boy, what did you do that for? Suppose they upset?"

John A. replied laconically, "Then I would go out and pull them in." Fortuitously, as Helen and John A. looked on, a summer breeze steered the girls' boat safely back to land.

On frequent occasions, John A. organized his sisters into games of soldier. He always played captain, because the position imbued him with the authority to assign various duties to his sisters to perform, such as cleaning pots or dusting cobwebs. On one occasion, he ordered Louisa and Margaret to march in a circle around him. When he found Louisa's marching skills wanting, he commanded her to stop. She refused, mocking his authority by skipping around the room. Incensed, John A. grabbed an old gun that hung on the wall and pointed it at Louisa, shouting, "Louie, if you don't be quiet, I'll shoot you!" Undaunted, Louisa called his bluff and continued to skip. John repeated the threat, this time with such ferocity that Margaret became terrified and cried, "Oh! Johnnie, Johnnie, put that gun down." John A. finally did so, but

John A.'s sisters: delicate Margaret (left) and rough-hewn Louisa (right).
(LAC C22818, C022817)

with great reluctance. Shortly afterwards, Hugh discovered that the gun was loaded.

As the family's sole surviving son, John A. enjoyed his privileges, but this stunt was dramatic even for him, and for several hours that evening, family members sat by the fire, silently shaken. However, just as he would do in the future in his role as a politician, John A. instantly switched his anger off, dissipating all the electricity that had built up in the room.

Though they usually acquiesced to all their brother's whims, John A.'s sisters both adored him. Margaret, or Moll, the eldest, possessed the fragile beauty of a porcelain doll. She was the feminine girl of the family, petite and blond-haired, with large blue eyes. Though vital and strong, she projected an air of helplessness and enjoyed performing chores such as polishing silverware or sewing and embroidering. She loved playing with her collection of wax-headed dolls. No one would have trouble envisioning her marrying and bearing several children. When

John A.'s clothes became ripped or torn, Margaret invariably volunteered to mend them.

By contrast, Louisa, or Lou, resembled her brother. She was tall, dark-haired, and homely, with a thick nose and heavy eyebrows that conveyed a physical sternness matched by her inflexible personality. Rather than play down her plainness, she revelled in it, devoting no serious effort toward prettifying herself with fancy bonnets, ribbons, or lace. In another day or another age, she would have been a woman who traded skirts for pants, and enjoyed bungee-jumping or sky-diving. She threw herself into hard physical labour, building up her shoulder and arm muscles by carrying heavy buckets of water to and from the lake, or spent hours vigorously digging through several levels of soil to plant a vegetable garden. She kept an inventory of the store's goods, and loved to deal with customers, weighing the groceries and counting change. The Bible was her favourite book. She liked games, particularly cards, checkers, or chess, with John acting as her worthiest opponent. Neither accepted defeat graciously.

Louisa's practical nature proved invaluable the day John A. arrived home from school to discover the front door locked and no one stirring inside. Hugh and Helen commonly asked the girls to skip school and help in the shop on busy days. As a result, John A. had never suspected anything was amiss when the girls did not show up in the classroom. In order to enter the house, he had to break a side window, and, upon investigating, he discovered the family members so ill in bed they were unable to rouse themselves. Mindful she must get up, or let the family starve, Louisa told John A. to carry her downstairs on his back and to lay her on the sofa before the kitchen fire. From there she instructed him on how to knead bread and cook dinner. Not surprisingly, female family members came to look upon John A. as the man of the house. In his book *Anecdotal Life of Sir John Macdonald*, E. B. Biggar quotes Helen Macdonald as prophesizing, "Mark my word, John will make more than an ordinary man."

For such a young man, it must have been oppressive to realize that his mother and two sisters were increasingly becoming his responsibility. Like other women of that period, their financial security and social status depended upon how much money the men of the family could bring into the house. Without money, John A.'s sisters faced earning a living as shopgirls or cooks. Through family contacts, they could perhaps do even better, obtaining positions as official hostessess, or becoming companions to wealthy widows who needed their dogs walked, crystal dusted, or prescriptions picked up at pharmacies. During the winter off-seasons, when homesteaders weren't ploughing fields or buying seeds to plant, no one knew how close the Macdonald family sometimes came to losing it all. During every other time of the year, however, Hugh managed to keep his financial head above water.

Scraping together the savings from his Hay Bay shop, in 1829 Hugh moved his family to the Stone Mills, thirty miles west of Kingston, close to where the Glenora ferry ran across the water between Lennox and Addington County and Prince Edward County. Here, Hugh leased a grist and carding mill, the machinery powered by water from the mysterious Lake on the Mountain. Then, as now, the lake lies sixty-five yards above Lake Ontario, but, without any apparent source, has a constant flow of clean, fresh water. Some Indian tribesmen, pondering the source of the lake's water, once offered gifts to its spirits. Others thought that the lake must be bottomless. Hugh's mill also included a house for a miller, stables, and sheds.

Hugh increased the family's income by manufacturing cloth. Business was so good, he hired an individual named David Wallace to run the carding machine, as well as a miller named Hudson to run the grist mill and maintain the machinery. Hugh kept the books and acted as the business's boss. It should have worked. It had all the potential to succeed, especially since the region was then experiencing an economic boon. However, it was never more than an "indifferent success."

As the rest of his family members settled into life at the Stone Mills, John A. was now living for at least half the year in Kingston, where he attended the Midland District Grammar School, run by headmaster Rev. John Wilson, a fellow of Oxford University, and his assistant, George Baxter. Though it cost the family much of their savings to send John A. to this school (with annual tuition rates as high as seventy pounds), they felt their investment in his future was their only chance to avoid social oblivion. The two most prestigious careers for young men of the day were the church or the law. At school, John A. formed an enduring friendship with Charles Stuart, the son of Anglican Archdeacon George Okill Stuart, the two generally distinguishing themselves by their love of practical jokes and their intellectual acuity. The two boys frequently boarded with two elderly women at 110 Rideau Street. The women must have proved too staid for such high-spirited young men, so they spent vast amounts of time at Lieutenant Colonel Macpherson's house, where they regularly scarfed down slices of pudding and fairy cakes.

John A. was a naturally gifted, rather than diligent, student. Less intellectually blessed classmates smarted at his ability to rise to the top of the class without any intensive studying. Even more annoyingly, he was perpetually late for class, each of his excuses more ingenious than the last, prompting George Baxter to tell John A., "You'll make a better lawyer than a clergyman." Friends trumped Baxter's prediction by urging John A. to employ his gift of eluding culpability by becoming a politician. Politics meant power, and John A. liked the sound of that word.

In 1829, John A. left the Midland District Grammar School to attend the John Cruikshank Grammar School in Kingston, a private co-educational institution run by Rev. John Cruikshank, a good Presbyterian and a man renowned for his "classical and general education." The move was motivated as much by social ambition as scholastic excellence. There were approximately twenty-five children in the class, ranging in age from six to seventeen. Many of them would become people of distinction. For example, Oliver Mowat, John A.'s first law partner, would later become the premier of Ontario, while John Hillyard Cameron would attend Upper Canada College.

As 1830 approached, the curtain began to fall on Hugh Macdonald's less-than-stellar career as a businessman. For close to ten years, he had kept his family from the metaphorical poorhouse, but barely. Now, the youthful zeal he had felt as a new immigrant to the country had calcified into deep discouragement. Nevertheless, by virtue of his church affiliations, social activism, and Helen's family connections, honours continued to come his way.

Most astoundingly, Hugh Macdonald achieved prominence by being appointed a justice of the peace for Upper Canada's Midland District. The Midland District, originally named Mecklenburg District when it was created in 1788 until it was renamed in 1792, was bordered on the east by the Gananoque River, and to the west by the Trent River, Kingston being its main town.

The position did not include a fixed salary, but a justice of the peace got paid on a "fee for service" basis. JPs met four times a year (in Quarter Session). So, in one of the family history's greatest ironies, the man who let his son's murderer go free adjudicated assault and theft cases for the local government of the district. For this job, Hugh enjoyed the title "Esquire." It must have been a welcome step up from "Shopkeeper."

II

THE APPRENTICE

In September 1829, at the age of fourteen, John A. travelled alone by stagecoach to the Law Society of Upper Canada in Toronto and upon arrival paid the ten-pound admittance fee to write the exam that permitted him to study law. The money did not come easily. Between intense periods of schooling, John A. had earned a small portion of it working in his father's Hay Bay store. The remainder was courtesy of a loan from Hugh.

The Law Society of Upper Canada, founded in 1797, sought to ensure that lawyers-in-training learned under the highest in ethical and technical standards. The society did not offer formal legal education to its students, however. Instead, they apprenticed with licensed lawyers during the day while reading law at night. At the end of their apprenticeships, the students returned to the Law Society of Upper Canada to write their final examinations, which entitled them to become lawyers in their own right.

On the ride home to Kingston, John A. drew his admittance card out of his pocket and noticed that it contained a typographical error: his last name, Macdonald, was spelled McDonald. Small errors like this irked him. They smacked of discourtesy.

As soon as he arrived back in Kingston, he immediately began studying law with a prominent thirty-five-year-old Kingston lawyer named George Mackenzie, whom he had met through his father. Mackenzie invited John to live with him and his wife, Sarah, in their elegant two-storey stone house on Barrack Street in Kingston. The following year, the Mackenzies moved to Princess Street to be closer to the more lucrative commercial district of town.

As a lawyer-in-training, John A. stole the spotlight from his father, Hugh, as the head of the Macdonald family. It was not a subtle usurpation of power and it was not meant to be. As the de facto head of the Macdonald household, he sometimes appeared invincible. At times, he felt it. But only at times. The rest of the time, he drank his doubts away at Kingston's taverns, which had no liquor laws. He was barely fifteen years old.

John A.'s weakness for alcohol wasn't news to Mackenzie. During the day, he instructed his protégé on mundane tasks, such as how to perform legal research, transcribe letters, and oversee discovery proceedings with clients. After John A. had spent the day in Mackenzie's law office, he studied in the couple's handsome living quarters in the evenings. In the Mackenzie's home, John A. found evidence of the opulent lifestyle a law practice could provide. Expensive, custom-made mahogany bookcases lined the parlour. Crystal chandeliers dangled from the dining-room ceiling. Walking back to his bedroom, John A.'s size-ten shoes sank into thick broadloom.

As an ambitious man himself, Mackenzie approved of John A.'s desire to rise as high and fast as he could in his profession, hoping one day to secure a position in public office. Mackenzie himself planned to run in the near future for the provincial legislature. It was less obvious to see how Sarah Mackenzie benefited from hosting John A. in her home, especially when he indulged in teenaged irresponsibility. One of his worst habits was failing to rouse himself from bed in the morning.

One day, when Sarah failed to awaken John A. by knocking on his bedroom door, she taught him a lesson by drawing a set of heavy curtains across his windows, plunging him into inky darkness. As John A. slept, Sarah went about her household duties. She even left the house to perform a couple of errands. Yet still John A. slumbered. Finally, as Sarah began to prepare dinner, she heard some frantic rustling and thumping in the room overhead. As she soon discovered, John A. had suddenly awoken, peeked out between the window curtains, and observed people on the street walking home from work. It was the last time John A. was ever late for work.

Mackenzie recognized John A.'s flair for the law, as well as his boundless confidence. In fact, John A.'s favourite motto was "Be to our faults a little blind, and to our virtues always kind." His only major blunder in Mackenzie's office occurred when he gave his opinion on a matter of law to a prospective client named Moore, only to discover that Moore's opponent had already formally asked George Mackenzie to represent him. Mackenzie had to drop the client.

In 1830, Kingstonians petitioned the legislature for a new bank (which would ultimately become the Commercial Bank of the Midland District), and George Mackenzie became the bank's first solicitor. As Mackenzie's reputation grew, so, too, did young John A.'s. For more than two years he worked diligently as Mackenzie's apprentice. As a reward for his good service, in 1832 Mackenzie appointed John A. branch manager of his office in Napanee, located twenty-five miles west of Kingston.

Without his family as an emotional buffer in Napanee, however, John A.'s confidence collapsed. In private, he became standoffish and distracted. At work, he was unyielding and repressed. Subordinates grumbled that the boy lacked the right stuff for the job. John A. wondered the same thing.

For the first time, John A. faced the possibility of failing. He isolated himself. Co-workers and friends soon nicknamed him the "Artful Dodger" for his uncanny ability to find closets or doors to escape through during crises. Napanee in 1832 was no

Kingston, after all. There was no hustle and bustle, steady foot traffic, or sophisticated commerce to stir the blood. Instead, it was a town with fewer than a dozen buildings in its entire downtown core. Among its residents were European stonemasons just completing the Rideau Canal, the five-mile-long man-made waterway connecting Ottawa to Kingston.

"I do not think that you are so free and lively with the people as a young man eager for their good will should be. A dead-and-alive way with them never does," George Mackenzie instructed John A. by letter, after he received news that his protégé was experiencing self-doubts. Instead of heeding the letter's instructions judiciously, however, John A. interpreted it as a licence to go wild.

Suddenly he was striding around town as if he owned it. He moved to an apartment in the Clarksville district of town with Tom Ramsay, a local merchant. Before long, John A. came to appreciate the benefits of simulating a strong moral conscience and intentionally rubbed shoulders with older, and often more affluent, residents at church services held at an old schoolhouse. The local minister, Rev. Saltern Givens, a Church of England missionary in Napanee during this period, recalls that John A. even took a prominent part in pitching the tunes each Sunday morning.

To fuel his growing self-confidence, John A. frequented the old Red Lion Tavern on the west side of the river, one of two taverns in town. The other tavern, named the Quakenbush, featured an addition to one side where the Fredericksburgh magistrates held local courts, such as the Court of Requests. Before long, a trio of bachelors, comprised of John A., Tom Ramsay, and Donald Stuart, the son of a judge, swaggered through town, turning it upside down with their bouts of "deviltry." Said one friend of John A. during this period, "He was much more famous for his knowledge of books, his fondness for boon companions, and his humour and strong liking for anecdotes, than for his professional knowledge and tendencies."

John A.'s cousin Allan Macpherson, Lt. Col. Donald Macpherson's eldest son, nicknamed the "Laird of Napanee," tried to monitor John A.'s behaviour as best he could, advising him on the merits of self-restraint, but John A. often let his advice go in one ear and out the other. Macpherson owned a saw-and grist-mill in town, and opened his large Georgian home to John A. whenever he wished to recuperate after a particularly heavy drinking bout.

Thomas Ramsay ran three or four shops in town, including a grocery store, and he shared John A.'s love of books, beer, and women. For relaxation, John A. often joined Ramsay behind the counter, weighing out tea and sugar.

Despite his peculiar looks, John A. did not lack for female companionship. Women revelled in his rapacious wit and sly social observations. He had his father's flair for flattery, and a disarming gift for self-mockery. However, apart from his mother and sisters, he rarely considered women as anything but pleasant diversions. Sometimes his lack of social graces landed him in trouble. At a local dance, he forgot his promise to dance the quadrille with a certain young woman. No matter how ardently he apologized to her, she refused to forgive him. In an act of supreme self-ridicule, he finally collapsed on the floor at her feet and, writhing in mock pain, cried out, "Remember! Oh, remember! The fascinations of the turkey." As guests erupted in laughter, the woman, flushed now with embarrassment, had little option but to forgive him.

During his time in Napanee, he courted a few local women, including a handsome widow several years his senior. Nevertheless, he was all ambition. For now, romance and marriage were far in his future.

When he applied himself, he was a clever lawyer, showing a flair for advising clients on real-estate matters. Yet he could also be lazy, sometimes lying in the tall grasses reading verses for hours, or watching clouds sail by.

Somewhere during this time, John A. appears to have leap-frogged from performing mere law-clerking duties to defending clients in court, a practice strictly forbidden by the Law Society of Upper Canada until a student reached the age of twenty-one. His mentor, George Mackenzie, simply looked the other way. Years later, while campaigning for public office, John A. bragged to journalists that one of his favourite cases during his Napanee period was successfully defending a client who had left a dead horse in the local Methodist Church, made all the easier since John A. admitted that he himself had participated in the practical joke. "It always taught me the weakness of circumstantial evidence," he explained.

John A. achieved early success in country courts because he willingly catered to small-town prejudices, and if necessary, spoke to jurymen using unsophisticated, local colloquialisms. Fellow lawyer and future law partner Alexander Campbell observed some of John A.'s performances in court during this period. In a hand-written memoir stored at the Archives of Ontario, Campbell noted, "He never became in my judgement a good lawyer, but was always a dangerous man to encounter in courts. His power before a country jury was always marked chiefly if not wholly owing to his knowledge of the jurymen and his appreciation of their habits of thoughts and ways of speaking. He was in tone of voice and manner as thoroughly a Bay of Quinté boy as if he had been born there. I have for instance heard him say to a jury in speaking of an assault, say of the defendant that 'he took & went & hit him a brick.'"

Lost in the euphoria of his early courtroom success was any concern for its legal implications. Quite simply, as one who had not yet been called to the bar, John A. should have been legally estopped from representing clients in court. That he may have done so shows his peculiar contempt for the law, even as he perfected its application. However, slips such as this were not unusual in an age in which frontier justice had quite recently been replaced by due process. Besides, breaking rules rarely slowed John A. down when he was intent on attaining a specific goal.

In the spring of 1833, John A. returned to Kingston to oversee George Mackenzie's law practice, as Mackenzie travelled to Montreal and Quebec on business. Entrusted with running a prestigious law practice in a big city was heady stuff for an eighteen-year-old, and John A. wrote Mackenzie a letter expressing his appreciation for the honour. "I am sensible of your attention to the duties of the office," he wrote. Mackenzie replied, "And I trust that I may have it in my power to mark my sense of your zeal and fidelity."

Mackenzie's faith in John A.'s fidelity was more misplaced than he might have believed. In the fall of 1833, John A.'s cousin, Lowther Pennington Macpherson, a lawyer in the township of Hallowell (later named Picton), located fifty miles southwest of Napanee, became ill with bronchitis and wished to travel to Britain to convalesce, inviting John A. to run his practice during his absence. His request may have been a way to test the extent of John A.'s clannish loyalty – as well as to seek repayment for his family's generosity to John A.'s family – but for John A. it was also a chance to make more money and carve out his own legal identity. Despite his gratitude to Mackenzie, John A. accepted Lowther's offer, and George Mackenzie reluctantly watched his star protégé depart, leaving an impressive number of satisfied clients behind him.

Back in Napanee, John A.'s good friend Tom Ramsay heard the news and hoped that Macpherson would amply reward his new employee by "a vigourous employment of those talents in his service which you so fully possess."

John A. felt emboldened in Hallowell, because he was living so much closer to his family members than he had been in Napanee or Kingston. Hugh, Helen, and the girls were at the Stone Mills, less than five miles away, always handy for a home-cooked meal. Hugh had bought a piano, and family singalongs became a regular pastime. When Lt. Col. Donald Macpherson had died in 1829, his widow, Anna, had moved from Kingston to Hallowell. So, for at least a brief period of time, Hallowell became a meeting place for the Macdonald-Macpherson clans.

In Hallowell, John A. exploited the social benefits his position yielded. He was appointed secretary of the Prince Edward School Board and first secretary of the Hallowell Young Men's Society. He also helped draft a petition for the union of Hallowell and Picton, which ultimately occurred in 1837.

John A.'s career was heading straight up, but he managed to bend the arrow before it hit its target. In Hallowell, his weaknesses were not professional, but personal, and he seemed blind to how much disrepute he could bring upon Macpherson's law practice through his private peccadilloes. The fact was, when John A.'s mind wasn't engaged in work, he drank openly and without apology. Family friend James Porter recalled that John A. was as fond of whisky as was his father, Hugh. No slouch at imbibing himself, Porter was often astounded at the volume of alcohol John A. consumed without losing his balance or slurring his speech. The morning after one of these drinking sessions, Porter would see John A. on the street. "And whenever I saw John A. on the street, why, bless you, he wouldn't wait for me to come and speak, but he would duck his head in that peculiar way of his, and come right across the street to shake hands. 'Damn it, Porter,' he would say, 'are you alive yet?'"

Perhaps also because he felt emboldened by having his family close by for moral support, while in Hallowell, John A. committed a series of almost fatal public-relations blunders owing to his penchant for cruel practical jokes. As it happened, he had formed a passionate dislike for a local hostelkeeper named Bob Hopkins, who had the disconcerting habit of riding his horse and buggy through the centre of town at breakneck speed, causing townsfolk to scatter. While Hopkins was away on business, John A. and some friends erected a rail fence across the road for Hopkins to crash into upon his return. As evening descended, John A. and his friends fell back into the grass stifling their laughter as they listened to Hopkins's buggy rattle down the street. As expected, Hopkins's horse galloped straight into the fence. Fortunately, for John A., Hopkins was uninjured, though his horse was maimed for life.

In his eagerness to find the culprit for the prank, the local magistrate, Justice James Shallow, arrested the wrong man. Though John A. knew Shallow had made a mistake, he did not immediately confess to the crime. Finally, wracked either by pangs of conscience or by the fear of exposure, John A. stepped forward to reveal himself as the brainchild behind the stunt. Using John A.'s burgeoning career as a lawyer as a mitigating circumstance, in the end, Justice Shallow declined to press charges against John A. for the crime. Instead of leaving the courtroom with a sense of remorse, however, John A. left with a sense of wry amusement. The young lawyer-in-training had won a lucky escape and learned nothing from it.

John A. committed at least one more memorable stunt in Hallowell, this one involving an unpopular Irish firebrand named Dr. Frank Moore. Moore, a Reformer, had a particular distaste for Conservatives, Orangemen in particular, and threatened to cure Conservative patients of their political ills by applying "a leaden pill." On July 11, 1834, John A., surrounded by a group of young men, stood chatting near the entrance of the Hopkins Hostel, when Dr. Moore entered the building. As Moore passed him, John A. surreptitiously pinned a long Orange ribbon to the back of Moore's coat. When the doctor discovered the ribbon, he flew into a rage. To diffuse the situation, John A. swiftly apologized. Later that same afternoon, Moore spotted John A. and his friends still gathered in front of the Hopkins Hostel, laughing. In a fit of paranoia, he concluded they must be laughing at him. Moore drew John A. aside and said, "Some puppy pinned an Orange ribbon to my coat this morning. He was not an Irishman, nor an Englishman, but a lousy Scotchman."

"Doctor, I apologized, and said I was sorry for what I did, but you must not speak in that way of my nationality, for I will not put up with it," John A. replied.

Undeterred, the doctor yelled, "Shut up, you puppy, or I will box your ears."

"You are not able," John A. shouted back.

As the doctor raised his leg to kick him, John A. caught his foot, threw him down, and began vigorously punching him (to the delight of bystanders). A local magistrate, as he pulled John A. off the doctor, whispered, "Hit him again, John!"

Days later, the Picton courthouse was the site of the case of *The King vs. John A. Macdonald* for assault against Dr. Frank Moore. Before a jury of his peers, John A. pleaded not guilty. After retiring for a short deliberation, the jury returned a verdict of not guilty. Moore wasn't so lucky. The next day, a jury found him guilty of assault against Mr. J. A. Macdonald, and fined him six pence for the scuffle, no doubt a pence for every punch.

John A. longed to move on from Hallowell, but even following his return from England, Lowther Pennington Macpherson's health continued to deteriorate so drastically that John A. was obliged to stay.

So far John A.'s life had been characterized by a series of fortunate near-misses. He had missed being assaulted by the servant Kennedy as a child, he had missed imprisonment for pranks he had committed in Hallowell, and in 1832 and again in 1834, he had missed the cholera epidemics that swept through Kingston. In 1832, he had been in Napanee, and in 1834, he was in Hallowell.

In her brilliant essay "Health, Emigration and Welfare in Kingston, 1820–1840," Kingston historian Dr. Margaret Angus traces cholera's spread during these years. As Angus records, by early June 1832 word arrived in Kingston that cholera had broken out among passengers on board ships arriving at Quebec and

Montreal. There was little doubt that passengers aboard ships bound for Kingston would also be carrying the disease. Cholera was primarily caused by a bacillus found in contaminated water supplies. The symptoms included nausea, vomiting, cramps in the hands and feet, dizziness, and often death.

At a public meeting held on June 14, Kingstonians adopted measures they hoped would prevent the spread of cholera throughout Kingston. They created a Board of Health to care for the sick. Nevertheless, on June 17, Kingston recorded its first death from the disease. To mark the event, citizens raised a yellow flag in the marketplace near the harbour. The *Chronicle* newspaper reported on June 18 that no boat was to enter the harbour until inspected by the health officer. Town officials posted notices announcing that any master who entered the harbour with a sick or dead person aboard his boat would be fined. The dead were to be buried five miles from town.

The 1832 epidemic passed over the houses of most Kingstonians due to brilliant foresight, excellent organizational plans by town officials, quick dissemination of information, and the erection of temporary medical hospitals in tents near the river's edge.

The cholera that attacked Kingston in 1834 was a different story, however. This was the deadly Asiatic variety, which usually killed its victims within twenty-four hours, despite doctors' frantic efforts to cure it by bleeding, cupping, or feeding milk to patients. Some citizens believed they could catch cholera simply through their fear of it. In some cities, fear that all immigrants might be carrying the disease grew so great that passengers were charged a "medical tax" before they could disembark.

As the second epidemic drew to an end, estimates of the number of dead in Kingston rose as high as twelve hundred people, almost a quarter of its population. George Mackenzie, John A.'s former mentor, had just been nominated as one of the Conservative candidates for Frontenac. He would never even get a chance to campaign. On the morning of Sunday,

August 23, 1834, he dressed in his best clothes and walked to St. Andrew's Church, tipping his top hat to the ladies before taking his pew. Within ten minutes of his sitting down, sweat began pouring down Mackenzie's face. His vision blurred. He closed his eyes but, upon reopening them, found his vision just as blurry. Mackenzie managed to sit through the entire service. Afterwards, he walked home, his gait unsteady, hands shaking, and teeth chattering. He grasped his front doorknob, stepped inside his vestibule, and promptly collapsed. His servants took him to bed. Within hours, his face had turned blue, the telltale sign of imminent death from Asiatic cholera. By early Monday morning, he was dead at the age of thirty-nine, leaving behind his wife, Sarah, and an infant son.

The minister of St. Andrew's Church, John Machar, almost buckled emotionally under the devastating shock of burying several of his friends on the same day. In his book *The Rock and the Sword: A History of St. Andrew's Presbyterian Church, Kingston, Ontario*, Brian Osborne quotes Reverend Machar's personal impressions of his activities during the epidemic:

> On the second day it prevailed, there were eight funerals in the Scotch burying ground alone and as in this country ministers attend all funerals of their people. I waited nearly all that day to receive the various funeral trains as they arrived, and at one time three bodies were laid side by side in their narrow resting place . . . [Some] of the most prosperous and most beloved of my congregation died; for the disease, this past season, was not confined to the lowest and most intemperate.

John A. had felt genuine affection for George Mackenzie, and grieved his death. Yet, business was business. He hastily re-established contact with clients he knew and secured contact with Mackenzie's current clients, including those in both Napanee and

Kingston. He had some big decisions to make. He could either remain working in Lowther Pennington Macpherson's office in Hallowell or open an office of his own in Kingston. However, at twenty, he was still too young to be called to the bar. He reluctantly remained with Lowther for almost another year, kicking like a racehorse at his enclosure.

To frustrate John A.'s ambitions even more, in 1834 the Conservatives had lost a general election in both Upper and Lower Canada. Upper Canada, the predecessor of modern Ontario, had originally come into existence when the British Parliament passed the Constitutional Act of 1791, dividing the old Province of Quebec into Lower Canada in the East and Upper Canada in the West along the present-day Ontario-Quebec boundary. Now, the British Toryism of the Anglican-based Family Compact, which had dominated the political, cultural, and social habits of citizens of Upper Canada, was diminishing in strength in Kingston, while it was simultaneously gaining strength in Toronto. At the same time, in Lower Canada (the southern part of modern-day Quebec), the French agitated for a greater voice in the Province of Canada's affairs.

In response to what they considered the French's pugnaciousness, while John A. was in Napanee on a business trip, he, Tom Ramsay, and Charles Stuart created a fake political organization they called the "Société de la Vache Rouge," the title combining Gallic flair with Highland Scottish bombast. Together the group travelled to the Stone Mills to visit with John A.'s family. There the group enacted a serio-comic burlesque, with John A. enlisting each friend and family member to assume a heraldic role. Charles Stuart became "Lord Lyon, King of Arms," while John A.'s mother happily chewed the scenery in her role as "The Lady Helen o' that Ilk." To lend queenly ferocity to her performance, Helen knighted those around her with a cardboard sword, laughing until she cried.

The entire performance took place beneath a banner that read, "Sans Peur et Sans Reproche."

At last, in the summer of 1835, John A. moved back to Kingston for good. There, he occupied his late Uncle Donald Macpherson's square-cut limestone house on Brewery Street. The house had been built in 1810, and was purchased by the lieutenant colonel as a rental property. John A. managed this and other properties for the Macpherson estate. He studied for his bar exam in his bedroom on the top floor, its windows facing south toward the city centre, the sloped roof threatening to decapitate him if he bolted to his feet without thinking. His relative and former employer, Lowther Pennington Macpherson, visited him here upon occasion. During one of these visits, Lowther carved his initials into a wooden roof beam, which remains there to this day. Within a year, Lowther would die on board a ship while returning from a failed rest cure in Jamaica.

John A.'s house on Rideau Street in Kingston.
(Metropolitan Toronto Reference Library)

The Brewery Street house (the name of the street was later changed to Rideau Street) was the first John A. inhabited on his own, at least temporarily, and it contained many attractive features, including a centre hallway, a fireplace on the main floor, and a cozy front parlour. The walls were painted a deep green, a colour certain to contain the heat in Kingston's icy cold winters. Heavy curtains across its windows protected the house from drafts. On the ground floor were four built-in cupboards in which John A. could store his books without them cluttering up the parlour's tables.

The house had one drawback, common for its time. The kitchen was located in the basement. As a result, by the time hot meals reached the main-floor dining room, they were often cold. This was a minor inconvenience, however. It's most important feature was that it stood on a fashionable street, in an upwardly mobile city, and John A. fervently believed that the appearance of success was as good as success itself.

Before long, Hugh picked up the scent of this success. He quickly packed up what remained of his failing business at the Stone Mills and happily returned with his family to Kingston, specifically to the Brewery Street house. John A. was overjoyed to have his family with him again. He needed them around to maintain his sense of balance and purpose. Without them, he habitually indulged in various vices, leading to accusations of intemperance.

Hugh had visibly aged, his sandy-brown hair was greying; his once compact athletic frame was paunchy and flaccid. His complexion was sallow and, when he wrote, his hands trembled. He'd had a bellyful of failure in his life, and had never reached what he considered his full potential. Now he saw in his son the realization of all his frustrated dreams. So Hugh gave up on a business career. He probably had some savings, but in his mature years he was also content to live off his son's earnings. Retirement proved easier to cope with emotionally than he had imagined, especially after he received a clerkship in the Commercial Bank, courtesy of Helen's cousin Frank Harper.

Viewing his call to the bar as a mere formality, John A. went ahead and opened his first law office on Quarry Street in Kingston. When he signed the lease to his office, he was still technically a minor, yet the owner of the building, Mr. Collar, either failed to notice or failed to make an issue of the oversight. John A. was already becoming a recognizable figure, striding through town in his natty – even slightly foppish – clothes, complete with silk bow ties, full-skirted coats, and gabardine pants, usually cut slightly too short, exposing the tops of his scuffed leather boots. He took over as many of Mackenzie's clients as he could, acquiring a few more through vigorous networking. At last, on August 24, 1835, he placed an advertisement in the *Kingston Chronicle* and the *Gazette*:

> John A. Macdonald, Attorney, & c. Has opened his office
> in the brick building belonging to Mr. Collar, opposite
> the Shop of D. Prestion, Esq., Quarry Street, where he
> will attend to all the duties of the profession.

On February 3, 1836, John A. travelled by stagecoach along the icy and treacherous road stretching from Kingston to Toronto to take his exams at the Law Society of Upper Canada. As few doubted, he breezed through the exams, finally graduating as a barrister of law on February 6, 1836. Within twenty-four hours, he returned in triumph to Kingston, finally able to remove the "etc." from his business sign. He was now fully in charge of his own destiny, and determined to move up socially, politically, and professionally.

John A.'s first employee was his old schoolmate Oliver Mowat, who was still as cherubic-looking as he'd been when the two boys attended class together at the prestigious John Cruikshank school in Kingston. Next to John A.'s reputation for deviltry, Mowat's metaphorical halo provided a welcome reassurance to nervous clients. As an articling lawyer, Mowat was answerable to John A. for his work performance, but he was not an employee who needed supervision twenty-four hours a day, or whom John A. needed to worry would abscond with the company's profits. Instead, Mowat was clever, conscientious, and dutifully appreciative of John A.'s superior authority in the firm, an important lesson for future junior colleagues to learn if they wished to remain in John A.'s employ.

The ramshackle office on Quarry Street sat on the third-busiest road in town, so it attracted plenty of foot traffic. The structure itself was remarkable for its plainness. The exterior was made of grey brick. The cramped and cluttered interior was mainly attributable to John A.'s messiness. Never known for his physical neatness, he often worked with his feet propped up on his desk and his papers piled up on the floor beside him. However, few clients underestimated the orderliness of John A.'s mind, or his ability to broker lucrative real-estate deals and complete corporate business transactions.

Eliza Grimason in middle age.
(Rare Books and Special Collections Division, McGill University Library)

Sixteen-year-old Eliza Grimason burst into John A.'s office in the summer of 1836, seeking advice about a shop she and her husband, Henry, wished to purchase on Division Street, once the site of All Saints' Church. Eliza was far from being the type of client John A.'s office actively solicited. Born to a lower-class family in Ireland, she was poor, uneducated – or "uneddicated," as she put it – illiterate, and bombastic, either oblivious to or contemptuous of society's rules concerning female propriety.

Even as a young woman she was matronly in build: short and stout, with full hips, the spitting image of John A.'s mother in her youth. Like Helen Macdonald, she could size up a man in sixty seconds with her penetrating gaze. She adored John A. on sight, and he her. The two would continue a close friendship for the remainder of John A.'s life. In time, Eliza would become one of his richest and most ardent political supporters – and, some suspected, even more.

It must have given John A. Macdonald, attorney at law, an enormous measure of self-confidence each evening as he walked home from work. Perhaps as he turned the corner to Rideau Street, he stopped and savoured his impressive accomplishments. Perhaps he paused before entering the front door of his house to catch a glimpse through the window of his family gathered together before the orange glow of the fireplace. He had earned what his father had bartered their homeland for – respectability and status – and he deserved all the rewards success had to offer.

John A.'s first project was mastering the art of self-marketing by joining as many societies and social groups as he could, among them the Orange Order, for which he acted as the recording secretary. There was also the Celtic Society, and the Young Men's Society of Kingston, where he delivered lectures on a variety of timely topics. Yet, it wasn't long before his fellow citizens realized that John A. flouted convention as often as he sought it.

Bucking the tradition of selecting "safe" and easily winnable corporate cases, John A. cannily chose to defend a client who promised to earn him lots of newspaper ink and transform him into a household name. Of all potential defendants, he chose an individual that Kingstonians considered the most repugnant: accused child rapist William Brass. John A.'s opponent in court was the stentorian-voiced new Solicitor General, William Henry

Draper. John A. knew he had no hope of winning the case, but this reality did not affect his courtroom performance. His grandiose eloquence and theatrical rhetoric moved hardened reporters to tears as he tried unsuccessfully to spare Brass from hanging. The day after the trial ended, columnists praised John A.'s impassioned performance as "ingenious and reflecting credit upon a young member of the bar." The press, hardened toward the defendant, nevertheless sympathized with John A.'s failure to spare his client from the noose. John A. had won over the most impressive audience of all – the press. Through this one case, he established his talent for defending the indefensible, while winning hearts along the way.

The Young Men's Society elected John A. as its president, with Oliver Mowat replacing John A. as the recording secretary. Step by step, John A. was establishing his reputation as a role model and man of influence and, by association, Mowat followed every step of the way. The first subject debated in the society's winter program was entitled "Are the Works of Nature Sufficient in Themselves to Prove the Existence of a Supreme Being?"

No sooner had these Kingstonians finished debating the existence of a Supreme Being in early December 1837 than they received reports that four hundred armed and dangerous agitators, led by the first mayor of Toronto, William Lyon Mackenzie, had gathered north of Toronto to seize the city and free it from its imperial yoke. As soon as they heard of Mackenzie's threat, a "little amateur army of farmers, mechanics and professional men," they marched up Yonge Street in Toronto and quickly put the rebellion down before it had a chance to spread. Nevertheless, panic erupted throughout Kingston, where citizens feared a similar attack.

Two months later, in February 1838, rumours circulated that American sympathizers of the Upper Canadian rebels were about to attack Fort Henry, the fortification rebuilt from the original in 1832 to protect Kingston's main trade routes, the St. Lawrence River, the Rideau Canada, and Lake Ontario.

In addition, the Lennox and Addington militia rushed to protect the town. They formed a heavy guard on all of the town's main streets. Roads were barricaded, and night patrols were instituted.

As a member of the Sedentary Militia (as were all able-bodied men in the province between eighteen and sixty years of age), John A. took literally the word *sedentary*. Much to his father's dismay, John A. failed to display the Macdonalds' warrior spirit but instead seemed content to march in circles through muddy fields holding a rusty musket, his companion "a grim old soldier who seemed impervious to fatigue." He turned down the chance to accept through social connections an appointment to the officer ranks, and insisted on remaining a private. He told officials that his higher duty was to support his family. John A.'s selective pacifism was probably fortunate; had he actually fired his weapon, he would no doubt have done more damage to himself than to his target. To placate his father, however, he did allow himself to be named as a member, along with Oliver Mowat, of an ad hoc group called the "Loyal Scotch Volunteer Independent Light Infantry Company," a title almost as absurd as John's A.'s "Société de la Vache Rouge." Instead of bearing a musket, he could always brandish his mother's cardboard sword.

It may not have felt like business as usual, but Kingston's officials still had administrative chores to complete. The first was to incorporate Kingston as a town, which occurred on March 11, 1838. Later that month, elections for seats on the Town Council were held. John A. was one of four lawyers who acted as reporting officers. Even in this simple task, however, he couldn't avoid controversy. In all, there were four wards, with an alderman and councillor representing each. John A. was returning officer for Ward 3. Polling throughout the evening had been slow. When John A. heard that officials had already closed other polls, he instructed supervisors that the poll he oversaw should also be closed if no voters turned up within thirty minutes. When no one did show up, John A. closed the poll, declaring two winning candidates: Edward Noble as alderman and Walter Cunniffe as common councillor. Before any confetti was tossed, however, the defeated candidates filed a protest, arguing that John A. had rushed to close the poll to manipulate the election's outcome, and they asked the mayor to establish a committee to investigate the situation. On April 22, Kingston's first mayor, Thomas Kirkpatrick, formed a committee to look into John A.'s actions. John A. was ultimately exonerated, and the election results were ratified, but a public perception of vote tampering would persist throughout John A.'s political career.

Fearing attacks by anti-colonialists, Kingstonians continued to brace for a fight and, on November 6, they finally got it. Led by Col. Nils von Schoultz, a motley assortment of "liberators" calling themselves the "Patriot Hunters" crossed the American border and landed near Prescott, just down the St. Lawrence River from Kingston. Upon their arrival, von Schoultz unfurled a banner that read, "Liberated by the Onondaga Hunters" and directed his men to take shelter in a nearby windmill. As soon as they heard about the presence of the Patriot Hunters, the Royal Navy sailed from Kingston to Prescott with two armed steamers and seventy marines. The British ships opened fire on the windmill, killing many of the men who were firing on them from inside. Finally, on November 16, the Patriot Hunters surrendered, but not before they had shot and killed several members of Canada's army, butchering with a bowie knife the body of one Lieutenant Johnston. One hundred and fifty of the surviving rebels were rounded up and forced to walk all the way to Kingston for trial. It was a humiliating defeat. Stripped to their waists, their torsos tied together with a rope, the Patriot Hunters, with von Schoultz leading them, half-walked and half-stumbled down the streets of Kingston as the townsfolk they sought to "liberate" jeered them.

Perhaps only John A., the defender of unpopular causes, perceived von Schoultz's expression of romantic fatalism as he passed the crowds of people that lined Brock Street on his way to jail at Fort Henry. Like John A., von Schoultz was tall, dark, and slim. He held his head high, and comported himself with dignity, despite the burlesque show that had broken out around him.

The better John A. understood von Schoultz's motivations, the more fully he could empathize with them. The Russian Army had forced Polish-born von Schoultz from his homeland. With tragic miscalculation, von Schoultz considered Upper Canada's relationship with Great Britain to be just as oppressive and on that pretext felt it his mission to absorb Upper Canada into the United States, where a more democratic sentiment would prevail. He realized his mistake almost as soon as he reached Upper Canada's shores, and accepted his court martial and sentence to hang with stoic dignity. John A. could not offer von Schoultz a defence, because von Schoultz was tried by a military court. The most John A. could do was to beg officials to execute von Schoultz by firing squad, rather than by hanging. Officials insisted on hanging von Schoultz, but agreed to John A.'s request to conduct the hanging at a special scaffold built at Fort Henry, rather than in a public square.

On December 8, 1838, von Schoultz was duly hanged. To compensate for his misguided invasion of Canada, he left four hundred pounds to the widows and orphans of the British militia who died at the windmill. Von Schoultz also bequeathed one hundred pounds to John A. in his will as thanks for his friendship. John A. never collected the sum.

The von Schoultz trial was an important milestone in the building of John A.'s public status. Yet, to the consternation of many Tories, it also showed Macdonald to be more of a liberal pacifist than a reactionary conservative. His non-performance in the theatre of battle during the rebel invasions of 1837, and his refusal to accept a post any higher than military private, further diminished any reputation as being more of a fighter than a lover.

Even more damning, the von Schoultz case was the second in which John A.'s defendant was found guilty, prompting William Henry Draper, the trial's prosecutor, to joke, "John A., we will have to make you attorney general, owing to your success in securing convictions!"

There was no question that John A. derived a perverse pleasure in tweaking the noses of Kingston's authority figures. Rather than buckle to public criticism, he further enraged Tories in town when he successfully defended eight rebels who had been involved in the December invasion. The eight in question were actually residents of Hastings County, and of Lennox and Addington County, who had wrongheadedly joined in the 1838 rebellion. John A. grew enraged when he discovered that a local magistrate had coerced these semi-literate men into signing affidavits of guilt, unaware that, by signing, they would be condemned to death. Declaring the process "an outrage to the administration of justice," John A. successfully oversaw the men's acquittals and return to freedom.

When fifteen rebel prisoners broke out of the county jail, John A. incurred the wrath of fellow Conservatives even further by successfully prosecuting Colonel Dundas of the 83rd division and his troops in Kingston for libel in wrongfully accusing their jailer, John Ashley, of being complicit in the prisoners' escape. John Ashley walked away with two hundred pounds in damages. John A.'s opponent in the case was no less than Attorney General Christopher Hagerman. This was heady stuff for a lawyer of only twenty-three.

Finally, six months after the von Schoultz trial, John A. drew to a close his career as a criminal attorney to concentrate on more lucrative corporate cases. He happily accepted election as a member of the board of directors of the Commercial Bank of the Midland District and shortly afterwards as the bank's solicitor, replacing Henry Cassady, the former mayor of Kingston, who had died unexpectedly of natural causes. This finally put money in John A.'s pocket, and inspired him to pursue a career in public service, just as his mentor, George Mackenzie, had been planning to do before his untimely death.

In the fall of 1839, Oliver Mowat, regarded by many clients as the conscience of John A.'s law firm, began to contemplate divorcing himself from John A. and moving to Toronto. There was no question he was jealous of his former school-mate's success. Every day he spent around the charismatic John A. reminded him of his social deficien-cies. He even confided to a friend that he had a deep-seated fear of "not being anybody" of importance. There had been early signs that the partnership wouldn't last. Mowat and John A.'s management styles had always clashed, with John A. sloppy and Mowat fastidious. Mowat was also a teetotaller, a liability in an office environment awash with

Oliver Mowat, one-time apprentice, then John A.'s political foe. *(Metropolitan Toronto Reference Library)*

snifters. He was grateful to John A., even fond of him, especially looking back on their childhood friendship, but he never felt beholden to him for his later success.

Despite Mowat's impending defection, the future still looked bright for John A.'s firm, especially now that he was solicitor for the Commercial Bank of the Midland District. To celebrate his climb up an important rung in the social ladder, John A. moved his family to a house on Queen Street, a high-class neighbourhood in Kingston. Thanks to his increased salary, he could also now hire a second legal apprentice. This time he chose seventeen-year-old Alexander Campbell, the late Henry Cassady's law student. Campbell was the son of a Scottish doctor who had emigrated to Montreal in 1822, then relocated in 1836 to Kingston. As with Oliver Mowat, John A. had met Alexander Campbell at the Midland District Grammar School.

Alexander Campbell was slim and spare in build, with closely cropped dark hair and a slightly stern expression. He loved nothing more than to mull over legal questions late into the evening with John A. and Oliver Mowat, turning cases upside down and inside out before arriving at course of action. Best of all, he was organized, and adept at keeping track of bills and invoices that mysteriously seemed to remain on John A.'s desk unopened.

Mowat passed his bar exam at the Law Society of Upper Canada in the spring of 1840. Afterwards, he turned down John A.'s final request to return to the Kingston firm. Instead, he formed the firm of Burns Mowat in Toronto.

In Kingston, John A. strengthened ties with his biggest client, the Trust and Loan Company of Upper Canada. Rumours circulated throughout town that Kingston was about to become the seat of government for both Upper and Lower Canada and, in response, attracted an unprecedented influx of immigrants. That meant new homes needed to be built, with existing ones rented to the new arrivals. John A. was eager to profit from the housing boom, and before long relocated his family to comfortable living quarters above his office on Store Street. At the same time, he bought a town lot on upper Brock Street in December 1840, and soon after began building a house for his family on the site.

He didn't forget his friends. When George Mackenzie had died, he willed his widow, Sarah, premises called the Artillery Mess House, which the Imperial government had leased from him for sixty pounds a year. To assist Sarah, John A. drew up a petition, accompanied by a personal letter to the military secretary, in which he argued in favour of Sarah's desire to raise the rent to eighty pounds per year. John A. had assembled an interesting and influential collection of co-signers, including John Mowat, Oliver Mowat's father, and H. Smith, a member of the legislative assembly for Frontenac.

Hugh Macdonald never saw the inside of the Brock Street house. He died suddenly of a cerebral hemorrhage on September 29, 1841, at the age of fifty-four and was buried at the Garrison Burial Grounds. He died proud of his achievements, and oblivious to his list of failures. He had financed his children through school, an exceptional achievement for those days, and had realized his ambition to build John A. into a legal superstar. Little could he have imagined, however, how relentless John A.'s desire for status would become, ending with him attaining the highest position in the country.

John A. was twenty-six when his father died. His mother was sixty-four, his sister Margaret twenty-eight, and Louisa twenty-three. With such an illustrious brother to fuss over, neither sister seemed in a rush to marry, which placed an even bigger burden on John A.'s finances.

One might have thought that Hugh Macdonald's death would have freed John A. psychologically from the pressure to succeed. However, just the opposite occurred. Indeed, his frenzied business schedule left him virtually no time to devote to his own health, and soon he paid the price.

In fact, within a month of his father's death, John A.'s own health took a frightening turn. One evening, he collapsed at his Store Street office, wracked by stomach pain, his forehead bathed in sweat. His family called a doctor, but he was unable to diagnose the exact nature of the illness. John A. had always suffered severe indigestion in the course of growing up, and had swallowed mints by the dozen to try to bring cooling relief to his burning stomach. This attack was different. It was severe, unrelenting, and exhausting. He spent several days in bed. Once he had recovered some of his strength, he made plans to take a break from his work and visit England and Scotland in January 1842, with his family's blessings. He had not seen his homeland since that day on the deck at Greenock.

The trip turned out to be a momentous one, and by the time he returned, his days as a bachelor were ending.

III

BACHELOR HUSBAND

Hugh Macdonald's death left the female members of his family sad but not rudderless, thanks to John A.'s income. For a time, however, Hugh's death did eliminate John A.'s largest impetus to succeed. As long as Hugh had remained alive, John A. could measure his professional success against his father's failures. Now that he could no longer nurse his childhood grievances, it was finally time for him to grow up. The process would prove more difficult than anticipated.

In 1841, Kingston became the seat of the Canadian government, so it was potentially a good time for John A. to make a political move. While Kingston's elite recognized John A. as a young man on the rise, few knew that, beneath his ambition, lay a deeply indolent procrastinator who liked nothing better than staying in bed for days on end reading trashy French novels. One colleague noted that he had "windows in every corner of his mind," but was unsure of what time of day he chose to look through them. As gregarious as he seemed, mastering the art of charming the public, remembering names, and recognizing faces and places with astonishing ease, he counted few people, particularly overly fastidious, "overwashed Englishmen," as true friends.

As the president of the St. Lawrence Warehouse Dock and Wharfage Company and the Manufacturers Life Insurance Company of Toronto, John A. earned enormous prestige in Kingston's business community. At the same time, he recklessly bought real estate for himself with money he removed from his law firm's bank account.

Finally, in 1842, when balancing his private and public personae grew too stressful, he collapsed. Without hesitation, his sisters and mother closed protectively around him as he took to his bed, complaining of indiscriminate stomach pains, for which he took over-the-counter medications such as "Beecham Pills for Bilious Nervous Disorders" and "King's Specific for the Permanent Cure of Dyspepsia and the Severer Forms of Indigestion." For chronic constipation, he tried "Syrup of Figs," made by the California Fig Syrup Co., which promised to "act gently yet promptly on the kidneys, liver, and bowels." When all else failed, he swallowed morphine tablets, which only bound his bowels up more. When doctors prescribed several weeks' rest, he obliged.

He decided to sail to England. Before he stepped on board ship, however, John A. summoned enough strength to join some male cronies in several rounds of the card game Loo. In Loo, a player is dealt either three or five cards and has to abandon the game free of charge or play the cards dealt him, the challenge being to accurately anticipate his opponents' moves. "Politics is a game that requires great coolness," John A. once told a friend. He played Loo the same way he would play politics, with little emotion, lots of stamina, and plenty of bluff. In the end, he easily scooped up the four-hundred-pound pot for himself. The game had lasted three days, but no one was watching the clock. With his winnings securely in his vest pocket, an exultant John A. boarded the *Caledonia* in January 1842 in the company of Thomas Wilson, a representative of the Commercial Bank in Montreal.

After a storm-tossed voyage, the *Caledonia* docked in London on February 17, and John A. spent two weeks touring Westminster Palace, the Tower of London, and other famous sites. Afterwards, he travelled by train to Chester, where Evan Macpherson's 68th Battalion was stationed. Together they reminisced about the days when Evan had formed a successful business partnership in Kingston with John A.'s father, Hugh. From there, John A. weighed his future travel options. "I shall direct my wandering steps wherever my fancy leades me thro," he wrote to his mother almost giddily. He spent time with friends in Gardyne. Then, after two weeks he returned south to Kendal in Westmoreland to meet Thomas Wilson and his father's former business partner Evan Macpherson. There, they fished in the Lake District.

After departing Westmoreland, John A. explored the scenic charms of the university towns of Oxford and Cambridge. His failure to earn a university degree had always bothered him, and one can only imagine his thoughts as the school's slightly patronizing students breezed past him in their caps and gowns, their arms weighed down with books. Perhaps in response, upon returning to London, he ordered almost an entire library of law books in Chancery Lane, the total cost amounting to one hundred pounds of his winnings.

He wrote to his mother on March 3, 1842, extolling the benefits of his first vacation. "Since my arrival in England, my health has been remarkably good. You would be surprised at the breakfast I eat. Wilson rolls his eyes as he sees roll after roll disappear & eggs & bacon after roll. My dinners are equally satisfactory to myself and expensive to my chopman. [Now] only fancy, my commencing my dinner with sole fried, with shrimp sauce, demolishing a large steak, and polishing off with bread & cheese & a quart of *London Stout*. [I] find it necessary to support myself against the tremendous exercise I take every day."

In Edinburgh, he continued to spend money as if it had just been printed. Having disposable income was a novelty for him, and he didn't want to waste his chance to purchase the best of everything for each member of his family. Unlike most men of the time, John A. actually enjoyed buying clothes, comparing colours, fabrics, and cuts. In Scotland, he visited the well-known tailor T. Buckmaster and purchased a black "silk velvet" Highland jacket and a soft Macdonald tartan kilt for himself, a fine wool Glengarry bonnet with plume of high heather for his mother, and fine wool tartan hose for his sisters. The total value of his shopping spree exceeded seventy pounds. Afterwards, he sent the gifts home by ship with special instructions as to their care. Convinced John A. was a man of means, T. Buckmaster not only gave him a discount on his order, but enclosed a free airtight coat case.

Thanks to Edward Wanklyn, a relative of Tom Wilson, John A. gained admittance to the state apartments at Windsor Castle. "Through [Wanklyn's] means I was lionized everywhere," John A. bragged to his mother. "Mr. Wanklyn obtained from Lord De La Warr an order to see the Queen's private apartments, so we saw all the domestic *Conveniences* of Her Majesty and I can assure you, things are as plain & snug as in the family of a private person. [Comfort] is in no case sacrificed for magnificence or show. [In] one of Scott's novels, he speaks of the unrivalled scenery of Windsor, and certainly the prospect of the terrace opened to my eyes a view which I could not before conceive."

To make the day particularly memorable, John A. walked "arm in arm" with the "very pretty girl," Margaret Wanklyn, who was also seeing Windsor Castle's interior for the first time. Margaret's companionship provided a boost to John A.'s ego, and the two spent the day "very agreeably engaged" in "comparing their impressions. *Our ideas sympathized wonderfully,*" John A. wrote home. As the King of Prussia had just visited the palace, its state apartments with their "paraphernalia of royalty" were closed. However, John A. got around this impediment. "By remarkable good fortune," he told his mother, "[Margaret and I] slipt in, and saw the whole magnificence of the Royalty of England. I shall not attempt to describe the fairlies as they will form the subject of a great many conversations when I return."

Accompanied by Margaret, John A. attended theatricals, including several Shakespearean revivals at the Drury Lane Theatre, as well as Robert Browning's *A Blot on the 'Scutcheon*. He also attended burlesques and vaudeville shows, and concerts and ballets at the Royal Albert Saloon on Shepherdess Walk, Hoxton, a theatre distinguished by having two stages built at right angles to each other, one facing an outdoor auditorium, the other a closed theatre. There were also, in John A.'s words, "a countless number of exhibitions of all shapes and sizes" occurring at the time of his visit. While attending these events, he made sure to collect all the catalogues, descriptive accounts of the exhibitions, as well as theatrical playbills for his mother and sisters to pour over upon his return.

To round out his trip, John A. and some acquaintances visited the House of Lords to watch the politicians in action. During his tour, he formed a casual friendship with a young lawyer named Leach. Before he knew it, a month-long vacation had stretched into two months, and John A. felt homesick, as well as "an uneasy desire to be at work." He wrote to Helen, "To a person obliged during all his life to be busy, idleness is no pleasure and I feel assured I shall return to my desk with greater zest and zeal than ever."

Before he returned home, however, he hired a cab to drive him to Manchester to liquidate the remainder of his winnings at Loo. Damask and some iron railings for his Brock Street house were among the items he bought. He also purchased paper hangings and chimney ornaments to send home. Prior to leaving, he attended a Bachelors' Ball at Manchester with Edward Wanklyn and, no doubt, with Edward's sister Margaret, who had made such a favourable impression on him earlier in his trip.

If anything stood out as remarkable concerning his trip, it was his failure to write home praising the virtues of his first cousin, Isabella Clark, the woman who would become his wife in less than two years. Isabella was the daughter of Helen Macdonald's stepsister Margaret and her husband, the late Capt. Alexander Clark, so she was already a member of the Macdonald clan.

Where and when John A. met Isabella remains sketchy. Either Isabella travelled to Scotland to visit him, or he took a side trip to a farmhouse situated three miles from Douglas, the principal city of the Isle of Man, where Isabella lived frugally "in relative obscurity" with her sisters, Margaret and Jane, on the money left to them by their late parents. One of the benefits of living on the Isle of Man during this period was its low income taxes.

Six years older than her husband, Isabella was considered over the hill for her time. *(LAC C004815)*

From the lack of evidence to prove otherwise, it's safe to surmise that Isabella did not initially make a strong impression on John A. For one thing, she was thirty-two years old to John A.'s twenty-seven, and a victim of the prevailing notion that she was well and truly "on the shelf."

Isabella's girlish demeanour seemed caricaturish in a woman her age. Yet she persisted in talking in a soft whisper, forcing visitors to lean closer to hear her. Her conversational topics were not particularly daring, in the manner of John A.'s mother, Helen, or sisters, Moll and Lou. Instead, she enjoyed flowery conversations about fabric patterns or family gossip. Just as significantly, she was no beauty, but possessed a narrow angular face softened only by the brown ringlets that cascaded down each cheek. Her strongest features by far, however, were her large, beautiful blue eyes, with an imploring expression that melted more than one observer's heart.

While John A. might have succumbed to Isabella's fragile femininity, no letters exist to suggest that he fell hard enough to propose marriage to her during his visit abroad. Instead, he returned home eager to build up his professional and political reputations.

In a possible attempt to force his hand, in the fall of 1842 Isabella left England and relocated to Kingston, for an extended visit with her sister Maria, the wife of John Alexander Macpherson (son of Allan Macpherson, the "Laird of Napanee") The trip was apparently undertaken on Isabella's own initiative. If she expected to find John A. as financially flush as he had been when she first met him, she was in for a shock. By the time she arrived, John A. already owed several hundred dollars to friends and banks for loans, including thirty pounds to Justice John McLean of the Midland District, before whom he had defended the alleged rebels of Hastings and Lennox and Addington Counties.

According to tax rolls of the time, John A. also owed money on both his Store Street property and his house on Brock Street. The Brock Street house was valued at ninety pounds, and the Store Street dwelling and office came in at ninety-six pounds. According to the census rolls for 1842, six people from Scotland and one Roman Catholic from Ireland occupied his house. Of the seven people, four were Macdonalds, two were servants, and the other may have been a law clerk. Since John A.'s family had moved into the Brock Street house before he had rented the Store Street property, he was assessed for both properties, placing an added strain on his finances.

The two-storey Brock Street house was located in a prestigious area of town. Shortly before moving into the house in August, John A. wrote Kingston's Town Council asking for permission to make some renovations to his property. These included erecting the iron railing that he had bought in Manchester around the front of the premises, and lowering the street pavement at his expense so it would not obstruct the gate to his house, or allow rainwater to drain onto the property.

While John A. polished his rising star, Isabella demurely settled into her sister's home in Kingston, where she waited patiently for John A. to call. Her nephew, James Pennington Macpherson, who was four years old at the time, recalled Isabella fondly during this period as possessing a "sweet gentleness of manner and tender sympathetic nature," who would "tell [him] fascinating fairy tales or to soothe [his] sorrows with her warm caresses." Anyone who truly knew Isabella, however, perceived the steel that lay beneath her passive exterior. To start with, she had fixed her sights on John A. as a future spouse, and she was not about to suffer the ignominy of returning to the Isle of Man as a spinster. While John A. contemplated his next move, Isabella announced to her family that another sister, Margaret, had met and married a wealthy military man named Greene and moved to Savannah, Georgia, with sister Jane moving in with them. So, unless John A. married Isabella, she had no home on the Isle of Man to return to.

Under these less-than-ideal circumstances, John A. dutifully began calling on Isabella, gradually developing a deep affection, perhaps even love, for her. Certainly, her willingness to listen to him expostulate about himself for hours probably endeared her to him even more. Then, too, as a rising politician, John A. knew it was expedient for him to appear in public with a respectable wife by his side. As far as sex was concerned, however, he possessed a split personality. Passionately attracted to females of questionable moral character, he also believed that sex robbed men of their ability to reason. "There is no wisdom below the belt," he'd lecture subordinates.

So John A. and Isabella entered into an uninspired courtship. Macdonald called on Isabella, drank tea with her in the company of the Macphersons, and strolled with her around town. Yet he did not rush to marry her. Instead, he made plans to heighten his personal profile in Kingston by seeking political office. In February 1843, he offered himself to the electors of Ward 4 in Kingston as alderman, assuring them through newspaper ads that he would spare nothing to fulfill the duties imposed on him. To John A., power was like catnip. It brought him influence over the affairs of his district, but also ensured future entree to even the most exclusive social circles.

If there was one thing John A. had learned from him father, it was how to curry favour. On March 23, 1843, he hosted an elegant reception at his Brock Street house for Canada's newly appointed Governor General, Sir Charles Metcalf. Members of Kingston's elite turned out for the event, the women dressed in their finest silks, the men in tartan kilts and Highland regalia. All of them recognized that John A. was a charismatic man on the rise.

Six days later, a less sartorially attired John A. waded through a sea of flying fists in a downtown tavern to accept his 156-to-43-vote victory over his Irish opponent, Col. Jackson. Ecstatic celebrants carried the men through the streets of Kingston on chairs. After a few steps, those carrying John A.'s chair lost their balance and dumped their precious cargo into a pile of street slush. "Isn't it strange that I should have a downfall so soon?" John A. joked as he rose and brushed himself off, further endearing himself to his electorate.

With his newly enhanced status, John A. experimented with social activism, lobbying to pass a law compelling homeowners to clean their chimneys in order to avoid fires like one that had almost levelled Kingston in 1833. Problematically, virtually every house in town had wooden shingles, and though homeowners were legally obligated to keep two fire ladders on their premises, the ladders were also made of wood.

As an elected official, John A. was now a public figure and, at twenty-eight, very publicly unmarried. To rectify this dilemma, on September 1, 1843, at 10 a.m., he wed Isabella Clark at St. Andrew's Church. Rev. John Machar, who had presided over the church since 1827, performed the ceremony, with Tom Wilson and Charles Stuart serving as witnesses. Allan Macpherson filled in for Isabella's late father by escorting her down the aisle.

No pictures exist of the wedding, however, like most brides over the age of twenty-five, Isabella probably followed the style of the period and avoided wearing white on her wedding day for fear it might clash with her sallower complexion. White also stained easily, so her dress may very well have been blue or green. In her hands was a bouquet of flowers – dried, rather than fresh.

John A. wore his complete suit of Highland dress and accessories, supplied by T. Buckmaster of Edinburgh, including a

The young bridegroom.
(FS Richardson/LAC C003813)

"fine silk velvet Highland Jacket, and Tartan Kilt." When the outfit had arrived from overseas, it even included instructions for dressing. As he and Isabella finished reciting their vows, they slipped matching twenty-four-carat yellow-gold wedding rings, etched with ivy leaves and daisies, onto each other's fingers. Reverend Machar approved of John A.'s choice in a wife. Machar was a strict moralist. In fact, just two months after John A.'s wedding, he refused to preach the annual sermon at the Kingston Society because a ball was scheduled to follow shortly afterwards. His mantra was for women to "respect themselves" and to "eschew immodesty." If little else, Isabella was the picture of propriety.

So, Isabella had landed her man – for the duration of the ceremony. However, the fairy tale ended as soon as the wedding carriage clattered up to the pavement in front of John A.'s Brock Street home. There, family members who had returned early to the house to organize the wedding reception, including Helen,

Margaret, and Louisa, excitedly swarmed the disoriented bride before she could even make it to the doorway of her new home.

No sooner was Isabella in the Macdonald family's custody than John A. reboarded the wedding carriage and travelled across town to join Alexander Campbell in cutting the ceremonial ribbon to the Princess Street law office named Macdonald & Campbell. The partnership agreement between the two men went into effect the same day. Never one to allow his private life to interfere with his public duties, John A. felt an enormous amount of secret pleasure fulfilling two official functions in one day. As Alexander Campbell expressed it in his hand-written memoirs, the social faux pas of dropping his bride to attend to business "may have amused John A.'s half-practical and half-romantic nature."

The partnership agreement was detailed and thorough. John A. would own two-thirds of the business and Campbell, one-third. The partnership did not affect the business coming from the Commercial Bank; as the bank's solicitor, that was exclusively the property of John A. John A. would reimburse Campbell for any frequent absences by paying him five hundred pounds over and above the amount Campbell earned as his share of the partnership. Macdonald agreed to take no more than six hundred pounds a year from the business, and Campbell agreed not to take more than four hundred pounds. Perhaps most importantly (and one can imagine Campbell requested this provision), all purchases, investments, and speculations made with funds of the partnership were to be placed in a joint account to be divided along the terms of the partnership. Finally, Campbell would be paid two hundred and fifty pounds per annum for his services, in addition to his agreed-upon share.

While John A. and Alexander Campbell were indulging in mutual self-congratulations, back at the Brock Street home Isabella carefully removed her wedding dress, replaced it with a plain one, wrapped her brittle flowers in coloured paper, and got down to the business of hosting her own wedding reception. Against Lou and Moll's conversational gymnastics, she possessed pitifully little skill. She had no real interest in politics, and didn't pretend to now that she had achieved her goal of snaring John A. Instead, she withdrew to a corner, perfecting her best Mona Lisa smile.

The Brock Street house was "large and commodious," and despite the marriage's dubious beginnings, filled with harmonious contentment for the first year and a half. Two horses, one named Mohawk and the other named Charlie, boarded in a barn located on the property. On fine sunny days, Isabella rode into town in the family's carriage, holding a parasol above her head, returning with sweets for the family dinner table. She knew better than to try to take side trips to John A.'s office, where her presence would have proved jarring and disruptive.

On frequent occasions, Isabella's nephew, James Pennington Macpherson, visited the couple at their Brock Street home, where he usually found John A. sipping sherry in the library. Whenever James drew close, John A. patted him affectionately on the head, then began reading a book as a large grandfather clock ticked loudly in the background. The two seldom spoke. Once John A. became absorbed in a book, it was virtually impossible to draw his attention away from it. Nevertheless, James found the atmosphere pleasing, since he had a corner to himself where there were "numerous illustrated books with such captivating titles as *King Arthur and His Knights of the Round Table*, and *The Arabian Nights Entertainment*."

James recalls that, if he met John A. on his way home from school, John A. would embrace him in a bear hug, then, feigning sternness, would pretend that James was a delinquent debtor who owed him money. John A. would then "liquidate this debt to the extent of the half pence he might have in his pocket," much to James's profound glee. "I grew to regard him, not only as the richest but as the most generous man I had ever known," he wrote in his book, *Life of The Right Hon. Sir John A. Macdonald.*

Pennington reveals that most of John A.'s family still considered Isabella an unknown quantity and worried that she lacked the strength to deal with her husband's social demands. The introversion that John A. had considered so coquettishly charming during their courtship quickly hardened into anti-social behaviour. Even friends from the Old Country found themselves unwelcome at her door. One evening, an elderly couple from Scotland showed up unexpectedly at the Brock Street house. The woman introduced herself to John A. as Isabella's wet nurse, and expressed a warm desire to see her. Despite John A.'s entreaties, Isabella refused to follow him downstairs to meet with her childhood caregivers. The two visitors ultimately left, crestfallen.

In November 1843, Montreal was formally designated as the next seat of government. Overnight Kingston's lucrative real-estate market dried up, as investors realized bureaucrats would be moving to their new home base. The move also meant that the value of John A.'s land acquisitions threatened to bottom out unless he could come up with an alternative lure for potential investors.

John Counter, the mayor of Kingston, hosted a boisterous meeting in early December, at which Governor General Metcalf was present. There, John A. stressed that Kingstonians deserved "a constructive programme from government, but all the municipal officials had done was to effect the ruin of Kingston." Raising one fist in the air, he pledged to continue to fight to make Kingston, "the town in which I have lived so long," a voice in provincial politics, and not merely a satellite city filled with empty buildings and broken dreams. The meeting was a rousing success, and established John A. as a Conservative MP-in-waiting, not to mention a savvy real-estate investor, intent on protecting his properties from total economic collapse.

By March 1844, Conservatives were ripe for an election and, to represent them, Kingstonians picked the one man they knew possessed as much charisma as he did horse sense: John A. Macdonald. More than two hundred and twenty people signed a document endorsing his candidacy. In response, John A. wrote in the April 3 issue of the *Kingston Herald*:

> With feelings of greater pride and gratitude than I can express, I have received your requisitions inviting me to become a candidate for the representation of Kingston at the next vacancy. [The] mode in which I can best evince my high sense of the honor you have done me is at once to lay aside all personal considerations, and accede to your request.

In order to accede to the request, John A. was prepared to put his marriage second. In response, after leading a peripatetic life filled with economic uncertainty, thirty-five-year-old Isabella suddenly dug in her heels, unwilling to accompanying her husband to whichever city government business might take him. In Montreal, she would have to be more sociable, and it would take relatives days, if not weeks, to visit in the event of an emergency.

Meanwhile, John A. remained trapped in limbo, still to be elected, yet itching to serve. Even worse, by June, most of the elected public officers had already moved their files and possessions to Montreal. Governor General Metcalf, for example, had left Kingston on June 20. With the election not scheduled to take place until October 14, John A. had to twiddle his thumbs in Kingston, attend to his law practice, and, when he had time, try to salvage his already-ailing marriage.

To pacify a discontented Isabella, he agreed to accompany her on a trip to Savannah over the summer to visit her sister Margaret

Greene. Due to the length of time it took to travel to Savannah by carriage, steamer, and bus, Isabella and John A. had no sooner arrived than they had to turn around and return to Kingston. Certainly, John A. grumbled throughout most of the trip. He had never been a great admirer of Americans, particularly Southerners, and regularly mocked their accents every time he had an opportunity to do so.

By September, Isabella and John A. were back home. They had barely finished unpacking their luggage when a set of personal calamities befell them. First, Helen Macdonald suffered a slight stroke, and then Louisa came down with a case of severe influenza. Isabella, meanwhile, began suffering mystifying migraine-like headaches, with painful pins-and-needles sensations afflicting her extremities. She took to bed, for hours at a time, then for days. But whereas Helen and Louisa gradually recovered from their ailments, Isabella did not. By the time the leaves began falling from the trees, it was clear the honeymoon between her and John A. was over. They had been married for less than two years. Very possibly, it had dawned on her that, in marrying John A., she had permanently tethered herself to an absentee husband who lusted for power more ardently than he lusted for her. The autonomy she'd enjoyed with her sisters on the Isle of Man had become a distant memory. Meanwhile, the more publicly recognizable her husband became, the more her marriage threatened to become a dog-and-pony show, each social engagement becoming fodder for newspaper gossips.

Undeterred by Isabella's discomfort, in late September John A. called a meeting at Metcalf's Inn to reconfirm his Conservative Party loyalty. Those assembled quickly endorsed John A. as their candidate. His opponent was Anthony Manahan, an Irish-Catholic firebrand.

The election took place at 9 p.m. on Monday, October 14. It was an open poll in which each vote raised cheers or jeers, and tavern keepers kept voters well supplied with whisky at the candidates' expense. After two days, the counting was double-checked, and the math was with Macdonald. He had won his seat by a vote of 275 to 42, and was now off to Montreal as the Conservative member for Kingston.

Within a week, John A. kissed his mother and sisters affectionately as he bade them goodbye at the wharf for the trip downriver to Montreal, while Isabella, still ailing, nursed her misery back at the Brock Street house. Alexander Campbell stayed behind to oversee the law practice, although his resentments would build as John A.'s absences stretched from weeks to months.

In his excitement to take his seat in the legislative assembly of Upper and Lower Canada, John A. had forgotten to reserve accommodation in Montreal, so he booked himself into a room in a boarding house located over a grocery store run by a man named Henderson, at the corner of St. Maurice and St. Henry Streets. Newspapers of the day lauded him for sacrificing his commercial success as a lawyer in exchange for selflessly devoting himself to a career in public service. Little did they understand what a small sacrifice this had been for him.

In Montreal, twenty-nine-year-old John A. explored the joys of being a bachelor husband by touring the city by gaslight. Thoughts of Isabella did not prevent him from frequenting taverns with dubious reputations, for which he seemed to have a penchant. It is perhaps no coincidence that during this period, he kept folded up in his wallet a favourite verse written by Irish poet and playwright Oliver Goldsmith. Entitled "On the Glory of her Sex, Mrs. Mary Blaize," John A.'s favourite stanza read, "She strove the neighbourhood to please / With manners wondrous winning / She never followed wicked ways / Unless when she was sinning." John A.'s sympathy for fallen women would remain part of his character throughout his life. Several decades later, when his Cabinet would end the practice of encouraging females to immigrate to the prairies as potential wives for prairie farmers, John A. would remark, "[We] must *protect* the Canadian whores."

On November 28, John A. took his seat as a parliamentary backbencher. The House's first order of business was to elect a Speaker, in this case Sir Allan McNab, a long-time member of the Family Compact, who won the position by just three votes.

John A. eased his way into policy-making issue by issue. The first petition he presented was on behalf of Henry Smith, the warden of Kingston Penitentiary. Smith sought an increase in salary. John A.'s second petition concerned incorporating the College of Regiopolis at Kingston, a Catholic institution separate from Queen's University, and asking the legislative assembly to pass an act enabling the college to hold real and personal property yielding annual revenues of five thousand pounds. The third petition, on behalf of Alexander Smith, boot and shoemakers, sought for a duty to be placed upon boot and shoes imported from the United States.

During his first session, John A. also introduced a bill to incorporate the Wolfe Island Kingston & Toronto Railroad Co., and moved the second reading of the Montreal & Lacine Railroad bill. For a neophyte, he was already scoring political points.

In his biography of John A. entitled *Reminiscences*, J. E. Collins noted that as John A.'s confidence grew, so, too, did his almost theatrical flamboyance. His quick and jerky walk invited silent jeers from his fellow House members and he would take his parliamentary seat almost uncertainly, resembling a "bird alighting in a hesitating way from a flight," the image enhanced by his "quick and all comprehending glance."

John A.'s biggest influence in his early months was William Henry Draper, who had arrived in Canada in 1820 when he was nineteen years old, studied law, then joined the office of Attorney General John Beverley Robinson in Toronto. Draper had soon carved out a successful career as a member of Parliament as the colonel of a York militia regiment, as Solicitor General, and then as Attorney General. Macdonald had in fact first met Draper as his legal adversary in the William Brass child rape case. Draper was Anglican and should have been popular with Toronto's Family Compact, but his moderate stance on several issues shook their confidence in his ability to enact the Compact's hard-line conservative policies. By aligning himself with Draper, John A. was courting the moderate side of the party, while at the same time trying not to alienate members of the more rigid Family Compact, which included Allan McNab and John A.'s school friend, John Hillyard Cameron. Ultimately, John A. recognized that the strongest bond that united the disparate elements of the Conservative Party was their allegiance to the British Crown. Toward that allegiance, John A. was unwavering. More than once he had said, "A British subject I was born, and a British subject I shall die."

High political ideals aside, when the session finally ended in January 1845, House members celebrated as if they were in a frat boys' dorm. Playful politicians threw dollar bills at one another or affixed paper pigtails to their coats as they chased one another around the room.

In contrast to the criticism of his peers, John A. received glowing reviews in the press for his parliamentary acuity. On January 21, 1845, the *Montreal Transcript* called him "a young man of prepossessing and gentlemanly appearance, with something frank and open in his bearing." The columnist further noted, "I understand that Mr. Mcdonald [sic] enjoys a good practice in Kingston, where his election shows that he is very popular. From what I have seen of him, I should say he is 'a rising man,' and not likely to disappoint the expectations of his friends."

The "rising man" of Montreal found a far different scene awaiting him in Kingston. For one thing, his home was in a state of emotional disarray. His mother was ill again, after suffering another cerebral hemorrhage that left her temporarily paralyzed on her right side. She recuperated quickly, thanks to Louisa's and Margaret's constant nursing. Isabella, meanwhile, also required round-the-clock care for her recurrent attacks of "neuralgia," which left her prostrate for much of the time John A. was away. Upon his return, however, she miraculously rallied. Even before John A.'s return, an exhausted Louisa set off on a rest cure to Coburg. She left no forwarding address. Although she felt physically better, Isabella did not appreciate her sister-in-law's defection. "We have heard nothing of her since she left. How would you like that?" Isabella wrote her sister Margaret Greene in a huff.

Now that her husband was home virtually full-time, with the exception of a few side trips on business to Toronto, Isabella excitedly planned a trip to New Haven, Connecticut, in June to visit Margaret Greene, who had travelled north from her home in Savannah. Isabella worried that Helen's illness, which had stolen the spotlight from her, might jeopardize the travel plans. "Mama is nicely again & may we feel the blessing. But, Oh! God it was hard to see her face so twisted," she confided in a rambling and disjointed June 11, 1845, letter to Margaret. "I am thank God *much* better, but my head is very confused & I am not sure what I say . . . [I] will get a red petticoat for you to wear with the yellow stockings."

She had taken for granted that Margaret Macdonald would accompany her and John A. to the United States as a companion and nurse. Already overwhelmed with caring for her sick mother, however, Margaret forcefully instructed Isabella that she would be unable to accompany her stateside. Isabella immediately complained to Margaret Greene of Margaret Macdonald's intransigence. A few days later, Margaret Greene wrote a letter to Isabella in which she hinted at the potentially dire consequences to Isabella's health due to Margaret Macdonald's decision. Isabella made sure to read her sister's letter aloud to Margaret and then awaited her response.

Feeling thoroughly on the defensive, and worried that her lack of co-operation might be misinterpreted as lack of affection, Moll wrote to Margaret Greene, trying to explain that no ulterior motives or dark feelings lay beneath her decision not to accompany Isabella and John A. to New Haven. "[I] feel the greatest reluctance at remaining so far from home as the attack Mamma had was accompanied by strong symptoms of paralysis," she explained. "Now that her [Helen's] alarm has passed away, you will not I hope, my dear Mrs. Greene impute my unwillingness to remain with Isabella to an alteration in my feeling of affection towards her but to the real cause my fears for my mother, perhaps they may be groundless, but who could tell?" Then, instead of staying the course, Margaret hesitated, lifted the pen off the page, and, losing her internal fortitude, offered a compromise. Conceding that Isabella was "unable to take care of herself," and that John A. was "nearly as useless as a child," she assured Margaret Greene that she would accompany Isabella and John A. as far as Oswego, but would need to return home immediately thereafter.

Miffed by what she perceived as Margaret's stubbornness, Isabella suffered a devastating recurrence of her mysterious illness. The problem was, nobody truly knew what was wrong with her. Doctors diagnosed her as suffering from everything from tic douloureux, a devastating pain in the fifth nerve of the face, to "uterine neuralgia." For menstrual cramps, Isabella almost certainly drank a popular solution called Styptic Balm, which contained the unsavoury combination of sulphuric acid, turpentine, tea, and water. For other pains, she uncorked her prescription of liquid opium, and drank liberally, until the pain abated and she was again in soporific bliss. Opium, also referred to as "God's own medicine," was available in every chemist's shop in Kingston. Most doctors liberally prescribed it to keep unruly women quiet. The drug could be drunk or smoked, though some applied it as a paste, ate it, inserted it in as a suppository, or injected it.

John A. could see the toll the drug was taking on his wife. By July, he was referring to Isabella openly as "the invalid." Having spent the bulk of the summer sitting by her bedside, listening to her groan in pain, he wondered if "her terrible disease" would prevent them from being able to travel to New Haven and then on to Savannah with Margaret Greene by summer's end. "It may be days – nay weeks – before she has rallied sufficiently to attempt any journey," he wrote his sister-in-law.

Yet, by the following day, Isabella's pain miraculously dissipated, though she continued to suffer numbness in one leg, and such an "irregularity in the action of the heart" that her husband sent for Dr. Sampson, a crusty old navy surgeon, to get to the root of her illness. Sampson had a reputation of being "magnificent in appearance, very clever, if abrupt, very kind, if blunt." He was immune to manipulation, and therefore one of Isabella's least favourite Kingston physicians. John A. had originally met Sampson in 1839 when as a twenty-four-year-old lawyer, he had attended a meeting at St. Andrew's Presbyterian Church at which the subject of a proposed college to be erected in Kingston was discussed. John A. had tried to pass a motion in the House. However, it wouldn't be until 1855 that Dr. Sampson was appointed the first professor of Clinical Medicine and Surgery at the Queen's University Medical School.

Sampson briefly examined Isabella and then enigmatically stated that he simply could not "relieve her." Upon analyzing this statement, several contemporary physicians conclude that Sampson believed Isabella was suffering from hypochondria. Quite simply, Sampson could find nothing organically wrong. None of her symptoms comported with any known organic conditions, including lupus, migraine, neuritis, trigeminal neuralgia, or tic douloureux. Instead, she seemed possessed by a potpourri of all these diseases, which also seemed to be exacerbated by failing to get her own way.

John A. was in a fog of fear. He was convinced Isabella was about to die. He wrote her sisters, Margaret Greene and Jane Clark. "I do not therefore hesitate to tell you, that unless God in his infinite mercy works an immediate change for the better, it is impossible for her to remain in her exhausted state for many days . . . [God] bless & protect both of you my beloved sisters and enable you to meet the impending anguish with fortitude & resignation."

As Dr. Sampson might have predicted, Isabella did not die. Rather, within six days of his visit, she was strong enough to accompany John A. to Oswego by steamer. The stunning speed of her recuperation was undoubtedly due in part to the fact that Margaret had capitulated about going and also had ultimately succeeded in convincing Louisa to return to Kingston and accompany the group to Oswego, leaving Helen Macdonald in the care of servants. Even John A. had initially failed to perceive the manipulative nature of Isabella's illness. Instead, he persistently feared losing her. One can only imagine the sight of Isabella, carried by servants like a Roman goddess on a litter all the way down to the gangplank at Kingston harbour, moaning at each jerk and sway. "The exhaustion produced by carrying Isabella down to the boat, was dreadful to witness. We thought she would die on the dock," John A. wrote to Margaret Greene. "The weather was so stormy that all our party were sick, Isabella dreadfully so, and yet strange to say her health and strength seemed to return to her, and here we now are safely landed and lodged at the Welland House."

Isabella and John A. didn't leave Oswego until late September. As a relieved Margaret and Louisa finally returned home, John A. and Isabella travelled on to Syracuse, then Jersey City, and eventually to New Haven, where they joined Margaret and Jane. There, Isabella finally relaxed, though she knew an even-more-arduous journey awaited her to Savannah, where she intended to spend the winter with her sisters. In New Haven, Margaret Greene introduced John A. to some of her influential friends and relatives, not to mention to the delights of fresh peaches and milk, as well as other "little delicacies," as John A. described them. They also took turns nursing Isabella. Winter was fast approaching, and John A. felt an urgent need to reach Savannah before the weather turned savage. Margaret Greene and Jane did not accompany John A. and Isabella on the last leg of their journey. Margaret needed to finalize the details of selling her New Haven home, and could not join the couple until the negotiations were completed.

Isabella suffered greatly during her trip to their first stop, Philadelphia, and as usual, her husband felt powerless to help her. Some dockhands strapped her to a chair, then carried her from the dock to a waiting steamboat. Upon reaching Philadelphia, another set of dockhands placed her back in a chair and carried her down the gangplank to the city's dock. There, the couple rented a hack to take them to their boarding house. The quarter-of-a-mile drive turned out to be so bumpy that, by the time she arrived at the boarding house, John A. noted Isabella "was obliged to subdue pain by opium."

The Macdonalds' stay in Philadelphia lasted longer than either expected, due to Isabella's grogginess from opium ingestion. For more than a week, the couple remained cooped up in their room, as the rain fell outside their windows. John A. never managed to escape the room unless "Madam Isa," as he came to refer to his wife derisively, fell asleep. He wished Margaret Greene and her sister Jane had been there to tend to their sister. "She never speaks of it, but I am perfectly conscious how much she suffers from being away from you, & without the aid of your untiring and judicious attentions, which were always at hand night & by day when needed," he wrote his sisters-in-law.

As the endless days passed, John A. despaired of anyone "seducing" him from his "allegiance" to his "Petticoat Government" (as he referred to Isabella's influence) until a friend named Mr. Robinson invited him to a *conversazione* of the Wistar Club at Dr. Randolph's home. There, John A. met "all the Science &

Belles Lettres of Philadelphia" in between nibbles of terrapin and swigs of expensive champagne. "Like the apostles my spirit was willing but my flesh was weak & required those creature comforts," he admitted. A few days later, he escaped again and "sauntered" through the "city of marble steps, broad brims & scrubbing brushes" to impulsively call on Mrs. Biddle, the wife of Thomas Biddle, a Philadelphia businessman whom he'd met at the Belles Lettres of Philadelphia evening. "I like her self possessed English manner very much," he confessed by letter to Margaret Greene, adding, "She is a ladylike & intelligent person and I regret having had so small an opportunity of knowing her."

John A.'s charm achieved its desired effect on women – so much so that they soon reciprocated his advances, without prior notice. One Saturday, "a sweet pretty woman" whose name he recognized called on John A. when he was away from his and Isabella's boarding house. Rather then feel relief at avoiding an awkward social situation, a few days later John A. set about trying to find her address, going so far as to ostentatiously riffle through the pages of the local telephone directory in Isabella's presence. "[But] the directory was vague & I was stupid, & so I did not see her again, much to Isabella's delight, who says she does not like my taking so much to your lady friends," he told Margaret Greene.

Was John A. drinking heavily again? His careless carousing suggests he was almost certainly doing so. In spite of Isabella's jealousy, he even began to write flirtatious notes to Margaret Greene. "By the way, sister," he wrote, "there is a latin proverb Noscitur a Sociis, which may be translated for the benefit of the country members, birds of a feather flock together. I always considered you a *Charming Woman*, but I did not calculate for all your friends being so."

Rather than curtail his effusions when he saw the negative effect they were having on Isabella, John A. became even bolder in his letters to Greene. "I have only to say, that you will confer a great favor on me by sitting down & writing me letters of credence to *every one* of your Yankee lady friends, and it will go hard but I deliver most of them. [Tell] Aunt Maxwell I am resolved to take her by storm, some day or other. I am resolved too, that she *shall* like me & be good to me, & give me some of that ginger bread, that I only got a taste of. Just enough to make me like Oliver Twist 'Ask for more.'"

By early November, John A. and Isabella were once again on the road. They had made it only as far as Baltimore in their seemingly endless trek to Savannah. Back in Montreal, the House was back in session and more than one of John A.'s peers noticed his absence. As for John A. himself, before he had even reached his destination, he was desperate to return to the corridors of power.

They wearily rode a carriage to the U.S. Hotel in Baltimore, where they attempted to check in. However, much to John A.'s anger, the hotel denied the existence of his reservation. Desperate for rest, John A. and Isabella climbed into yet another horse-drawn carriage and thundered across a heavily rutted road to another hotel. By the time Isabella reached the second hotel, she was in "physical agony." As soon as the couple entered their room, she practically ripped open her "blister box of medicines." With a mixture of fear and fascination, John A. watched her shakily apply opium oil "in large quantities" to her extremities, and drink it from a tiny flask. The entire trip to Savannah was turning into a disaster, with no end in sight.

Finally, "taking the Pilgrim's staff in her hand," Isabella, with John A. at her side, boarded a steamer down the Chesapeake Bay to Norfolk, where they then transferred to a James River steamer. From there, they took a side trip to Wilmington, Deleware, for a rest. Once in Wilmington, they checked into the Franklin Hotel. The house was "tolerably quiet & clean," and despite the fact the owner's name was "Battle," John A. remembered him as a "messenger of peace."

From Wilmington, they took another steamer to Charleston and finally, exultantly, glided by another steamer into Savannah, in John A.'s words a "city of sandy streets" and "circular drive-ways." The couple boarded a bus at ten-thirty at night and jiggled uncomfortably along the uneven dirt road to a local boarding house. They took the first accommodation they could find: "two rooms in the rear of the basement story." Though Isabella suffered a "furious attack" of what John A. referred to as "tic" shortly after checking into their rooms, she resisted the assistance of her blister box. John A. feigned pleasure at securing temporary lodgings, but beneath his exterior calm, he was impatient to return to Montreal to do the work he felt destined to do.

To compensate for his frustration to not yet being able to return home, John A. accepted an invitation from friends of Margaret Greene to attend a local "Whig meeting," where Sen. John Macpherson Berrien (senator for Georgia and one-time Attorney General for the United States) was speaking. John A. felt Berrien was all bluster and no bite, and told his relatives so. "He is evidently an able man, with great fluency and force of expression, but has the great fault of American speakers (with, I believe the single exception of [Daniel] Webster) of being too theatrical in his manner, & turgid in style." After the two-hour meeting ended, John A. did not allow his low opinion of Berrien's speaking style to prevent him from accepting an invitation to sip peach brandy at Mr. Burroughs's house, Mr. Burroughs being Mr. Berrien's father-in-law.

The following day, John A. found three letters from Margaret Greene at the town's post office, in which she included the names of even more individuals throughout town. But John A. had no intention of staying for any length of time. As yet, he hadn't even made any steps toward securing lodgings for Isabella at Mrs. Hardy's boarding house – one of the best known in the town. He worried about how she would be able to care for herself without him near her, and he wrote to Margaret, urging her and Jane to leave New Haven and come to Savannah as fast as possible, so they could nurse Isabella during the winter while he was away "among the frosts and snow of Canada, sucking my paws like any other bear." He expected to be home by the beginning of December, only two weeks away. He regretted leaving, yet yearned to return to the familiar though "cold comfort of Canada again."

John and Isabella had committed a blunder of the first order by travelling to Savannah without any definitive itinerary or any idea of who might care for Isabella upon their arrival. No matter how many nurses John A. hired to care for her until Margaret Greene arrived, it was going to cost him money – money he didn't have, though he was still pulling in three-quarters of the earnings of his law firm, thanks to Alexander Campbell's dogged work.

As it turned out, Margaret Greene and Jane didn't arrive in Savannah until the middle of January. Margaret had suffered an illness, and the negotiations over the sale of the house had gone more slowly than she'd hoped. As soon as they arrived, however, John A. felt compelled to rush home to Kingston, as well as to discover what political business he'd missed in Montreal. Rather than make Isabella's heart grow *fonder*, however, John A.'s absence only made her heart grow *stronger*. In Margaret's and Jane's company, Isabella's health improved exponentially. She sat up, spoke, and ate hearty meals. She even accepted the use of the "comfortable carriage" of family friend Mrs. Kollock for tours of town. Indeed, Isabella's restoration to health was so miraculous that John A. dared hope that she might yet return to him in "complete health, strength, and spirits." A darker secret, however, lurked beneath the surface of the Macdonalds' marriage, one at which Dr. Sampson had only hinted. Isabella's illness may have been hysterical in nature, with the stress of living with the Macdonald women exacerbating her feelings of alienation from her own family.

Each positive letter from Margaret Greene must have made John A. wonder again whether he might be a contributing factor in his wife's illness. By February 27, 1846, he was back in Kingston, but by now his long-repressed demons had finally caught up with him. He was drinking heavily again. He disappeared from Kingston. Several biographers of John A.'s, including Dr. Donald Swainson in *Sir John A. Macdonald: The Man and the Politician*, claim that, emancipated from his wife's sickroom, John A. joined a young lawyer named John Rose of Montreal for a bizarre visit somewhere just south of the U.S. border to let off steam. The story made the rounds of society gossips in its day, although it wasn't until several years later, after a written account of it landed on the desk of Britain's future colonial secretary, Lord Carnarvon, that Carnarvon made it public. He told acquaintances the following:

> When quite a young man [Sir John A. Macdonald] and Sir John Rose, and a third, whose name I forget, went into the States and wandered about as strolling musicians. Macdonald played some rude instrument, Rose enacted the part of a bear and danced, and the third did something else. To the great amusement of themselves and everyone else, they collected pense [sic] by their performance in wayside taverns, etc.

If the story is true, within a few days, John A. was back on the wagon and back in Kingston. His professional bridges were not yet blazing, but they were smouldering. As fast as he tried to smother one fire, another one broke out. He assured Alexander Campbell that he would make time to handle the portion of the legal cases he was required to take care of under their terms of co-operation, but his diligence lasted no longer than a month. By the end of March, he was back in his seat in Parliament, resuming where he had left off.

Even this return to relative normalcy, however, was tempered by John A.'s continuing disputes with Alexander Campbell over reparations. Not only had John A. got himself into grave debt, he had betrayed the trust of Campbell once again by using company

funds to pay his personal expenses, endangering the reputation of
the practice and of Campbell. Under the partnership agreement,
the debts of one had to be covered by the other partner. And yet,
even now, John A.'s charm achieved the near impossible. To
compel his exceptionally capable partner to stay, John negotiated
a new contract in which he agreed to pay Campbell five hundred
pounds up front, as compensation for his long absences. Campbell
was also to earn profits from the Commercial Bank, business that
had previously been exclusively John A.'s. Humiliatingly, John A.
also agreed to take no more than six hundred pounds out of the
company profits for personal use over each year.

After he had had his fingers slapped, John A.'s professional
life looked up, while his personal life remained unfulfilling. To a
man of John A.'s passions, it must have seemed absurd to the point
of farce that he ended up marrying an invalid, who flourished best
when high on narcotics and out of his presence. Isabella lingered
in Savannah for more than a year. Finally, when she sensed her
husband could endure no more procrastination, she informed
him she felt sufficiently improved to travel to New York for
Christmas of 1846, where the two finally reunited.

It didn't take long for Isabella's passion to dissipate. After a
sweetly romantic interlude with John A., she suddenly experienced a relapse of the excruciatingly painful symptoms that had
plagued her during their trip to Savannah. Over the holidays,
they stayed in the dimly lit quarters of her boarding house. For
hours he sat reading books, while, on the rain-slicked streets
below his window, shoppers hurried to buy last-minute gifts.
Soon, he would have to decide whether to stay or to go.

IV

ADDICTED TO LOVE

John A. faced a dilemma in January 1847. Should he remain by the side of the ailing Isabella in her New York boarding house, thus imperilling his chances of political advancement, or should he return to Kingston? The answer seemed remarkably easy. He returned to his brideless Brock Street house in Kingston, where at least his sisters Louisa and Margaret could care for him.

By now, John A. supposed that much of Isabella's "sciatica" originated from her reclining in bed for hours at a time in one position. Nevertheless, he noted wryly that distracted by good news, she could rally with extraordinary speed. For example, at the same time that she proclaimed her pain most acute, she seriously considered accepting an invitation to travel to Swampscott, Massachusetts, to visit a beloved old friend named Mrs. Field, whom she'd known since childhood. "I really wonder now how I ever had the courage – the self-denial – to obey the doctors in New York, and sometime refuse her," she wrote to her astonished sister Margaret Greene.

Was Isabella's health improving by remaining in New York? Not really, but she certainly was inflicting intense loneliness on her husband. In Savannah, she had seen with her own eyes his eagerness to seek out and flirt with her female friends and relatives. Accordingly, she tugged the reins of his metaphorical bridle hard enough to remind him she was very much of his life, if not in it. Plagued by debt collectors, political responsibilities, and Isabella's incessant emotional neediness, John A.'s strength often buckled, leading him to view himself a condemned man. "Like a thief on a treadmill, I must step on, or be dragged," he noted in a letter to Louisa.

During his absence in New York, Queen Victoria had appointed John A. as a Queen's Counsel. He was pleased with the honour, informing Margaret Greene by letter that he now had the "Mighty right of wearing a Silk Gown, instead of a Stuff one," and earned "rank and privilege" over his brethren. He had not lobbied for the position, which made the honour all the sweeter. The problem was that he effectively had no wife with whom to share his success.

On January 11, 1846, Isabella rallied sufficiently to write "in her own trembling handwriting" a sentimental Happy Birthday note to her husband. Still, John A. didn't budge from Kingston to visit her. Ultimately, there was only one piece of news that finally persuaded him to re-enter the city he referred to derisively as the "American Babylon." Isabella was pregnant.

To John A., New York was no place for his first child to be born. Ever since the Fenian invasions of the 1830s, he considered the city a festering pool of Irish discontent. In 1845, a second wave of Irish inhabitants had sailed to New York to escape the Great Famine. Now they crowded into neighbourhoods like Sweeney's Shambles in the city's fourth ward and Five Points in the sixth ward, which Charles Dickens toured in the 1840s and in his book *American Notes*, described as "loathsome, drooping, and decayed." Dickens learned that without skills, young men turned to crime, and women to prostitution, earning the nickname "nymphs of the pave." Even Manhattan tolerated what it termed its "underclass." During the evenings, homosexuals and cross-dressers spilled onto the streets out of dance halls.

On April 5, John A. and Isabella's sister Maria Macpherson finally arrived in New York to provide reinforcements for John A.'s exhausted sister Margaret, who had travelled ahead and had been nursing Isabella for the past several weeks. For John A., it was desperately difficult to hear his wife cry out in pain when she suffered "critical attacks" of "uterine neuralgia" that ran down one side of her body due to *his* baby's increasing weight. In spite of her physical agonies, during John A.'s absence, Isabella had managed to find a doctor who suited her tastes; in short, one who acquiesced to her every demand. John A. loathed Dr. Washington's "obsequious" tactic of "worming his way into Isabella's good graces," particularly his indulging her request to allow only two visitors at a time into her dark, depressing room, which reeked of the sweet scent of opium-powdered sherry. Despite her delirium, Isabella was acutely aware of the strain she was placing on her family members. When Margaret Macdonald briefly "lost her usual presence of mind" when Isabella writhed in agony, Isabella instantly noted her distress and panicked, being soothed only by Maria's ministrations.

As an unfortunate by-product of her drug ingestion, Isabella struggled against lapsing into paranoia – without success. She misinterpreted one of her sister Margaret's letters, thinking it accused John A. of "cutting" Nathanael Greene, the son of Margaret Greene's brother-in-law, also named Nathanael Greene. When she verbally lashed out at John A. over what she interpreted as a social snub, he was flabbergasted. "I have no recollection of seeing Mr. Greene but once, and that was when I had the pleasure of conversing with him in his own office on Beaver St.," he tried to explain to her, adding, "If I met him at any other time, I must either have not seen him at all, or not recognized him. Should he be under that impression that I did act in this way I beg of you, in justice to me to write to him that I am not conscious of having done so."

Assured by doctors that there was nothing more he could do, within a month, John A. again returned to Montreal. With each of his absences, his party had grown fonder toward him. On May 6, the Honourable William Morris, who had joined the legislative council after the union of Upper and Lower Canada in 1841 as receiver general, offered his position to John A., while he moved on to become president of the executive council. Before he accepted the position, John A. had many factors to consider. By accepting the job, he had to face forfeiting his two-hundred-and-fifty-pound income from his law firm, Campbell & Macdonald. The second was the strain a minister's life would place on a wife and child. After all, Isabella was never going to be the kind of hearty woman capable of braving the rough-and-tumble political campaign trail.

There was no denying that John A. made an odd choice for receiver general, especially since he had never proved himself adept at either paying or collecting his own bills on time. Despite these drawbacks, on May 9, 1847, John A. officially accepted the post. After all, if he was going to be answerable to higher-ups in the party, he wanted to approve of just who those higher-ups would be. "I like to steer my own course," he argued.

Unimpressed with his promotion, the *Globe* newspaper of Toronto dismissed John A. as a "harmless man" and a "third class lawyer" who, after two sessions in Parliament, "had barely opened his mouth during the whole time." The *Montreal Gazette* of May 12, 1847, was even less charitable.

> The intrusion of a young lawyer into the situation of Receiver General appears to our eyes, and if we are not very much mistaken, will appear also to those of the public, a blunder of the most stupid kind. Although practically there may be very little for the Receiver General to

do, still the office is one which ought not to be held by a lawyer, and we are totally at a loss to conceive what could have induced His Excellency's advisors to recommend Mr. Macdonald to fill it.

Less than a month later, John A.'s mother suffered another "spell," or mild stroke. "Such attacks are not uncommon in the aged people and are of course to be guarded against," he wrote to her from Montreal with an external calm that belied his internal distress. He told Helen he would "look with anxiety for another letter from Margaret tomorrow informing me of your being convalescent."

His mother's health was hardly his only worry. Isabella was nearing her due date, and each cryptic letter he received from her caregivers was gloomier than the last. Isabella was conscious. She wasn't conscious. Doctors feared a spontaneous abortion. There was no cause for alarm. Then, in mid-June, all communiqués suddenly ceased, throwing him into a panic. . . . ["I] am becoming very anxious. Pray let Marg write me whenever she hears from Maria as I will otherwise get but few acounts about Isabella," he begged his mother, who herself was still struggling to rally from her own illness.

As much as he may have wished to rush to Isabella's side, John A. forced himself to remain in the House. As the ministers around him engaged in tumultuous parliamentary debates, he distractedly sat at his desk doodling notes to Margaret Greene. "Our House is at this moment making all kinds of speeches [sic]," he wrote. "The great struggle for power & place is going on, and it is impossible to say what may be the result."

As soon as Parliament was prorogued on July 29, John A. rushed to New York. When he arrived two day's later, he found Isabella suffering severe contraction-like pains. These pains were almost certainly not uterine neuralgia (a vague medical term applied to all pains, including menstrual ones, that occurred in the uterus), but a forewarning of actual labour known as Braxton Hicks syndrome. Dr. Washington tried to convince Isabella to walk slowly across her room to relax her abdominal muscles and speed up labour, but each attempt ended in Isabella's tearful pleas for fresh doses of opium.

On August 2, John A. informed his mother by letter that Dr. Washington had finally pronounced Isabella to be in full labour. He wrote, "She suffered for some hours tremendously, when we called in Doctor Rodgers a phycian [sic] celebrated for the use & application of the Lethean or somnific gas. She was too weak & her nerves in too disordered a state to give her enough to set her asleep, but from time to time, enough was administered to soothe her considerably."

Despite having imbibed, injected, and applied opium paste to her body, as well as inhaled the Lethean gas within a twenty-four-hour period, Isabella continued to writhe in agony. At other times, she drifted in and out of reality. By the morning of August 3, she appeared near death with prostration. Just before sunrise, John A. called for Dr. Washington. Upon examining Isabella, he decided that enough dilation had occurred for him to apply the forceps to the baby's head, Isabella being too weak and "quite unable to deliver herself," John A. wrote to his mother.

At eight o'clock in the morning, Dr. Washington finally delivered a male baby. "Is the baby alive?" Isabella whispered, after falling back on the bed.

"Yes," Dr. Washington replied.

"Is he deformed?"

"No," he said. With her worst fears allayed, Isabella gazed at John A. and, in their supreme moment of intimacy, instructed him to write a letter to Margaret Greene in Savannah asking her to suggest a name. Failing to recognize a slight when he'd been dealt one, a deliriously happy John A. searched for a notepad and dutifully did what he had been told. The same day, he wrote a letter to his sister Louisa, describing his newborn son. "His eyes are dark blue, very large & nose to match. When born his length was 1 foot 9 inches & was strong & healthy, though thin, though as Maria told Dr. Washington, that was not to be wondered at, seeing he had been living on pills so long."

Isabella was so weak from blood loss and drowsy from drugs that she was unable to hold her newborn son. Shortly after the baby's birth, she asked her sister Maria to whisk him off to Kingston to live with her and be wet-nursed by a friend of the family, just as Isabella herself had been wet-nursed. Ironically, this was the best decision she could have made. Had Isabella breastfed her son, she would certainly have re-exposed him to the opium and alcohol she was using to medicate herself, the same combination that had no doubt poisoned her baby's bloodstream, leading to his low birth weight.

John A. knew nothing of these side effects. From visual inspection, his son looked healthy. However, like any typical father, he was concerned about his baby's welfare when in another caregiver's hands, even if that caregiver was his sister-in-law Maria. "We have only heard *once* about Baby since he left us," he wrote Margaret Greene two weeks after his son's birth. "He was then well. I presume he was quite well 4 hours ago, as we have a telegraph now to Kingston & any illness would at once be communicated to me. I shall write to Maria to send you a lock of his hair." The letter has a fretful subtext to it. For the relentlessly power-seeking John A., temporarily losing physical custody of his son to Isabella's family must have seemed unbearable. Isabella had even denied him the chance to name his own child. As a kind gesture, Margaret Greene tactfully chose to name the child John Alexander.

As the weeks dragged on, John A. remained cooped up in the small room in the boarding house in New York with Isabella and the ever-obsequious Dr. Washington. Isabella had begun suffering sciatic pains down her left side again, which Dr. Washington leeched, sitting on a small stool beside her bed. John A. noticed Washington's pallor as his exertions stretched into hours. He began to sweat profusely. He took periodic breaks to rest, only to return looking more exhausted than ever. By August 30, he was dead. It was an extraordinary irony. As one of his last acts prior to his death from an inflammation of the bowels, Washington had asked a friend named Dr. Johnston to arrange for Isabella's care.

John A. wasn't going to tether himself permanently to a woman he suspected was malingering. By September, he had made a decision. He was going home to resume his governmental business. "Our Isabella was a good bit agitated at my leaving her," he admitted to his sister Louisa.

He left anyway. Back home, John A. faced the difficulties Isabella's protracted recovery had caused in his family. His mother was still recovering from her stroke; Louisa was laid up with a bronchial infection; and Margaret was racing around the house trying to nurse both her sister and mother simultaneously. That left no one to travel to New York to care for Isabella. Even Isabella's sister Maria Macpherson could not spare the time to return to New York, since, in addition to being entrusted with raising John Alexander throughout his first months of life, she had a husband and two other children to care for. In Savannah, Margaret Greene and Jane Clark were also ailing and unable to travel north to see their sister. As a result, Isabella sulkily hunkered down alone in New York over the winter of 1847–48.

John A. knew his political success came with a high personal price tag. "I feel quite solitary & miserable living in lodgings alone," he wrote to Margaret Greene from Montreal. "I would spend a pleasant winter, if Isabella were only here, as I have just enough work to keep me from ennui, and not so much as to absorb my attention." John A. also wanted to admire his newborn son, yet he gratefully deferred responsibility for the boy's upbringing on his sister-in-law Maria.

Isabella knew perfectly well how much her husband wanted her to return home. Yet she refused to journey back to Kingston. Private whispers turned into public roars among Kingston's social doyennes. "I can only hope that Isa may rally so as to be able to travel homewards. If not I must look for some respectable person as a sort of companion for her during the winter," John A. wrote as the season wore on. With great reluctance, he finally hired a caregiver to tend to his wife during her "convalescence," but worried that doing so would drive him into irrecoverable debt. He may have been right. At this point, his income from his Kingston law firm was insufficient to compensate for having accepted a ministerial post. "I am in a nice mess," he confessed to a friend.

His "mess" got only messier when Isabella made a startling admission. She did not wish to return permanently to the Brock Street house, where she would be among "his" clan, including his sisters and mother, and not with "her" clan, such as her sister Maria. If John A.'s sisters and mother saw Isabella's admission as a slap to their pride, they did not say so, though it was becoming common knowledge that they found Isabella a drain on his pocketbook and emotional reserves.

As one with delicate sensibilities, Isabella argued that the Brock Street house was too noisy, because there was a stable located behind it. If the clip-clop of horses' hooves wasn't bad enough, then surely the pungent aroma of fresh manure was enough to discourage domestic bliss. To strengthen her argument, she reminded John A. that masons and carpenters were already constructing a Catholic church and a bishop's residence across the street.

Though he was an adroit lawyer, John A. knew he'd lost his case. His sentence consisted of buying a new house for himself, Isabella, and baby John Alexander, in addition to continuing the lease of the Brock Street house for his other family members to live in. To do this, he needed to raise money – fast.

It was also more imperative now than ever to hire another staff member to handle the influx of cases at the offices of Macdonald & Campbell in Kingston. As a result, on November 10, he hired Alexander Morris as a law clerk. Contractually, Morris was hired for a term of five years "to keep the secrets of the said Honorable John Alexander Macdonald and readily and cheerfully obey and execute his [lawful] and reasonable commands." However, perhaps because of overwork, Morris remained for only nine months. The break was not acrimonious, though. Even after his departure, he and John A. kept in close touch, and Morris would eventually serve in John A.'s Cabinet.

John had more than money worries plaguing him. Prior to Isabella's return, he had to seek re-election to the legislative assembly. In January 1848, he was one of the few Conservatives Party members to escape a savage trouncing at the hands of the Liberal Party. The Conservative Party's strength was cut in half and its remaining membership consisted of nothing but stalwart Loyalists. French Canadians rejected the Conservative cause. Even Conservative leader William Draper had quit politics altogether in May 1847 due to divisions between moderates and Family Compact members in the party. Now the country was in a Depression, driving the party further aground.

By March, the entire Conservative Party had resigned. It was time to regroup, rethink, and replan, as the Liberal Party, led by Robert Baldwin and Louis LaFontaine, formed a new government. John A. was about to trade in his dysfunctional governmental family to rejoin a dysfunctional nuclear family, beginning with his own wife.

While Margaret, Louisa, and Helen remained at the Brock Street house, John A. rented Bellevue House, a visually stunning

Bellevue House, where John A.'s first child mysteriously died. *(LAC C010746)*

"Eyetalian Willar," as he humorously referred to it, in the more exclusive westerly area of Kingston. Constructed entirely from stucco-covered limestone, the L-shaped three-storey house featured a tower and finial, slated roof lines, and windows with decorative shutters and small balconies, which earned it the nickname the "Pekoe Pagoda." Its most striking external feature, however, was its landscaped grounds and gardens. In the early fall, Indian corn rose to eight feet in height. Edible nasturtium plants grew in profusion. Servants hauled water from a well by shoulder yokes. When the leaves fell from the trees, the surface of Lake Ontario glittered like thousands of tiny diamonds in the distance.

Upon learning that suitable accommodations awaited her, Isabella's symptoms abated sufficiently for her to agree to return from New York. "You know however headlong I always go," she wrote her sister Margaret, without recognizing the irony in her own statement. It had taken almost two years to persuade her to either cross or circumvent Lake Ontario. She and John A. had now been apart for almost three years – three years in a marriage of only five year's duration. Under those circumstances, the word *headlong* certainly did not apply.

Finally, in late June, John A. accompanied Isabella on a vessel crossing the lake to Kingston. During the trip, she suffered a sustained coughing fit that "shook her grievously," in John A.'s words. When she drew her napkin from her face, she noticed that it contained small specks of blood. Although everyone knew this as the first signs of tuberculosis, in a spectacular suspension of disbelief, John A. chalked her cough up to being "a cold." Even Dr. Hayward, who accompanied the couple on the trip, reported to Dr. Johnston, her doctor in New York, that he considered the bleeding, which was unaccompanied by pus, a consequence of a lung irritation exacerbated by the fatigues and excitement of her journey. As soon as Isabella arrived in Kingston, Dr. Johnston wrote confirming Dr. Hayward's diagnosis. Neither doctor had observed any ulceration or permanent affection in her lungs. Yet, as days turned into weeks and the hacking cough continued to come and go with alarming frequency, John A. sensed something more serious might be wrong. "[The doctor] says it arises from the tenderness of the lungs, but that he discerns no symptoms of ulceration or permanent affection – but I fear. I fear," he wrote Margaret Greene.

Margaret and Louisa had worked feverishly to supervise the cleaning-up of Bellevue and had ordered new furniture for the comfort of Isabella and John A. Due to the severity of her symptoms, Isabella slept in a morning room located on the main floor. Situated on the east side of the house, it was the first room to catch the morning light, but because she suffered photophobia, Isabella usually kept the shutters closed. There were other benefits though. As Isabella ate her food off a tray in the morning room, she could keep John A. within eye and earshot as he ate his dinners alone at the dining-room table.

Not long after Isabella and John A.'s return to Kingston, Maria brought John Alexander to Bellevue for a reunion with his mother. "She has now one source of interest which was denied her, the society of her boy," John A. confidently declared to Margaret Greene shortly after the boy's arrival. "At first he was shy & uncomfortable in her room, which is in some degree darkened and as she could not dandle him, or toss him about, a ceremony which the young gentleman insists upon from all who approach him. He is now however, great friends with her, and sits most contentedly in the bed with her, surrounded by his toys, which he throws about, much to her inconvenience I am sure, tho' she will not allow it."

As a daily ritual, servants carried John Alexander down a steep flight of stairs from his upper-landing nursery to Isabella's bedroom for several ten-minute visits. The boy saw his father for a few minutes in the morning prior to John A. leaving for his law office, and upon his return in the evenings. For the rest of the day, the boy relied for companionship on servants, his nurse, and John A.'s family members, such as his doting grandmother, Helen, whom John A. supposed "dreams of him all night" and "talks of him all day."

As the weeks passed, however, the atmosphere within Bellevue became claustrophobic, and John A. couldn't refrain from likening Isabella to a nineteenth-century carnival act called the "Invisible Lady," who was reputed "to have no human organs except a brain and a tongue." The "Invisible Lady," a female ventriloquist, sat encased in a wooden contraption on stage and threw her voice "miraculously" to audience members, using a selection of concealed acoustical devices. Those in receipt of her commands instantly felt the need to comply, or pay the consequences, usually dire.

As John A.'s "Invisible Lady," Isabella's complaints may have been more benign than those expressed by professional scam artists, but they were incessant, and frayed the nerves of servants and family members alike, especially John A.'s. His pen dripping with acid, he wrote Margaret Greene, "The Invisible Lady's voice, orders, & behests are heard & obeyed all over the house, & are carried out as to the cupboards which she never sees, & pots & pans that have no acquaintance with her. Not a glass is broken or a set of dishes diminished, but she knows of, and calls the criminal to account for. In fact, she carries on the whole machinery, as well, to appearance, as if she were bustling from *but* to *ben* in person."

Visitors to the home, including Maria Macpherson's son, James Pennington Macpherson, recalled the relative contentment John A. and Isabella enjoyed shortly after they were married. Now the Macdonald home was nothing more than a sanatorium, where Isabella lay endlessly recuperating from her latest relapse. Her illness adversely affected almost every member of her and her husband's family. Even worse, each day, Isabella seemed weaker, rather than stronger, so weak in fact that, one night in July 1848, she nearly drowsed off with John Alexander nestled against her side. Had she actually dozed off, she might easily have rolled over and suffocated the boy, or accidently knocked him off the bed, which stood several feet off the ground. Fortunately, she did not fall asleep, but, as she noted in a letter to her sister, Margaret Greene, his brow was moist and he seemed feverishly flushed. "He is not well & oh darling darling sister my very soul is bound up in him. God pardon me if I sin in this. But did I not purchase him dearly?"

On August 2, the entire Macdonald clan assembled to cele-brate John Alexander's first birthday. "He is in high spirits and in capital condition. Certainly there never was a child who has got through his first year with less trouble or illness of any kind," John A. observed in a letter to Margaret Greene written the pre-vious day, oblivious to Isabella's concern for his "cold." By September 21, the boy was dead.

To say John Alexander's death shocked the other members of the Macdonald family was an understatement. James Pennington

Macpherson recalls his mother, Maria, explaining tearfully that John Alexander had died of "convulsions." Within days of his death, she had visited Bellevue to "bid a last sorrowful farewell to the little white-robed figure lying so still and quiet in its tiny cot in a darkened room." Others whispered that the boy had suffered a fall down a flight of stairs.

There is, however, at least one other cause of death worth considering – that John Alexander, the boy who had smiled and crowed "from one end of the day to the other," may have died from SIDS, or sudden infant death syndrome. According to Dr. Josephine Faveraux of the Addiction Research Foundation of Ontario, the rate of SIDS increases in infants and toddlers born to mothers addicted to opiates, especially if alcohol has also played a part in the equation.

John Alexander's newspaper obituary was short and to the point. "Infant son of the Hon. John A. Macdonald."

As a result of John A.'s standing in the community, embalmers performed their work in Bellevue, and for several nights, John A. stayed up with the boy's white-robed body. The ladies covered all the windows with cloth and strung black crepe across the front door. The tall case clock in the front hallway, and those in all the other rooms, were stopped at the time of the boy's death, and all the mirrors were draped in black to keep the boy's spirit from making a permanent home on the premises.

After a short service at the house, pallbearers carried John Alexander's small body feet first from the house for the last time, and buried him alongside Hugh Macdonald's at the Garrison Burial Ground.

During the fall of 1848, John threw himself into legal business he had in Toronto. He journeyed back and forth to Toronto, possibly as much to escape Isabella's oppressive scrutiny as to work. Prior to his departure, he noted that the farthest Isabella could travel was "from the bed to the sofa." While in Toronto, he began to drink heavily yet again, and remained there for more than two weeks. Whenever he sobered up, all he could envisage was how far Isabella's condition might have deteriorated during his absence.

On returning home, however, he was in for a shock. Isabella's health had not deteriorated, but actually improved dramatically. In an effort to surprise him, she had practised sitting up in a chair. On his first night back, she asked a servant to bring a small table into the parlour so she and John A. could dine together before the warmth of the fire. On other occasions, despite attacks of neuralgia in the head, she allowed him to "draw her into dinner in a chair," where they would discuss matters of the day. Still, John A. noted that to treat tics she took large doses of opium, whose effects left her in John A.'s words, "weak languid and miserable."

For the remainder of the fall of 1848, John A.'s personal life settled into a semblance of normality. The pain in Isabella's joints did not seem to affect her manual dexterity. She could sew and knit with skill, mostly baby clothes for her nieces and nephews, and scarves for her numerous relatives. John A. worked with Alexander Campbell at the law firm from 9 a.m. until 5 p.m. As stable as this life seemed, it must also have been vexing. Did clients see him as a lawyer who was also a successful politician, or a successful politician who was also a lawyer? Being a politician may have been good for his law business, but it tore John A. in two separate directions. He was no starry-eyed idealist. If given a choice, he no doubt would have abandoned his private law practice altogether, in exchange for the highest level of political power.

Isabella seemed to derive no personal satisfaction from helping John A. climb the political ladder, but she did appreciate the status his success conveyed, including the close relationship John A. had established with many in the medical profession thanks to his support of the creation of a medical school at Queen's University in Kingston. In 1841, upon announcing the union of

Upper and Lower Canada, Queen Victoria had granted a charter for the opening of Queen's University, along with its associated medical college.

The Macdonalds' tranquil interlude didn't last long. Parliament was scheduled to meet again in January 1849. Isabella begged John A. not to go, arguing that she was still too distressed over John Alexander's death. John A. went anyway, arguing that to do so was a "matter of necessity." As an affectionate gesture, on his first day back in Parliament, he wore a waistcoat Isabella had stitched for him. It didn't bring him luck.

When John A. returned to Montreal, he faced a fractious House dominated by Reformers, led by the audacious Louis LaFontaine, joint prime minister with Robert Baldwin of the united province of Canada. As if suffering through a national depression wasn't bad enough, many spectators in the House felt as if they were watching the foundations of the old colonial system tipping toward permanent destruction. The mood inside the House stayed reasonably calm, however, until Lafontaine and Baldwin proposed a bill to use ninety-thousand pounds in public funds to compensate those persons in Lower Canada who had suffered property losses during the rebellions of 1837 and 1838. Author Donald Swainson speculated the Tories felt that the Rebellion Losses Bill was "not compensation for loss but reward for treason." Ultra Tories and English-speaking residents of Montreal particularly raged over what they perceived as an injustice, apparently unaware that persons in Upper Canada had already received compensation over the years through a series of bills passed by the Tory-held House.

John A. kept his counsel and peered "with his all seeing eyes" around the room, as pandemonium over the bill erupted in the House. In the gallery, spectators flung their wooden chairs over the balcony in disgust. It was a long way from the quiet gardens of Bellevue. Macdonald's jaw must have tightened as he listened to brash Irishman William Hume Blake (Liberal Solicitor General for Canada West) lecture the house for hours on rebellion losses. Blake's speech was passionate, assertive, and obnoxious. He accused specific members of the House of instigating the rebellion, but reserved his most direct attack for Conservative member Allan McNab. McNab leapt to his feet to deny the charge. His supporters in the galleries also leapt up, exchanging fisticuffs with dissenters, as "ladies tumbled over the low barriers." However, nothing deterred Blake, who continued reading self-serving excerpts from newspapers and dispatches, omitting vital details that conflicted with his viewpoint, and generally discrediting each document by reading it in piecemeal fashion.

When he could bear it no longer, John A. rose to address Blake personally. "I should feel obliged by the honourable member reading all the words," he said.

"What does the honourable member mean?" Blake inquired.

"I want the honourable member to read the whole of it," Macdonald explained. "I shall do it for him myself, if he wishes. Is it parliamentary, in reading documents, to leave out whole sentence and parts of sentences?"

"I shall read any part I like," Blake declared pugnaciously.

John A. sat back calmly in his seat and started writing a note. He motioned a page over to him, handed him the note, and grinned. The raucous debate within the House raged on. As soon as Blake read John A.'s note, he blanched. It was a threat. Not merely a threat, it was an invitation to a duel. John A. sprinted out of the room. Blake followed. As soon as the Speaker learned of John A.'s threatening note, he cleared the gallery floor, armed the sergeant-at-arms with a mace, and dashed up and down the corridors in search of John A. and Blake. He quickly found John A. Blake, however, appeared to be in hiding. By the end of the evening, police had both men in custody, and John A. finally withdrew his threat.

The final debate on the Rebellion Losses Bill took place on February 22. John A. spoke until late in the evening. He opposed the bill, but was aware of the powerlessness of the Tories to overcome it.

By the time Governor General Lord Elgin, who had arrived from Britain in 1847, signed the bill in early April, John A. had secured a leave of absence and was once again rushing back to Bellevue on "urgent private business." The leave was officially for two weeks. Not only did he have to rescue Isabella from yet another "attack," but he also had to save his own law firm, which was teetering on the brink of extinction due to Alexander Campbell's dissatisfaction with the avalanche of work he had to wade through each day in John A.'s absence. As it turned out, John A. had left the legislative assembly just in time to avoid witnessing a catastrophe first-hand. On April 25, the ultra-conservative members of the Tory Party, in response to the Rebellion Losses Bill, torched to the ground the Parliament Buildings in Montreal, destroying twenty thousand irreplaceable books.

Isabella's health had withstood John A.'s absence in the spring and early summer. She now had two full-time servants waiting on her, in addition to a cook and a housekeeper. As John A.'s return stretched from two weeks into the entire summer, her condition improved even more, very possibly because she had also temporarily reduced her dependence on opium. In June, an elusive and much younger brother named John arrived from Philadelphia for a visit. His arrival naturally enticed other family members to gather, including Isabella's sister, Maria Macpherson. Throughout the early summer the family enjoyed lazy afternoons sipping tea on the outdoor porch, as Maria's children weaved in circles around the wicker furniture. The threat of tuberculosis seemed a distant memory, since Isabella had not spit blood into her hanky for several weeks. Without drugs to slow her thinking, she engaged in spirited and lively conversations. With the assistance of others, each day she took a few tentative steps. However, John A. shared in

Isabella's bed, sitting room, and opium den at Bellevue House. *(Parks Canada)*

letters to Margaret Greene the information that, by late afternoon, her energy tended to flag and "the agitation of partying made her quite ill." At midsummer, she suffered a severe attack of dysentery that reduced her to "the very lowest state of prostration." With the exhaustion that followed, she was unable to "raise her hand to her head." "The whole gain of this spring is gone & we have not more than two months & a half of summer left," John declared wearily in a letter dated July 24. Rather than suffering from dysentery, however, Isabella's gastrointestinal system may simply have been responding to opium withdrawal. Once she resumed its use, sometime in late summer, her dysentery disappeared.

Was living with a sick person beginning to make John A. sick? A cholera outbreak had swept through the province. Suffering nightmares about his mentor George Mackenzie's fate, John A. fretted that everyone in the house would also contract the disease. When Isabella's brother John showed "premonitory symptoms of cholera," John A. made him see a doctor. John was so ill that he convalesced for five or six days on the drawing-room sofa. Maria also fell ill and retreated to bed. In this environment, it was hard to imagine anyone achieving relaxation, much less Isabella. Nevertheless, the crisis passed and, by the end of August, both John and Maria were back home, leaving John A. to cope with Isabella.

Remarkably, by early fall of 1849, she discovered she was again pregnant. The odds were stacked against even a healthy forty-year-old woman of the period becoming pregnant, but the odds in Isabella's case were virtually insurmountable. Although she wouldn't have realized it, her pregnancy cast doubt on the theory that her original physical complaints were organic in nature. As Dr. James McSherry put it in his essay "The Illness of the first Mrs. John A. Macdonald," Historic Kingston, 1986, "It is difficult to imagine any medical condition which would produce such gross deterioration in physical well-being while preserving menstrual function and fertility."

Now, when he needed money the most, John A.'s legal partnership with the overworked Alexander Campbell was about to dissolve. In an attempt to appease Campbell, he drew up a two-year partnership agreement in which each partner received half the profits and bore half the losses. Campbell considered the offer, but balked at the last minute. "I feel that I have been doing too much and getting too little," he bluntly told his friend. Indeed, Campbell was at this point receiving only a third of the firm's profits and he had never yet been paid four hundred and twenty pounds for additional work he'd performed. Campbell also felt John A. exploited their friendship by neglecting to pay bills on time. The firm's debts totalled eighteen hundred pounds, solely because of John A.'s expenditures. Campbell drove the last stake through John A.'s heart, however, with his final sentence, in which he alluded to defects in John A.'s character rather than merely on his business deficiencies. "Your absence from home and your necessities have been I think the *main* although not by any means the only cause of the annoyances that have arisen." In the end, John A. bought out the partnership for £1,250. No doubt, the cheque bounced.

Without Campbell providing him with a financial safety net in Kingston, John A. needed to curtail his expenses. He immediately moved his practice from an office he had leased on Princess Street into a smaller one at 343 King Street, a less prestigious area of town. All the while, he was spinning debts like china plates. He mortgaged his Brock Street house, where his mother and sisters continued to live, and moved a pregnant Isabella and their servants into the west half of a handsome two-storey stone house at 180 Johnson Street, near Sydenham Street.

Isabella occupied the largest room on the ground floor, complete with a fireplace. In that way, she would be able to see and hear most of what occurred on the main floor of the house and possibly much of what went on on the second floor. She had two servant girls to tend to her needs and, though she had a four-wheeled carriage at her disposal, she rarely used it. At sunset she liked to sit by the large front window and watch John A. walk through Selma Square and the quiet Regiopolis College grounds surrounding Queen's University on his way home from work.

Ever so gradually, John A.'s finances improved. Thanks to his Trust and Loan Company income of £1,500, his china plates never crashed. For much of the fall, he had to slog through piles of deeds, liens, foreclosures, loans, wills, and the other minutia of a general law practice. Isabella made sure he paid attention to his health by taking sitz baths and hydrotherapy and drinking "tumblers of *aqua pura*." His mother's health had also improved dramatically, so much so that she frequently came by the house to keep Isabella company. That winter the weather remained sunny and cool, rather than cold. Feeling less fatalistic than he'd been in years, John A. wrote Margaret Greene, "I have a strong feeling that our circle will not soon again be narrowed. The rod cannot be always smiting."

He was wrong. On November 13, Isabella's sister Jane, who lived with Margaret Greene in Savannah, died at the age of thirty-seven. Upon learning of her sister's death, a devastated Isabella suffered a renewed attack of neuralgia, followed by Braxton Hicks contractions. In fact, her contractions became so severe that, in January, doctors gathered in her room to await the baby's birth. Isabella moaned, groaned, and twisted with pain. The family summoned a midwife. A nurse sat ready. The moment of birth seemed imminent, then passed, then again seemed imminent, then again passed, a process that exhausted everyone present.

John A. tried to walk to the office, but could only concentrate enough to work half-days or less before rushing home again to see how Isabella's "illness" had progressed. He wrote Margaret Greene, enclosing Isabella's instructions should she not survive childbirth. "[Isabella] had given me many directions about herself and her offspring, which any evil happen, & having done all that she can do, is now content. It is her wish, as it is mine, that in case the child should be girl, you should name it. Should it be a male, Isabella says she will accept it as the return of her firstborn and will give it the same name." He added dejectedly, "Isa's in God's hands, and there we must leave her."

Finally, after possibly the most protracted labour of the Victorian period, on March 13, 1850, Isabella finally gave birth to a "fat and coarse" baby boy. "We have got our Johnnie back," John A. gushed. "I don't think he is so pretty, but he is not so delicate." While Isabella was anxious to name the baby John Alexander, because she considered him almost the "same being" as her late son, good sense prevailed. "Mamma, Maria, Mrs. Greene & many others have a prejudice against the renaming a child," John A. wrote his sister Margaret. "What his name may be therefore we will leave to be settled until you come up." In the end, everyone settled on the name Hugh John.

Isabella and John A. kept a journal of their child's progress. Oddly, however, they did not write these notations in a brand-new baby book, but in Hugh Macdonald's Memorandum Book, the same one in which John A. had recorded his brother James Shaw's death so many years before. The couple's notations read: "Wednesday, March 13, 1850 – My darling Isa has a fine boy. Saturday, June 1 – Darling Baby Christened by Dr. Machar 'Hugh John Macdonald,' Thursday, June 13, 1850 – Baby 3 months old began to play with sponge in his bath. Monday June 24, 1850 – Baby vaccinated by Dr Muir at 5 o'clock. July 14, 1850 – Baby in second length

A baby portrait of young Hugh John Macdonald, 1852. *(LAC C004814)*

clothes. Wednesday, September 18, 1850 – Dear Baby got a tooth. Friday, October 18, 1850 – Baby had 4 teeth this morning. Tuesday, Dec. 17, 1850 – Baby's gums lanced second time – 8 teeth coming at once."

Just when John A.'s life produced good news, bad news invariably waited nearby. In this case, Helen Macdonald suffered yet another stroke. She again recovered, yet each time she suffered an attack another physical faculty began to fail. In spite of it all, she bore the repeated onslaughts with unfathomable good spirits and optimism, especially now that she had a grandson on which to lavish her attention. Her two daughters, Margaret and Louisa, now in their thirties, were still of marriageable age, but probably too old to give birth to children of their own. As with Helen, Margaret and Louisa spent much of their time nursing relatives, including Isabella.

Soon, even worse news beset John A. Charles Stuart, Macdonald's "foremost and truest friend" from their days at the

Midland District Grammar School and best man at his wedding to Isabella, was dying of consumption at only thirty years of age. John A. swilled liquid courage prior to each of his visits with Stuart. He playfully scolded Stuart for failing to take his medications. But his good humour was gaiety in the gloom, and soon John A. broke down. He wrote to his sister Margaret, "How long he may live, I know not. His fate is decided. He *may* live until autumn. He *may* die tomorrow. For my part, I fear the worst. When I go to bed at night, I fear to hear of his death in the morning. He refuses to take all advice & all medicine except from myself, & I get thoroughly scolded & abused for the peremptory manner in which I play the Doctor." Uncharacteristically, John A. took stock of his life. "[Tho'] yet a young man, many, very many of my companions have disappeared and my firmest & best friend is about to leave me."

Even less cheering to John A., the Conservative Party was sick to the core. When Lord Elgin signed the Rebellion Losses Bill, members of the party had pelted him with hundreds of eggs and stones, while others poked sticks though portraits of the Queen, which hung in the Parliament Buildings they later burned down. Ultra-conservatives battled with members of the party's moderate wing. Some Conservatives unthinkably favoured annexation to the United States. Once the party's orgy of hate abated, Toronto and Quebec City became the new seats of government, perhaps on the principle that a moving target is harder to hit.

Surprisingly, however, when the legislature sat in Toronto on May 14, 1850, John A. was absent. He didn't explain his absence; he just didn't appear. At last, in early June, he materialized in the red-brick Georgian structure on Wellington Street in Toronto that served as the seat of government to hear a debate among the Reformers, the Clear Grits, and the Tories concerning whether Crown lands reserved for Clergy Reserves should be employed for secular uses. Within days, however, he received yet another summons home. Isabella had again taken a turn for the worse. By June 28, he was back in Kingston, "excused on account of sickness in his family."

Isabella's call had been another false alarm. By July, John A. finally returned to the House, but remained uncharacteristically mute. Financial survival was now his primary concern, and he would ruthlessly use any means to achieve it, even if it meant putting the government at his private disposal. One of his biggest clients, the Trust and Loan Company of Upper Canada, had unexpectedly plunged into financial difficulties. John A. had to find a way to save the company – and by association, himself – from the poorhouse. In late 1850, he sponsored a private bill, seeking to amend the Trust and Loan Company's statutes of incorporation to include interest-rate hikes. Thanks to these interest-rate hikes, the company could attract much-needed British capital.

Fortunately for John A., his bill whizzed effortlessly through a House whose members were distracted by bickering over petty procedural issues. With its passage, the company came closer to averting financial disaster.

By fall, John A. sailed for England to scout out new financial contacts. He hadn't crossed the ocean in eight years. This time, he was doing so in style, as an esteemed representative of the Trust and Loan Company of Upper Canada. According to an old Arab saying, "Throw a lucky man into the sea, and he will come up with a fish in his mouth." John A. did better than that. He learned to swim with the sharks.

V

JUMPING OFF THE TREADMILL

As his ship steamed toward England, the country in which he always felt most passionately at home, thirty-five-year-old John A. Macdonald finally ruminated about his accomplishments. He had charted what he thought was a seamless course toward success, yet he still felt like a stranger in a strange land. He'd married respectably but not happily. Isabella quite literally moored him to her bedside through coquettish cajoling, begging, and finally unseemly pleading. She showed none of the physical and emotional fortitude of the Macdonald women, and for that reason alone, John A. must have possessed some resentment toward her, no matter how effectively his imperturbable facade might have disguised it.

With the exception of the first year and a half of her marriage, Isabella's drug addiction had deprived her family of peace of mind and left them feeling like perpetual failures at "relieving" her pain. Yet exactly what ailment did she suffer from? Neuralgia? Sciatica? Migraine headaches? Most of her doctors had treated her body, but few, except Dr. Sampson, had even remotely considered how much her mind might have been affecting her body.

In the mid-1850s, French psychiatrist Dr. Paul Briquet diagnosed a new condition affecting women of thirty years of age and older that was sweeping through Europe. In increasing numbers, women were presenting pain without any apparent physical cause. Rather than define the women as "crazy" or "hypochondriacal," however, Briquet theorized that women who felt out of control over their emotional environments could literally make themselves sick, often severely so, the intensity of the ailments growing and diminishing in relation to their levels of stress. These women indulged in endless doctor-shopping, and like Isabella, they controlled their worlds from the confines of their beds. If one chose to notice, when surrounded by John A.'s family, Isabella became the "Invisible Lady" who was "heard but not seen." When surrounded by her own, she frequently rallied.

Certainly, Isabella experienced an astonishing restoration to health during her extended visit with her sisters Margaret and Jane in Savannah in 1846. John A., meanwhile, had played the bachelor husband in Montreal. But Isabella's improved state deteriorated soon after John A. reunited with her in New York in late 1846, and she became pregnant with Hugh John. Upon receiving this news, she sank into yet another period of intense suffering.

Meanwhile, her struggles with tuberculosis, finally diagnosed, placed the health of all the members of her family in danger and did little to improve her condition. She never opened the windows wide. Indeed, she seldom even ventured outside to breathe fresh air. Instead, she insisted on John A. staying near her, nursing her, loving her, and ceaselessly worrying about her. Eventually, in order to forget the trial his marriage had become, John A. drank excessively, in public and in private.

Despite this overindulgence, John A.'s charismatic allure for both sexes only increased as he matured. The mismatched pastiche of plaid pants, striped shirts, red silk vests, cashmere coats, and porkpie hats made of rabbit fur would have appeared ridiculous on anyone less lean and jaunty. If he ever brushed his hair, he must have done so with his hands, for it burst about his face like black steel wool.

In his book, *Reminiscences*, Tory backbencher-turned-Liberal minister Sir Richard Cartwright recalls witnessing an interlude in the House between John A. and a member of the Opposition party that illustrates John A.'s curious appeal to both men and women. "I was passing through a set of alcoves on my way to the supper-room when I saw [John A.] with his head on the shoulder of a certain stalwart Grit member from Western Ontario," he writes. "The pair made a rather remarkable tableau, and as I passed I heard his companion say to Sir John, 'Ah, John A., how I love you! How I wish I could trust you.'"

John A.'s trip to England was a turning point, and when he returned to Kingston, he hoped to be if not a new man, then at least hopefully a richer one, with money in his pockets, and a second chance to make a first impression on political friends and foes.

Conditions had certainly improved since John A.'s first voyage across the Atlantic. Now he travelled first class, enjoying the finest in whisky, clarets, and sherry. His quarters were small but luxurious, with plush velvet furniture and curtains and silk wallpaper from Venice. If he wished to work in bed, one of his favourite pastimes, he could do so by gaslight.

John A. went to England to entice the British government to rescue the struggling trust company, and in this way to make some money for himself in the bargain. It was a clear conflict of interest, but if that fact bothered him, John A. never showed it.

John A.'s ship docked in June, but it took two months, and a letter of introduction from Lord Elgin, for him to gain access to Colonial Secretary Earl Grey's inner sanctorum. John A. possessed no particular love for Elgin, but he had learned how to manipulate him. Only through his unique skill at playing both ends against the middle could he obtain Grey's assistance in raising financial backing from the British government.

Thanks to his trip, John A. ultimately raised a healthy financial infusion of five hundred thousand pounds for the Trust and Loan Company.

While in England, he quickly learned to savour the good life, attending champagne receptions, where caviar was served in crystal serving dishes and attractive young ladies vied to dance with the rising young star of Canadian politics. At the same time, he loved the rough-and-tumble banter of a barroom or tavern in which he could reel off his legendary tall tales. Alexander Campbell remarked in a letter, "I dare say you are very busy from night until morning, and then again from noon 'til night. I take it for granted – another glass of champagne and a story of doubtful moral tendency [are] elements in the political strength of a Canadian ministry not to be despised."

When John A. returned to Kingston in the late fall of 1850, he was a richer and certainly relieved man. The potential catastrophe of losing his largest corporate client was gone. Even better, Isabella wasn't suffering any imminent health crisis, and Hugh John, although hyperactive and nervous in temperament, was the light of John A.'s household.

So, for at least a few months a semblance of domestic calm prevailed, and the clouds appeared to be clearing for him in the government as well. In 1851, after co-premiers Louis LaFontaine and Robert Baldwin retired, Francis Hincks and Augustin-Norbert Morin headed up a new Liberal government. The Conservatives had not performed well in a late-fall election, John A. being an exception. Not only had he retained his seat in Kingston by a wide majority, he had also swept the entire Midland District, including Lennox and Addington County. Shrewdly, he succeeded by failing to ally himself with extremists on either side of his party.

The seat-of-government question would loom large in the coming parliamentary session. Though he hadn't ignited the fires that gutted Montreal's Parliament Buildings in 1849, John A. probably would have been happy to sit on a nearby wall and light his cigar in their flames. As much as he enjoyed the social pleasures Montreal had to offer as the government's capital, he was looking forward to moving his family to a less incendiary site that courted both French and English voters equally.

At the beginning of 1852, John A.'s old mentor William Draper had retired, and "bilious, gouty" Allan McNab became head of the Canada West Conservatives. John A. hungered to lead the party, but he didn't want to *look* hungry. Instead, he charmed his way into the centre of the public circle. His irresistible knack for self-mockery delighted even his most grizzled opponents in the House. For example, while attempting to gain support for a bill to license doctors, he had the House members laughing uncontrollably as he described the physical calamities he encountered while self-treating himself for lumbago. His physical contortions left his audience draped over their desks with laughter.

As for other assets, unlike many of his fellow party members, John A. could read French, understand it, and speak it reasonably well. Moreover, he had a message for those British inhabitants of Lower Canada who felt the French could be ignored. In a letter to the *Montreal Gazette* on January 1, 1856, he wrote:

> No one in his senses can suppose that this country can for a century to come be governed by a totally unfrenchified [sic] government. If a Lower Canadian British desires to conquer he must 'stoop to conquer'. He must make friends with the French, without sacrificing the status of his race or language, he must respect their nationality. Treat them as a nation and they will act as a free people generally do – generously. Call them a faction and they become factious. [The] truth is, that you British Lower Canadians can never forget that you were once supreme – that Jean Baptiste was your hewer of wood and drawer of water. You struggle, like the Protestant Irish in Ireland, like the Norman invaders in England, not for equality, but

ascendancy – the difference between you and these interesting and amiable people being that you have not the
honesty to admit it. You can't and you won't admit the
principle that the majority must govern. The Gallicans
may fairly be reckoned as two thirds against one third of
all the other races who are lumped together as Anglo-
Saxons – Heaven save the mark! The only remedies are
immigration and copulation and these will work wonders.

John A. Macdonald was a restless leader-in-waiting. No one
in the Conservative Party, except McNab, could deny it. But for
the time being, he had to bide his time and let the parliamentary
game play out.

Back in Kingston, Isabella continued to dwell in her nether-
world between sickness and health. Perhaps more than at any
other time in his marriage, John A. exhibited dwindling patience
toward the family squabbles that
broke out around him, especially
among Isabella, Louisa, and Moll,
who had differing ideas concerning
Hugh John's upbringing. John A.
clearly exploited his sisters' devotion to him by wheedling them into
nursing Isabella, Hugh John, and
Helen. He saw little of his son due
to the demands both his parliamentary and law office duties imposed
on him.

Rev. James Williamson,
Margaret Macdonald's
husband and Hugh
John Macdonald's surrogate
father and mentor.

(Queen's University Archives)

Finally, Margaret Macdonald
grew fed up with John A.'s dependency on her and, in an act of emancipation, accepted a marriage proposal

from Rev. James Williamson, whom John A. nicknamed "the preacher."

With an expression so dour it froze the timid at fifty feet, Williamson had been a Presbyterian minister, but retired in 1842 in order to enter the teaching profession. Despite his lugubrious expression, students soon referred to him as "Billy," and he earned a reputation as a well-respected professor of mathematics and natural philosophy.

Like John A., Williamson also had a tragic past. In 1844, he had married a woman named Margaret Gilchrist from Edinburgh. In June 1847, Margaret gave birth to a son the couple named James. Within a week, however, Margaret died, leaving Williamson to raise their son alone, hardly a fashionable state of affairs for an ambitious man seeking academic status. Williamson also supported his elderly mother, who was still living back home in Scotland. Williamson tried to hire nurses to take care of James, but they often proved insufficient to the task, or had sticky fingers.

Margaret's father, Jo Gilchrist, also exerted pressure on Williamson to return to Scotland and preach from a country parish, rather than risk his child's financial future by working for an uncertain academic institution such as Queen's University. Williamson stuck it out in the wilds of Canada, in spite of Jo's perception that Canada was a place filled with "primitive half breeds" and "heathen harlots."

The harder Williamson tried to maintain custody of his son, James, in Kingston, the more Jo Gilchrist pressured him to let the boy grow up in Scotland. Williamson, however, had no intention of passing him around to his in-laws like a collection plate.

Jo Gilchrist, however, proved obsessively persistent. He bluntly told James that he was sending Margaret's youngest sister, Elizabeth Gilchrist, to Kingston to bring baby James "home" to Edinburgh. Economically beaten and emotionally defeated,

Williamson had reluctantly handed over his son to his sister-in-law's care. The two had left for Scotland in the spring of 1848, never to return to Canada.

John A. was so preoccupied with grabbing the political brass ring that he only fleetingly considered how Margaret's marriage to Williamson might affect her duties toward her own family. While it was true that Williamson had informed John A. by the summer of 1852 that he intended to request Margaret's hand in marriage, a wedding date had never been set. John A. welcomed the news, but asked Williamson to make sure that prior to marrying Margaret, he should find "a careful person – some respectable widow – more a companion than a mere servant" to attend to Helen Macdonald's needs. Williamson agreed, and the two men parted warmly.

It was therefore with some anger that, on October 12, 1852, John A., who was then serving in Parliament in Quebec City, received a telegram from Louisa Macdonald announcing that the wedding between Williamson and Margaret would be conducted at Kingston's St. Andrew's Church on October 19, a mere week away. From a Victorian viewpoint, this amounted to an elopement!

John A. was a man who did not like surprises, unless they were his own. He was shocked that neither Williamson nor Margaret had revealed how hastily they planned to wed. "I had no intimation from [Williamson] that there was an intention to hurry the marriage," he wrote Louisa in a fury. "In fact, I learnt nothing more from him than the fact of the engagement, with which I expressed my satisfaction."

He saved the bulk of his anger for Williamson. Williamson had ignored John A.'s specific request to find a trustworthy caregiver for Helen prior to marrying Margaret. John A. was also annoyed that, in marrying Williamson so fast, Margaret was foisting Helen's care solely onto Louisa. He immediately wrote Margaret a stern letter, in which he stressed his displeasure at seeing Louisa exploited by her own sister.

Despite his dissatisfaction with Margaret's choice of a wedding date, however, John A. promised to "Strain every nerve to be up on the 19th," to attend Margaret's wedding. In the event he didn't make it; however, he wired Louisa twenty-five pounds to buy a wedding kit for the couple.

It was lucky John A. could raise even twenty-five pounds to buy a wedding kit. Once again his fortunes had taken a downward slide. In addition to investing in a series of dubious stocks, John A. was still smarting over some land-speculation disappointments he had recently suffered. In the summer of 1852, he had bought 9,700 acres of land in a sheriff's sale in Canada West. After questions regarding the legal clearing of titles and other problems, John A. had quickly flipped the properties "for a tolerable good sale." But tolerable was far short of what he needed to keep his family's heads above water.

To give Margaret some respite from the demands of her family, Williamson leased a large and comfortable stone house on Queen Street, just around the corner from Helen's home on Barrie Street. In retaliation, John A. decided that since James's house was just around the corner, Margaret could easily travel back and forth in order to see to her mother's needs, without undue inconvenience to Williamson. As Margaret well knew, coming from John A. the request to tend to their mother wasn't subject to negotiation.

To provide some economic safety for his family, on December 26, 1852, John A. purchased two thousand pounds' worth of life insurance from the Colonial Life Assurance Company's office. For the next few years, John A. had plenty of money coming in, but he also had massive amounts of debt.

If John A.'s finances were tight, Williamson's were even tighter. Within four months, Williamson and Margaret reluctantly relinquished the hard-won independence they had briefly attained. They moved out of their Queen Street house and into the house on Barrie Street with Helen and Louisa. Margaret resumed caring for Helen whenever Louisa felt unable to carry the responsibility alone. It was a trying time. Since John A. was paying most of the bills, Louisa felt it was her prerogative to order James and Margaret around as if they were her servants. Every day that she suffered under her sister's arch scrutiny reminded Margaret that, even by marrying, she had failed to obtain the autonomy she so craved.

Meanwhile, John A.'s bills kept piling up. He responded to most of them with the usual excuses, including "No funds" or "Insufficient funds." On at least two occasions, however, his exasperated law clerks got a little more creative. "Can't do it Sir 'tis hard times for money and we don't pay such things here," wrote one. Another staff member scribbled across an invoice, "The Hon Mr. Macdonald is now absent [and] has not provided for the payment of this Bill in his absence." One can only imagine a day in the life of one of John A.'s law clerks as they cringed waiting for another creditor to call, worrying about whether they themselves would receive a salary.

Despite his debts, throughout 1852 and early 1853, John A.'s life had at least taken on a stable rhythm as he travelled from Quebec City, where Parliament now met, to the Brock Street house in Kingston, where little Hugh John and Isabella resided, and back again.

In the House, he devoted his energies to sowing divisions in the Reform Party, now led by George Brown, who introduced the notion of Representation by Population. Brown, who had examined census figures taken in 1851, knew that the population of Canada West was now greater than that of Canada East. As editor of the *Globe* newspaper, Brown wrote voluminous columns on the subject, his contention being that the citizens of Canada West should enjoy a more powerful voice in government than citizens of Canada East, based upon strength in numbers alone. John A. did not endorse the Rep by Pop plan, as it was colloquially known, because he knew it would alienate the French Canadians – the very French Canadians he wanted so desperately to lure to the Tory side in upcoming elections.

He spent months trading barbs with Brown, but by May of 1853 John A. left Quebec City before Parliament adjourned. After such a promising start to the session, he suddenly felt tired, cynical, and discouraged by the lack of progress made by the Conservatives. He had watched George Brown's Rep by Pop plan, polarizing the English and the French inhabitants of the Province of Canada, discouraging a union of the two cultures into a productive partnership. Thanks to Rep by Pop, cultural and religious divisions threatened to erupt into violence.

These tensions exploded in June, when Father Alessandro Gavazzi, an ex-Roman Catholic friar turned evangelical Protestant, delivered an anti-Catholic lecture at Wesleyan Chapel on St. Ursula Street in Montreal. During his address, a riot broke out. The military inexplicably began firing on members of Gavazzi's audience, killing some and wounding others. In response, Montreal's Protestant population sought to arm themselves against what they termed "Catholic thuggery."

This was just the kind of publicity John A.'s moderate Conservatives didn't need. John A. tried his best to soothe both the English and French communities, without great success. Soon the *Montreal Gazette* defined the Conservative Party as "moribund" and "incapable of resuscitation." The summer of 1853 staggered its way into fall, with the Conservative Party in the doldrums. Then, just as suddenly, a storm of gossip began blowing around Francis Hincks, co-leader of the Liberal Party. As it turned out, Hincks had embroiled himself in a fraudulent financial scheme involving municipal debentures and the Toronto, Simcoe, and Huron Railway, through which he illicitly earned ten thousand pounds.

John A. knew a winning poker hand when he saw one and placed all his bets on bringing down the Liberals by hammering away for months on Hinck's ill-considered actions. After all, the

Hinck's scandal diverted the public's attention from the Gavazzi incident. By the time Parliament reconvened in June 1854, John A., in an interview with the *Globe* newspaper, boldly accused all of the members of the Liberal Cabinet of being "steeped to the lips in corruption" and that they "have no bond of union but the bond of common plunder." The Liberal government was split into two factions, comprised of moderates (Hincks supporters) and radicals (supporters of George Brown and the Clear Grits).

Macdonald pounded away at Hincks's disgrace and the inability of the Liberal Party to govern effectively. Hincks did not resign. Instead, with Lord Elgin's permission, he prorogued Parliament. Within less than two weeks, an election was in full swing.

John A. won Kingston easily, inheriting moderate Reform supporters disenchanted with Hincks. Even George Brown of the *Globe* admitted that, if forced, he would choose John A. over Hincks. John A.'s political platform for the election was simple: he would rid the country of "corrupt rulers."

His strategy worked. Macdonald won the election 437 to 265 votes. Only the divisions between moderate Tories and ultra-Tories continued to prevent the Conservative Party as a whole from gaining seats in Parliament. The party had failed to win enough seats to dominate the House. Newspaper reporters hinted that John A. was so tired of trying to unite his party that he toyed with resigning altogether. It was truer than most people thought. "The party is nowhere – damned everlastingly," he told Alexander Campbell.

By early September, however, John A. was buoyed by the sight of a rapidly splintering Liberal Party, culminating in Hincks's resignation on September 8, 1854. Conservative Party members were jubilant, no more so than its leader, Allan MacNab, who shortly after Hincks's resignation appointed John A. Attorney General for Canada West. Though Allan MacNab still officially led the party, he entrusted John A. with building a Cabinet or coalition to form the backbone of *his* vision of a Progressive Conservative Party, or a Liberal-Conservative Party. Everyone had recognized, even MacNab, that John A. was the leader-in-waiting.

In addition to his political progress, as Attorney General, John A. was now earning £1,250 a year, enough to rescue him from rabid bill collectors. Still, he continued to possess extravagant tastes. When he bought books, he bought them by the dozens, and rarely, if ever, did he pay a bill in full when he purchased anything.

Back in Kingston, John A. had invited a bright young attorney named Archibald Macdonnell to become a partner in his firm. In addition to handling real-estate matters and general legal cases, Macdonnell's main skill was diverting bill collectors. Incredibly, Macdonnell even lent John A. his own money, making him an eventual creditor in his own employer's office.

On a personal level, John A. faced a painful dilemma. He wanted his wife with him. But not a sick wife. He wanted his son by his side. But not *in his way.* He knew he was close to gaining recognition as the leader of the Liberal-Conservative Party and that, as soon as he attained that goal, his social calendar would fill up with endless dinner invitations. The St. Andrew's Society and the Freemasons would always welcome his presence. Isabella had good days, sometimes very good, but her health was never consistently good, and when a fresh attack hit, she always relied on her old standby: opium. It would simply be impossible for her to attend public events. John A.'s loneliness was exacerbated by the fact that the seat of government continued to move from Quebec City to Toronto, meaning he had no home base.

Then, too, Hugh John was forced to play musical houses between the Brock Street house, in which he lived with Isabella and two female servants, and the house on Barrie Street, which now housed Helen Macdonald (who was suffering strokes at a rate of once a year), Louisa, James Williamson, and his wife, Margaret.

John A. sent home money to pay for Hugh John's clothing. He monitored his academic progress, picked his son's reading list, and at one point even bought him a rifle, but father and son saw little of each other. To Hugh John, his father was a glittering but distant star in the constellation of Canadian politics.

James Williamson saw in Hugh John a surrogate for the son he had lost to his in-laws. As a result, he became the boy's surrogate father. In turn, Hugh John turned to Williamson for approval. While Hugh John shared his father's love of reading, he nevertheless incurred his father's displeasure by spouting Williamson's anti-French rhetoric.

The stronger Williamson and Hugh John's relationship became, the weaker Williamson's relationship became with his own son. In vain, young James tried to spur his father to write or visit Scotland more often. In 1852, he had written, "Dear Papa, Don't be afraid that I will ever forget you I remember you quite well playing with me here and I remember you every night in my prayers. I hope I will receive the gold dollar in the next letter you send to grandpapa. I am gathering up to buy Black's Atlas. Write me very soon again. P.S. I send you twenty kisses J.G.W."

Whether out of bitterness at his father-in-law, or because he lacked subjects to write about, Williamson wrote his son with infuriating infrequency, which his son did not fail to notice. "My dear Papa, I have been wondering why you had almost forgotten me as I only received one letter from you this year," he wrote in 1853. As a final resort, Williamson sent his son newsy updates on the growth of Queen's University, but in return received disdainful letters from his son, who couldn't understand why his father could not express more intimate feelings.

Williamson also endured the bitterness of his sister-in-law, Elizabeth, who resented the favouritism she sensed Williamson showed toward Hugh John over his own son. She wrote: "Our darling pet [James] is in perfect health, but full of spirit, and may I tell you he does not like you to hold up to his example the little boy McDonald [sic], he always sits angry at it, and thinks you like McDonald's better than him. Our darling is one in ten thousand and is held as an example to most boys."

By now it must have dawned on every Macdonald family member – distant or not – that in some small way they were contributing toward one goal: ensuring that John A. would achieve the highest public office in the land.

As 1855–56 progressed, John A.'s political fortunes peaked. That year George-Étienne Cartier joined the Tory Cabinet. The following year, Allan MacNab was deposed as leader of the Tories, and John A. finally gained recognition as the leader of the Canada West Conservatives.

John A. didn't gain party leadership without criticism. Some saw him as metaphorically kicking the cane out from under old McNab's hand, without a trace of conscience or regret. In fact, just prior to the House motion to force McNab's departure, John A. and Sidney Smith, a member of the Reform Party, almost traded blows in the refreshment room of the House when Smith accused John A. of conniving to force McNab from office.

Other critics saw John A. as a dilettante. Liberal minister Richard Cartwright observed, "He is fond of pleasure and has an almost boyish exuberance of animal spirits, and a pro-curatism, and want of earnestness in any pursuit which will always prevent him from being a successful leader. His instincts are all good, but he takes the world too easily to be much depended on."

John A. knew what others thought about him, but he shook their criticisms off. He knew politics was a game of capitalizing on opponents' failures, and he had made the most of the Liberal Party's fractured status to gain momentum for the Conservatives.

He was also happy to learn that, for the 1856–57 session, Parliament would meet in Toronto. He was determined to have Isabella and Hugh John join him there, where they could finally achieve some stability and unity as a family.

Prior to their departure, Louisa asked John A. if she could move into his Brock Street house while he was gone. The atmosphere in the Barrie Street house was so contentious with the clash of egos that Louisa despaired of anyone ever reaching a consensus even about something as simple as how to butter a piece of bread. John A. exploited Louisa's fondness for him by encouraging her to direct the household. If Louisa minded, she didn't say so. In fact, she enjoyed the power her closeness to John A. provided her. As a middle-aged spinster, she may have also recognized that the closest she would come to possessing parental authority was ruling John A.'s households in his absence. This awareness led her to throw her weight around, sometimes so objectionably that Williamson had suggested they should find alternative living arrangements, an idea that convinced Louisa to ask John A. if she could move into the Brock Street house.

In a letter of September 21, 1855, however, John A. cautioned Louisa to stay on the good side of the Williamsons, and discouraged her from rushing to move out. "Even if it is finally decided that Isabella is to go to Toronto," he wrote, "I have been unable to go there to make arrangements for her reception so that it will be the middle of October before she can be moved."

With the exactitude of a military manoeuvre, in October 1855 Isabella was carried by stretcher on board a train bound for Toronto and placed gently on a settee. Along the way, each screech of the brakes and each high-pitched train whistle shattered her calm reserve. Were it six years earlier, she would certainly have found it virtually impossible to travel from Kingston to Toronto, except by boat, since she would have had to bounce along deeply rutted roads by horse-drawn wagons, as John A. had done when he travelled as a young man to the Law Society of

Upper Canada to pass his bar exams. By the 1850s, however, Toronto had become a railway hub. The Oshawa, Simcoe & Huron, the Grand Trunk, and the Western railway lines all met at Union Station on Front Street.

Although a healthy person could walk briskly from Union Station to John A.'s boarding house on Wellington Square, Isabella, John A., and Hugh John hired a cab for Isabella to ride in, though it was expensive to do so. Horse-drawn omnibuses also travelled along the city's major streets for those who couldn't afford cabs. Yonge Street, Toronto's main artery, even operated horse-drawn street railways, a precursor to streetcars.

Toronto was a burgeoning city: politically, culturally, and economically. Its population of forty-four thousand, consisting predominantly of English, Irish, and Scottish settlers, flooded into the city so fast that housing construction could barely keep up with the demand. Newly built subdivisions and free-standing structures dominated the downtown core. There were also plenty of taverns, where weary working men could spend a happy hour or two before heading home to their boarding rooms and flats. The city was divided into seven wards named for saints, including George, Andrew, David, Patrick, Lawrence, John, and James. The core of the city fit into roughly a four-square-mile block, stretching from the Don River, west to Bathurst Street, and north to Gerrard Street. Due to a series of fires, the mayor placed a ban on building houses out of wood, so bricks had become the more popular choice. When John A. was perturbed, he liked to walk. He would have had no shortage of routes in Toronto.

The city's churches and government buildings were constructed near the centre of town, including the City Hall at Queen and Bay Streets, St. James' Cathedral, the St. Lawrence Hall, the York County Courthouse, the Mechanics' Institute, and St. Andrew's Presbyterian Church. Several prestigious schools also dotted the scene, including the University of Toronto, the

Anglican Trinity College, St. Michael's College for Roman Catholics, and the Presbyterian Knox College.

John A., Isabella, and Hugh John shared a rented apartment in a house in Wellington Place, a new housing development with all the modern amenities at the western border of the city. Unfortunately, the apartment's rooms were dark and extremely small, with narrow windows failing to allow in much daylight. In comfort, it was the polar opposite of Bellevue House, with its lush lawns, fragrant summer breezes off the lake, and outdoor patio. To Isabella's especial annoyance, the incessant clip-clop of horses' hooves resonated on the woodplanked roadway outside, as clouds of soot floated through her open window.

John A. had not lived alone with Isabella in close quarters since the first months of their marriage. Unfortunately, the physical closeness they possessed in Toronto seemed to drive them further apart rather than drawing them closer together. To cope, John A. drank. As his visits to the numerous taverns close by his office on Bay Street mounted in number, so, too, did his liquor bills.

Back at Wellington Place, Isabella was incapable of travelling anywhere without extensive preplanning. She relied exclusively on a variety of pills, alcohol, and medicated creams and ointments to alleviate her various symptoms, which seemed to change by the minute. She could not even leave her bed to play with her son. She brooded, complained of pain and pressure on her chest, coughed up specks of blood, and fell back on her pillow, her energy spent. As a result, for the first few months of the Macdonalds' residency, Hugh John was shuffled throughout town, living with whichever friends and family members could take him in, including John A.'s friend John Rose from Montreal, the family of David Lewis Macpherson (a member of the legislative council), and the Lewis Moffats.

At night, Hugh John visited his father to play Beggar My Neighbour, also known as Beat Jack Out of Doors, a card game based on eliminating opponents' cards until they had to capitulate.

Already, Hugh John showed a competitive spirit and a relentless desire to win, both qualities his father did not fail to notice. "He knows the value of the cards as well as I do, and looks after his own interests sharply," he wrote proudly to Helen.

Ultimately, cooped up in this unnatural environment, delicate, small-boned Hugh John, too, became ill, suffering painful physical episodes eerily similar to those experienced by his mother. John A. himself feared the boy had inherited his mother's fragile constitution. Upon examining him, however, doctors chalked up his condition to "fuss." They prescribed special bland diets for him, and hot baths to soothe his nerves. Rather than assimilating into this new city, Hugh John reminisced endlessly about Kingston, about his Grandma Helen, and about "the preacher." He showed no inclination to walk or exercise as other children did. To make sure his education didn't suffer, an exasperated John A. hired a tutor for him. By the spring of 1856, the tutor was spending more than two hours a day at the apartment.

Back in Kingston, the family dynamic wasn't much more cohesive. Louisa, Margaret, and James had all moved into the Brock Street house shortly after John A.'s departure. Six months later, flames consumed it, and the cause was never found. Following the conflagration, Louisa and Helen moved in with Maria Macpherson, Isabella's sister, who also lived on Barrie Street, while the Williamsons moved into a house on Collingwood Street. Within months, however, all but Maria reunited at a new residence at 194 Johnson Street.

In March 1856, John A. severely sprained his arm and kept it wrapped in flannel for weeks. The pain preyed on his mind. He was forty-one years old now, and less able to bounce back physically the way he had as a young man.

As for Isabella, unable to bear Toronto for more than a year, in the late spring of 1857, she returned to Kingston, where John

A.'s family could nurse her. Her defection was a result, in part, of her awareness that she could not endure the rigours of an election, which was scheduled for December. Hugh John accompanied his mother out of Toronto, rendering John A. once again alone and lonely. In part to distract himself from his failure to sustain a functional family life in Toronto, and in part to work, John A., accompanied by John Rose, sailed for England on board the *Anglo-Saxon*.

On July 28, 1857, the ship docked in Liverpool. Within forty-eight hours, he and Rose were rabble-rousing in London. Despite John A.'s prowess as an imbiber, Rose could usually match him drink for drink. Both were notorious experts on how to let off pent-up emotional pressure, and must have cut quite a swath after they finished their daily work promoting financial and railway projects for the Canadian government, particularly the building of a railway between Halifax and Quebec City.

By August 1857, England's salt air had again renewed John A.'s spirits, and he began making his obligatory courtesy calls on relatives. He visited Evan Macpherson and his wife for dinner. Around the same time, he also had dinner with Isabella's two brothers, John and William, bringing them up to date on her condition. A few days later, he stopped off in Paris, where he bought a Highland dress for Hugh John, in which he expected "Hughie" would "bare his bottom with due Celtic dignity."

Upon his return on November 30, instead of stopping off in Kingston to look in on Isabella, John A. headed straight for Toronto and immediately checked into the Rossin House Hotel, located at the southeast corner of York and King Streets. There he and John Rose got busy campaigning. John A. began furiously writing letters to candidates, aldermen, and anyone else who might be able to drive the Tories over the top in an election that was just three weeks away. He even wrote to Reform-member-turned-Conservative Sidney Smith, promising to forward his name as a possible judge, if he retired from the race to make way for a stronger candidate. "The Orangemen in Toronto have taken the bit in their teeth, and it is really now impossible to say what they will do," he wrote to Smith. The Orangemen. Weren't they John A.'s people? Smith had just learned an ominous lesson. John A. was not afraid to turn against his own to win converts to his cause. Smith took the bait and retired from the race.

With the election to retain his seat in Kingston facing him, John A. shuttled by train between Toronto, a city he tolerated, and Kingston, a city he loved, but that housed the disgruntled members of his meddling family. In fact, while in Kingston, he chose not to stay with his wife and child at all but selected instead a more unorthodox refuge: Eliza Grimason's tavern.

In 1856, Eliza had convinced her husband, Henry, to lease property on Princess Street from its then owner, John A. Macdonald. The property, which included a tavern on its ground floor and hotel on its second floor, soon became John A.'s campaign headquarters while he was in Kingston, and, in the weeks leading up to the election, Eliza held many a raucous fundraiser on its premises. As the Grimasons profited from John A.'s fame, he kept their lease locked in at a reasonable three hundred pounds a year.

In exchange, Grimason House, as it become known, became "the shrine of John A.'s worshippers with Mrs Grimason as its high priestess." Most nights, local farmers tied their horses up in a stall to the rear of the tavern and shambled through a back door toward their favourite benches. Kicking off their muddy boots, they unwound over their a pint of ale or lager, or maybe a shot of rum. On regular nights, a full-course meal, including Irish stew, yams, pie, and a bottle of wine, cost twenty-five cents. A glass of whisky cost only five cents. Along with their meals, patrons usually got friendly lessons in Tory politics from the proprietress. Fact is, had any of them revealed themselves as Grits, Eliza would have probably chased them out of the tavern with a broom handle.

On election nights, Eliza served alcohol for free, ensuring that her customers would be well inebriated when they later cast their votes for John A. In his book, *Anecdotal Life of Sir John Macdonald*, biographer E. B. Biggar wrote, ["Eliza's] influence became no small element in an election and it was said she could control a hundred votes."

Eliza Grimason's interest in John A. didn't stop with her merely admiring his fine way with a phrase. Whenever he was in town, she attended private political meetings, the only female in his life to do so. To the astonishment of those present, at one of these meetings, she walked past a throng of men, kissed John A. on the cheek, and retired to bed, without saying a word. If John A. was attending a political picnic, Eliza showed up in her horse-drawn carriage and personally chauffeured him and his party members back to town.

John A. often stayed overnight in two rooms that were always set aside for him in the hotel room above the tavern, one room in particular containing a king-sized brass bed. When he arose in the morning, Eliza cooked him breakfast on a large cast-iron stove. On Sunday mornings, she often had to awaken him early, so she could get him to church on time.

As Eliza's and John A.'s strange relationship intensified, John A. often bestowed gifts on her, the most notable one being a Regency-style cradle carved out of oak and mahogany, in which he had reputedly been rocked as an infant. There are no records to confirm exactly when John A. gave Eliza the cradle. However, it was undoubtedly shortly after one of her three pregnancies, which would place it during his marriage to Isabella.

Under the circumstances, the gift was breathtaking in its indiscretion. Even if John A. and Eliza were never physically intimate, the crib lent credibility to the notion that they might have been, especially at a time when the public considered a man forward if he visited a woman alone. As a further show of his

John A. is said to have given this cradle to
Eliza Grimason as a gift. *(Parks Canada)*

devotion, John A. kept a framed photo of Eliza on his office desk,
alongside a photograph of . . . his mother.

It must have seemed to John A. that all his childhood dreams,
his pranks, his ambitions, his hours of study under George
Mackenzie had led to this election, and never had he felt more
unsure of his own personal and political future. Despite all his
efforts in Parliament, there was no question that George
Brown's Reformers, with their insistence on representation by
population, were sweeping Canada West. The best John A.
could hope for was the Tory Party making a strong showing in
Canada East.

On December 10, John A. spoke in front of Kingston's City
Hall during the nomination meeting. His opponent, a man
named John Shaw, who had just completed his anemic speech,

faded into insignificance the minute the charismatic Macdonald sprinted two steps at a time up the stairs to the stage. John A. didn't lecture his audience, he just spoke to men and women as colloquially as he would to members of his own family. Kingston, he reminded them, was still *his* town, his home, the place where his heart would always be.

That message was enough for the voters to know who they wanted. On election day, John A. beat his hapless competitor, John Shaw, by 1,189 votes to 9. For daring to challenge the supremacy of John A. Macdonald in Kingston, voters burned John Shaw in effigy.

Disturbingly, however, the Conservative Party's popularity did not spread throughout Canada West. There, George Brown's Reformers dominated the election, winning not only in North Oxford, but Toronto, making John A. feel less at home in the city than ever.

George Brown clearly held the balance of power now in the House, and he had obtained it by suggesting the Tory Party was seeking to sublimate the interests of the British in Canada West in order to coddle the French factions in Canada East, a tactic they insisted had originated with none other than John A. Indeed, they could produce his *Montreal Gazette* letter to prove it.

John A. must have dreamt he was climbing a glass mountain. By publicly embracing the French, he had tried to unite Canada West and Canada East. Instead, he had alienated one faction from the other. Meanwhile, Brown had hammered his Rep by Pop proposal into Canada West's consciousness through his relentless *Globe & Mail* newspaper editorials. His message was simple: Canada West had more people, so it should have more say over the province's future.

John A. had no trusted companion in whom to confide his disappointment over his party's election results. Even if she had been well enough to be with him during the election, Isabella was no longer capable of communicating in a cogent manner. She did not write. She did not even have the strength left to lift a pen.

John A. had not intended to return to Kingston for Christmas Day, preferring to remain in Toronto to count the returns from a few straggling constituencies. However, he unexpectedly had a sickening foreboding, this time so powerful that he immediately hurried to Kingston to investigate the true state of Isabella's health. A hush filled the air as he turned the key and entered the Johnson Street house. He stared up the staircase directly ahead of him, but saw no one. Sunlight licked the sides of locked window shutters. The eerie silence pressed against his eardrums. Then he heard the rustle of a skirt, and Louisa appeared at the end of the hallway. She helped her brother remove his coat as the two walked into Isabella's room on the main floor. There Isabella lay, as white as the sheet that covered her, yet curiously composed, as if her whole life had been a dress rehearsal for this moment. She was alive, but barely. The omnipresent "blister box," filled with powders, vials, and ointments, remained untouched – the most ominous sign of all. For three days, John A. sat vigil at her side, until she finally drifted away on December 28.

Her obituary that appeared on the front page of the December 29, 1857, *Kingston Daily News* read: "On Monday, the 28th inst. of December, Isabella, wife of the Hon. John A. Macdonald, in the 48th year of her age. Friends and acquaintances are requested to attend the funeral without further notice, from his mother's residence, Johnson Street, to the cemetery, on Wednesday, the 30th inst. at three o'clock."

Isabella's sister Maria arrived to oversee the preparation of Isabella's body for viewing. All clocks in the Johnson Street house were stopped at the time of Isabella's death. Again, family members hung black crepe across the front door to signify that a death had occurred, though viewing of Isabella's body was by appointment only. For three days, Isabella lay in the parlour of the house. At night, John A. sat by the coffin, bathed in candlelight, alone with his thoughts. There was little to buoy him. His mother was still alive, true. That was a comfort. Louisa, of course was always at his side, as were the Williamsons, James and Margaret, who had practically raised Hugh John since Isabella's final illness.

On the day of her funeral, servants scattered hay on the street outside to muffle the sound of the horses' hooves (the sound so abhorred by Isabella) as they approached the house to transport her body to Cataraqui Cemetery, approximately a fifteen-minute drive away.

John A. had not arrived home in time for Isabella to speak with him, but she left pieces of herself with almost careful deliberateness throughout her bedroom. Her embroidery covered many of the furniture's seat cushions and pillows. Her lists of groceries and sundries lay on her bedside table, along with the other minutia of her world.

Seven-year-old Hugh John struggled to contain his emotions. In many ways, his mother had remained a wraith-like figure in his flesh-and-blood world. No doubt he both loved and feared her otherworldly fragility. On the other hand, he had seen little of his father, except through a distorted lens that made John A. appear larger than he was.

It had been a mild winter. The grounds of the seventy-acre Cataraqui Cemetery were thawed enough to allow a grave to be dug. As the Macdonald family stood vigil, cemetery staff lowered Isabella's coffin into the earth alongside her son, John Alexander, and her father-in-law, Hugh Macdonald, whose bodies John A. had moved from the Garrison Burial Ground in 1850, shortly after he bought the Cataraqui family plot.

Isabella's death boosted John A.'s flagging political fortunes. As brutal as this was, it contained a painful truth. Public sympathy garnered good ink. The 1857 election had been a catastrophe for the party, but John A. and George-Étienne Cartier were still co-leaders of the Macdonald-Cartier Canada West Conservatives, and John A. was not going to allow his party's defeat to deter him from personally rising to the top of the political heap.

Six days after Isabella's death, he returned by train to Toronto. He had little baggage except those papers he had been working on when he'd had the presentiment about Isabella's decline.

Hugh John was safely back home for good in Kingston with Williamson and Margaret, with John A. paying the bills for his upbringing. Within two years, John A. would draw up a more formal arrangement with Williamson.

John A. might have looked like the same man upon his return to Toronto. He may have even sounded the same, complete with jaunty witticisms and studied laconic responses, but one thing had most assuredly changed. John A. was now a single man, and he meant to make the most of it in the shortest time possible.

VI

PARTY ANIMAL

B y today's standards, John A. was a sexist. By the times in which he lived, he was courtly and charming, a real catch because he had what most women admired – power. "John A. had the devotion of women in remarkable degree," biographer John Willison observed. "It is rarely indeed that a political leader touches the hearts of women and only those who do it have that strange quality of attraction which we call magnetism."

For a woman to snare the recently widowed John A., she first had to pacify his formidable mother, Helen, and sister Louisa. Both protected him as ferociously as mother bears. Hugh John Macdonald, John A.'s delicate but determined doppelganger son, with his long curly red lashes, freckles, and thick ringlets of auburn hair, rounded out his father's protective scrum. There was just one more hurdle: John A.'s unrelenting ambition.

Throughout January 1858, John A. split his time between his Toronto law office and the House. His brain was firing on all cylinders. In fact, relieved of suffering almost daily apprehension of Isabella's death, he completed volumes of work he normally assigned to associates or put off until his hangovers abated. He completed some of his work in the comfort of his apartment in the luxurious four-storey Rossin House Hotel. There, John A.

rented a suite, with a private bath, sleeping quarters, and a parlour where he could entertain male and female guests alike. When he could no longer afford the costs of the hotel, he moved into bachelor quarters in a townhouse owned by Mr. Salt on Bay Street. John A. moved out of the Rossin House Hotel just in time. A month after his departure, flames from a fire that broke out in the ironically named Temperance Saloon snaked across the street, setting the venerable hotel ablaze.

While at his quarters at Mr. Salt's townhouse, John A. reviewed several criminal sentences that were up for appeal. He commuted death sentences against eight railway men for committing aggravated assault with intent to murder against their foreman. A postal employee, who had received a life sentence for stealing twenty dollars from the mail, saw his sentence reduced to five years, as long as his conduct in prison remained "praiseworthy." In general, John A. supported penal rehabilitation over punishment.

An expert at reviewing the fates of convicted criminals, John A. rarely examined his own past misdeeds, particularly those he'd committed in Napanee and Hallowell. His "criminal record" would have listed more than merely benign childish pranks. After all, he had stolen fish from a neighbour, maimed a horse, imperilled the life of its driver, committed assault, and placed a dead horse in a house of worship – evading punishment each time.

His personal insensitivities were sometimes just as devastating to his victims. He had almost certainly been emotionally unfaithful to Isabella, and perhaps physically with Eliza Grimason or the ladies of the evening in Montreal in his early days in politics. At the very least, he exacerbated Isabella's sufferings in Philadelphia when, despite her disapproval, he flagrantly called in on her lady friends, then threw stories of their charm in her face.

Furthermore, by alluding to Isabella's "petticoat government," and likening her to a carnival performer who could project her voice in distant directions, he was deriding her. It's reasonable to suspect that John A. resented Isabella for the manner in which her vague illness had delayed his ascent to political heights, drained his pocketbook with medical costs, and, with the exception of her tuberculosis, exploited the arbitrary nature of her illness. If he had truly loved her, he did little to demonstrate it as she lay dying in the weeks leading up to Christmas Day of 1857. Instead, up until virtually her last breath, he stayed in Toronto, orchestrating his campaign to assume his de facto leadership of the Liberal-Conservative Party.

Shortly after Isabella's death, John A. engaged in an affair with Mrs. Elizabeth "Lizzie" Hall, the pretty, wasp-waisted widow of John A.'s friend, Judge George B. Hall of Peterborough. Judge Hall had once represented Northumberland North in the Legislative Assembly of 1844–47. After Hall's death in 1856, a grateful John A. had administered his estate, and even organized the schooling of the Hall's two small children. Lizzie, meanwhile, fell in love with John A., first out of a sense of gratitude, then out of lust. Soon rumours flew that the two would wed.

For propriety's sake, as well as to spare her children's feelings, Lizzie destroyed most of the letters she and John A. exchanged, and the relationship seems to have been of a reasonably short duration. From out of the ashes, however, one letter survives, containing sentiments that leave the reader in no doubt concerning the depth of Lizzie's passion for John A. "My beloved John," she wrote,

I hope I shall have a letter from you today, my darling, as I shall not be able to hear from you another week as I am intending to leave here for Buckhorn tomorrow. [Mr.] Boucher went to town yesterday. [He] is holding court today so no hope until I return from the backwoods where I only intend to stay a week. So, you will have no letter for that time. If that is a privation to you, what must I feel – a fortnight without hearing from you. I cannot bear to think of it. [The] horses are ready. I must stop. Goodbye my own darling. Love your loving Lizzie.

Other women also threw themselves at John A. during his widowhood. He was linked to Jean Haviland, a sister of Thomas Heath Haviland, the Lieutenant Governor of Prince Edward Island, but the affair petered out before it could take hold.

The sitting of Parliament over the winter of 1858 was a desultory session. John A. spent most of his time trying to rebuild his support in Canada West, but to no avail. Meanwhile, Opposition leader George Brown was nipping at John A.'s heels and frenetically trying to destroy John A.'s fragile government.

Ill with delayed shock over Isabella's death, and lonely for his son, John A. relaxed by napping on the couch during weekend trips to a friend's Davenport Road house on the outskirts of Toronto. There were times when he felt like a perpetual-motion machine, unable to stop, but with no fixed address to call his own. He seriously considered retiring "with honour," writing his sister Margaret, "I find the work and annoyance too much for me." The truth was, he was bored and longed to make mischief. He was about to get his wish.

In July 1858, John A. announced to the members of the House that Queen Victoria had selected Ottawa as the permanent seat of government. Upon hearing the news, Reform Leader George Brown pounced, determined to bring down John A.'s Conservatives by stoking the anger of French members from Canada East, who wished to see Quebec or Montreal as the capital of the Province of Canada, instead of Ottawa. Brown figured that, if he could convince enough of the French in John A.'s party to desert the Conservatives on this issue, he could bring down the government. He was right. In July, a number of French Canadians in the Liberal-Conservative Party voted with Brown's

Reformers to renounce Ottawa as the nation's capital, the final vote being 64 to 50.

To the shock of the House, as a gesture of allegiance to the Crown, John A.'s Liberal-Conservative government resigned. Following this, a gleeful George Brown asked Governor General Sir Edmund Head to dissolve Parliament and call a new election, but Head refused. Instead, Head decided to keep Parliament in session, and prevailed upon Brown to form a new government. Taken aback by Head's decision, Brown hastily formed the Brown-Dorion government, failing to take into full account the fact that his party had no platform and, outside of the seat-of-government question, little popular support in the House. Also, by accepting Cabinet posts, members of his government automatically forfeited their seats and had to seek re-election. One day after creating the Brown-Dorion government, Brown realized with sickening clarity the truth of the saying, "Be careful what you wish for." Several of its members had already left his government to campaign for office. After only two days, the Brown-Dorion government collapsed in a non-confidence vote. Soon after, Brown himself resigned.

Unsure of how to proceed under such extraordinary circumstances, Governor General Head turned to George-Étienne Cartier to form a government and Cartier wasted no time in doing so, starting by appointing himself as premier of Canada East. Cartier then appointed John A. as Attorney General. John A. discovered that, under clause seven of the Independence of Parliament Act, "if any one of the principal officers of government should resign his office and within one month accept another one, he should not be obliged thereby to vacate his seat in parliament." Using this tactic, the entire Liberal-Conservative cabinet shuffled portfolios for twenty-four hours, with John A. becoming postmaster general, then shuffled to their original portfolios, without incurring the expense of a by-election. Under the Independence of Parliament Act, this "double-shuffle," as it became known, was all perfectly legal. But was it ethical? To those in the House who called the entire adventure a "swindle," John A. feigned righteous indignation. "It is a charge that I am a dishonourable man, a charge that the representative of our sovereign, myself, and all my colleagues, if they have any concern in the matter, are alike dishonourable conspirators, and here in my place in parliament, I say it is *false as Hell*." History fails to record how broadly John A. was smiling when he mouthed these words.

Not everyone in his party admired John A. Some critics speculated that, without the likeable Cartier by his side, Macdonald would not have enjoyed more than half of his party members' loyalty. When asked why John A. had lost some of his sheen, Richard Cartwright wrote, "A good many things had combined. In the first place, he had been leading a very dissipated life from 1856."

After his demoralizing defeat, George Brown left government for good. Thereafter, he used his paper, the *Globe*, to rage against The Wizard of the North, as he dubbed John A. According to the *Globe*, John A. was "evil," he was "conniving," and he was "ruthless." Brown raised the prickly issue of Representation by Population again. It was one of Brown's most effective mantras – especially in Canada West – whose inhabitants Macdonald largely dismissed as uncouth and uncultured land-speculators out for a quick buck. Brown argued that Canada West was richer and more progressive than Canada East, and should have a strong say in matters of education, railway development, and taxation. He maintained that Canada West was sick of paying their tax dollars to subsidize John A.'s efforts to woo Canada East.

John A.'s "double shuffle" had almost certainly driven Brown toward a nervous breakdown. Indeed, it sometimes seemed as though Brown replayed his humiliation at John A.'s hands repeatedly, to relive the pain. As a man perpetually obsessed with his own sense of failure, Brown eventually incurred money problems, but he was not the only one.

John A. had sacrificed a lucrative income to attain political office. His comparative penury had adversely affected the lifestyle he and his family could have enjoyed had he concentrated on purely commercial pursuits. Thanks to his law partner, Archibald Macdonnell, John A. still had his law firm on Wellington Street in Kingston to fall back on, but faced with the expense of raising Hugh John, he knew it was essential that his political gamble pay off. He had forfeited his own personal happiness for power and still had only known a fraction of what power he could achieve. With the exception of an unhappy marriage and a few broken dalliances, he hadn't fared much better romantically. Rootless now, he set off in search of personal diversions.

On a Friday morning in July 1859, he boarded the steamer *Ploughboy* for an excursion to Sault Ste. Marie. Newspapers reported that, just as the vessel arrived at Lonely Island in Georgian Bay, a part of its machinery snapped in half and, for safety's sake, the vessel had to cut off its steam. Since the *Ploughboy* lacked masts, she began to drift whichever way the wind and waves took her. Several crew members lowered anchors into the lakebed, but they failed to take hold. Other crew members offered to board an open boat to Owen Sound to secure the aid of the steamer *Canadian*. Before they could find help, however, the *Ploughboy* drifted to the most dangerous part of the coast, lying just west of Chabot Point. By Sunday morning, the vessel was within fifty yards of a precipitous rockbound shore, with a heavy swell setting in toward it, and a gale blowing her directly upon the breakers. Forty-five yards from land, on a lee shore, and in one hundred and eighty feet of water, the anchors finally caught bottom, preventing the ship from smashing to pieces against the shore.

A shaken John A. wrote his sister Margaret on July 7, "You will see by the papers what a narrow escape we had. None of the party will again be nearer their graves until they are placed in them.

The people behaved well – the women heroically. I am none the worse of the trip. The Governor General will be here tonight and I hope therefore in a few days to get away to Kingston. Love to Mamma, Hughy and Loo not forgetting the Parson."

The near shipwreck so affected John A. that he immediately wrote out a will, which he had delivered to Louisa on August 10. The document specified that, after Helen's death, he was bestowing an allowance of seventy-five pounds a year on both Louisa and Margaret, and instructed Louisa to pay Margaret for any expenses she incurred on behalf of "Hughy," until he reached age twenty-one. Should Louisa survive Margaret, she was to receive one hundred pounds a year and guardianship of Hugh until he reached twenty-one. Once Hugh reached twenty-one, the two sisters would divide the remaining capital among themselves and Hugh.

Despite miraculously surviving a catastrophic shipwreck, John A. was depressed rather than exhilarated. He vacationed on the beaches of Maine with Louisa and Hugh but was called to Parliament two days early. He desperately needed an infusion of the kind of life-affirming energy only one person in his life had been able to give him – his mother – but whenever he visited, he could see her slipping away, each stroke removing another piece of her past. Louisa, meanwhile, continued to tussle with Margaret over other household affairs and who was entitled to instruct servants as to their duties. When Louisa felt she wasn't getting her way on an issue, she frequently pestered John A. to intervene.

In 1860, James Williamson moved John A.'s family to Hazeldell, a spacious stone cottage on the western border of Kingston. The house sat amidst vast tracts of uncultivated land and featured a wide front porch and elegant French doors on each wing.

James Williamson leased the house from Sarah Mackenzie, the late George Mackenzie's widow, who had lived in the house since 1843. The move surprised James Williamson's relatives in

Scotland, particularly his father-in-law, Jo Gilchrist. "We have been wondering what has been the cause of your again removing to another house – Are you to be no longer a lodger but the house's holder? Does Mrs. Macdonald go along with you?" he wrote.

Though eighty-three and frail, Helen Macdonald still had her pride. She refused to allow Williamson to treat her like a freeloader. Consequently, she insisted on paying him rent, as well as reimbursing him for money he spent directly on her. Helen was so determined to pay her own way that she drew up a formal contract with Williamson, dividing their costs accordingly. She agreed to pay Williamson a yearly rent of twenty-six pounds for the house, garden, poultry yard, and a "yard that he has leased from Mrs. MacKenzie," the rent frozen for the duration of her lifetime. In addition, she agreed to pay ten pounds of a male servant's wages, six pounds for cutting wood, and four pounds for half the price of the horse's food.

As the months passed, James Williamson and Margaret found Louisa's myriad complaints wearing. They knew her main annoyance boiled down to one thing: her lack of power over the house. Rather than seeking to compromise with her sister's husband, she emasculated him, engaging in childish turf wars. In an effort to save some money, Williamson planted his own vegetable garden on the property. Louisa, who fancied herself an equally skilled gardener, balked at asking Williamson for a tract of land on which to grow her own flowers and vegetables. Instead, she sat brooding in her bedroom.

At ten years of age, Hugh John was thin and pale, with limited physical endurance. What he lacked in stamina, he tried to make up for by achieving high academic grades. "Tell Hugh that I am extremely pleased at the report of Mr. May. [Hugh's teacher]," John A. wrote Williamson. "Tell him that I am quite proud of it and that I have shown it to all my friends. Let him go on & prosper and he will make his mark in the country yet." He sent his son several gifts, usually books, yet perhaps the boy reminded him too much of Isabella, for he rarely spared the time to visit with him. What affection he gave the boy came by proxy through Louisa.

As James Williamson piously counted the family's pennies in Kingston, John A. used what money he had or could borrow to enjoy life in Quebec City. In 1860, beneath a giant gas-lit chandelier, he hosted an extravagant Valentine's Day ball for eight hundred guests in the Music Hall of the St. Louis Hotel in the city. The ballroom's walls featured flowered wreaths, handmade by the Sisters of Charity. A fountain in the centre of the room gently sprinkled perfumed water onto disgruntled men and delighted women. Two alcoves nestled beneath the galleries contained life-sized figures; in one was the God of love, Cupid, and in the other, Canova's statue of the "Dancing Girl." A large bust of an unsmiling Queen Victoria dominated the front of the room, not far from a statue of "The Three Graces," which, delightful as they were, lent the room the air of a high-class bordello.

Still, everyone who was anyone was there. Politicians, society mavens, clergymen, judges, anyone who might prove useful to John A.'s future made the cut. The only people absent were John A.'s family members, too weighed down with the responsibilities of caring for Helen and Hugh John to accept their invitations to the event. John A. had once remarked, "If a man desires peace and domestic happiness, he will find neither in performing the thankless task of a public officer." He forgot to mention the toll a public officer took on the life of his family.

A giddy John A. had spared no expense for the Valentine's Day gala. The entire bill for the affair totalled £1,606.70, with supper alone priced at £520. If one thing proved true, it was that John A. now knew his liquors. Among those consumed at the event were champagne, sparkling moselle, sherry, Best port, and Allsops ale, all a far cry from the five-cent whisky Eliza Grimason served in her tavern in Kingston.

Like a carefree schoolboy, John A. sprinted gaily throughout the room, bestowing valentines with "pretty little remarks" on the women, as an orchestra adorned with the Prince of Wales's plumes played Viennese waltzes. Following dinner, he left a lasting impression on his guests by rolling out a gigantic pie, out of which flew four and twenty birds.

That summer he was to host a visit to Canada by the Prince of Wales, the eighteen-year-old son of Queen Victoria, later to be crowned King Edward VII. This was no small honour to Canada, to the Conservative Party, and to John A. in particular. As a result, his handlers had to coordinate every aspect of the trip.

John A. wished to showcase his sartorial splendour. Prior to the prince's visit, he practised wearing the British Civil Uniform

John A. in rabbit-fur hat.

he would be expected to don during the visit. The uniform was made of dark blue cloth, with gold braid, a cocked hat, and a sword. George Brown gleefully drew the attention of *Globe* readers to the inconvenience of the uniform for someone who overimbibed. "A great deal of time has been wasted by John A. Macdonald in learning to walk," he noted, "for the sword suspended to his waist has an awkward knack of getting between his legs, especially after dinner."

On August 10, John A. arrived at the Gaspé on board the steamer *Queen Victoria* to await the arrival of the prince's ship, *The Hero*. *The Hero* finally sailed into port on Sunday at 7 p.m., just as the sun was setting and the bay was at its most picturesque. The following day, John A. lunched with the prince as the ship sailed toward Quebec, arriving on August 18. As the prince stepped off the ship onto the dock, he was met by a phalanx of public officials, all like John A. wearing their official, and very heavy, uniforms, which made them "as hot as pigs in armour," according to the *Globe*.

A triumphant John A. led the prince on a tour through Quebec City, where they attended several public events featuring much official bowing and scraping. On August 21, the prince bestowed honours on selected individuals at the Parliament Buildings. Afterwards, the group first sailed west and then rode the rails to Montreal, where the prince opened the Victoria Bridge. There was much popping of champagne corks and delicacies served whenever the prince's retinue arrived at a new destination. Through marital misfortune and financial obligations to his family, John A. had been deprived all his life of luxuries like this, and he savoured every aspect of the prince's opulent lifestyle with the same wide-eyed boyishness he'd displayed nineteen years before when he and Margaret Wanklyn toured the Queen's private quarters at Windsor.

As a highlight of the trip, the prince, John A., and other dignitaries rode a boat named the *Kingston* down the Lachine Rapids, an Indian pilot at the wheel. Soon, the churning waves beat, tugged, and nearly capsized the boat, drenching those on board. Upon rounding a turn, the boat thumped toward a massive rock, terrifying them all. Without betraying a hint of anxiety, the Indian pilot, holding the future of the British monarchy in his skilled hands, spun the massive steering wheel at exactly the right moment, the boat skimming within millimetres of the rock into calmer water. The prince, simultaneously terrified and exhilarated, whooped aloud as the boat neared shore.

On Monday, September 3, John A., the prince, and several ministers travelled up the Ottawa River by steamer and canoe to Arnprior, then drove inland to the village of Almonte, where they boarded a special southbound train travelling to Brockville. By the time the party arrived in Ottawa it was so dark they had to read their speeches by lantern light. Later that night, the party drove to the St. Lawrence River, where the *Kingston* awaited them.

In a dramatic display of loyalty, as the ship sailed along, firemen galloped on horseback along the riverbank, carrying lighted torches. The prince also noted that, despite the late hour, citizens placed candles in the windows of their homes to honour his presence.

So far, the trip had been a personal triumph for John A., as well as for Canada in general, but John A. knew trouble lay ahead. The closer the *Kingston* steamed toward Kingston, the tenser he got. His greatest fear, not unfounded, was that the numerous Orangemen who lived in Kingston and faithfully supported the Conservative Party would place ostentatious Orange Order signs, banners, and posters across the streets and any other place they chose to welcome the prince to Upper Canada. The problem was, even though displaying banners and signs was legal in Canada, it was illegal in the United Kingdom. That meant, should the prince be confronted by them, he could not leave his ship.

While he made sweet talk with the prince in public, behind the scenes, a desperate John A. sent advance parties to Kingston and Toronto to try to convince his fellow Orangemen to compromise and remove their banners from the roadways. Some did. But, much to John A.'s displeasure, the hard-liners held firm. Since no law in Upper Canada prohibited them from displaying their signs, they decided to do so, John A. be damned.

As the steamer neared Kingston harbour on the afternoon of September 4, the prince and members of his entourage could easily see a large Orange arch, Orange banners, and a dock full of overwrought Orangemen trying to entice the prince to leave his vessel. Faced with a stalemate, the *Kingston* remained docked in the harbour overnight.

Torn between his loyalty to the Orangemen who had helped elect him and to appeasing the prince, John A. abandoned the ship to join his disgruntled Orange supporters, sending shock waves throughout Upper Canada. Fellow ministers in the Conservative Party found it inconceivable that John A. would leave the prince midway through his trip. Yet that is precisely what he did. The *Globe* castigated John A. for abandoning his royal guest.

Mortified as John A. was by the dilemma in which he'd been placed, he was also angry that the Orangemen had tried to force the prince to publicly ignore the law. By the time the prince left, French-speaking Canada had left a better impression on the prince than its English-speaking counterpart.

The fallout from the botched visit lasted well into the fall. To mitigate the damage, John A. embarked on a month-long speaking tour to Brantford, St. Thomas, Hamilton, Toronto, Guelph, and all parts in between to explain methodically and clearly the reasons behind the prince's refusal to disembark from his vessel, and the constitutional machinations that had mandated it. John A. was particularly concerned about the reaction in Toronto, where fully 15 per cent of the male population were members of the Orange Order. John A. needed these votes when the next election came around, so he did some serious bootlicking during his trip. He played up the positive aspects of the prince's trip in such a winning way that audiences soon lined up to hear him speak. John A. had adroitly averted a major political catastrophe, and he had once again used his charm to do it.

While John A. was criss-crossing Canada West wooing future voters with his unmistakable charm, back home in Kingston Louisa and Helen Macdonald were again embroiled in an ugly dustup with James Williamson. In response to Williamson's authoritarian manner, Louisa displayed her characteristic irritable contrariness. She tried to act as a proxy for John A. at the head of the Macdonald dinner table, but found her attempts quickly trumped by Williamson. Louisa also feared for her mother's health. By now, Helen's health vacillated wildly. Some days her ankles swelled to twice their size, while her head throbbed unremittingly. On other days, she seemed more like her old self. Without John A. to reassure her, Louisa's mood grew dark, and she slowly began to lose her place within even the small world she inhabited.

On October 2, 1860, John A. attempted to ease Louisa's "discomfort" by suggesting that she should move out and find a house of her own. Distracted by putting out political fires, John A. uncharacteristically blundered by believing he himself had leased Hazeldell rather than Williamson. Under the circumstances, it was an incomprehensible oversight. He wrote Louisa, "If I understand the thing rightly the Lease of the House & grounds from Mrs. Mackenzie is to me. If this is so the best way would be for the Professor to lease the premises & you to pay him whatever expenses he has been put to. If I am wrong & he leases the grounds then you should make some arrangement by which to leave & look out for a house. Do this at once & let me know exactly the terms of your bargain."

It must have taken every fibre of Margaret Macdonald's gentle nature not to write to her brother complaining about Louisa's behaviour. After all, Margaret and Williamson had sacrificed their marital privacy to welcome Louisa, Helen, and Hughey into their house. Margaret and Williamson not only doted on Hugh John as a surrogate son, but also helped him complete his homework assignments and oversaw his moral training. During all this time, Margaret suffered from frequent lung infections, which she underplayed in light of Louisa's numerous complaints.

In the fall of 1860, Archibald Macdonnell gave Hugh John a pony. John A. accepted the gift, with a condition. He told Louisa that Hughey must "wear the waterproof I sent him, but he must ride daily." To augment Macdonnell's gift of the pony, John A. increased his household expenditures to include funds to buy grain and hay. He also sent a draft for one hundred pounds for Louisa and Moll to divide between them. However, the truth remained that, despite his good intentions, if pressed John A. was probably not able to list his own son's likes and dislikes, favourite foods, or ambitions for the future.

On the surface, John A. liked to try to appear imperturbable and jocund in all things, but increasingly he worried about whether he would ever be able to share his life with anybody again. In a letter to his sister Margaret, he confessed, "I am now so much accustomed to live alone, that it frets me to have a person always in the same house with me."

There were times when his spirit simply gave out, and he took to his bed, unable to explain his absence from Parliament. He drowned his sorrows in alcohol. Following one of these protracted absences, Governor General Head sent his aide-de-camp, Lord Bury, to John A.'s boarding house to order him back to the House. Bury got more than he bargained for.

When he arrived at John A.'s apartment, Bury literally pushed past John A.'s elderly housekeeper and entered John A.'s bedchamber, where he found John A. sitting up in bed, reading a novel, a half-filled decanter of sherry on his bedside table. "Mr. Macdonald, the Governor General told me to say to you that if you don't sober up and get back to business, he will not be answerable for the consequences." Macdonald frowned but did not budge from his comfortable position. Instead, he angrily asked Bury, "Are you here in your official capacity or as a private individual?"

"What difference does that make?" Lord Bury replied.

"Just this," John A. snapped. "If you are here in your official capacity, you can go back to Sir Edmund Head, give him my compliments, and tell him to go to hell. If you are here simply as a private individual, you can go yourself!" Startled, Bury beat a fast retreat. He had achieved his objective, however, and by the following day, John A. returned to the House.

Even the usually mild-mannered James Williamson resented John A.'s habit of poaching on his and Margaret's servants. His anger reached its apex after John A. sent driving equipage to Hugh John so Williamson's servant could harness Hugh John's equipment to Williamson's sleigh. Margaret, who seemed always to end up in the middle of household disputes, informed John A. by letter that Williamson felt frustrated by John A.'s request to share his servant with Hugh John, when he had been hired specifically to look after Margaret and Williamson.

If John A. felt Williamson had chastised him, his letters fail to show it. When he responded to Williamson, his tone contained a mixture of extravagant courtesy seasoned with a dash of patronization. "Now, I can quite understand that your servant has enough to do already, and I would not think of course of employing his services," he assured Williamson (writing to him directly, rather than through Margaret, in effect, showing that, unlike Williamson, he was not hiding behind Margaret's skirts). As a compromise, he asked Williamson to find a "lad in the neighbourhood" who might perform the services Williamson's servant would not. "I should think there would be no difficulty in getting a lad for that purpose," John A. wrote. "If there is no lad to be got, I will, if you have no objection ask Mr. A.J. to take charge of the pony & sleigh. So that Hughey can go up there & get the turn out when he wants to show off his driving."

Williamson probably felt relieved to have avoided the sharp end of John A.'s tongue. Others did not avoid it. Whatever anger John A. spared Williamson spilled out onto the floor of the House, much to the astonishment of members of both sides of the aisle. The catalyst for his rage came in the pudgy shape of his former law student – and friend – Oliver Mowat. Mowat had initially joined the Conservative Party and then, to John A.'s horror, crossed the floor to join George Brown's Reform Party, convinced by Brown's Rep by Pop proposition. John A. openly mocked Mowat in the House for flip-flopping on the Rep by Pop issue, even openly quoting transcripts of Mowat's original, strongly worded objections to the scheme. Instead of engaging in a jocular debate with John A., however, Mowat accused him of falsifying his quotes, and thus lying to the members of the House.

As soon as Mowat finished challenging John A.'s honesty, and the Speaker had stepped down from his chair, John A. stood up, strode furiously across the aisle until he was inches from Mowat's face, and shouted, "You damned pup. I'll slap your chops!"

Fat as he was, Mowat still miraculously managed to dodge John A.'s upraised fists. Almost immediately, however, Mowat would seek revenge, in a way he knew would prove most humiliating to his former boss.

By May 1861, the parties plunged themselves into another election. Out of sheer spite, Mowat offered himself as a candidate against John A. in Kingston, an unthinkable act on the part of any other politician. Kingston was the heart and soul of John A.'s constituency, its citizens as dear to him as his own extended family, and now Mowat was trying to steal those family members away.

Mowat tried to embarrass John A. at every turn. When John A.'s team reserved the town hall for a Monday-night meeting, he discovered Mowat's team had already secured the hall for that morning, attracting a surprisingly large turnout. When Macdonald held his meeting as scheduled that night, Mowat's people heckled John A., engaging in fistfights with his supporters. The following day, Mowat held a meeting at the city park in Kingston. Meanwhile, John A. planned ward meetings, one of them to take place in the same district grammar school that he and Mowat had attended together as children. Before the grammar school meeting could proceed very far, however, Mowat's people arrived and hurled stones at the school's windows, while others charged up the school's staircase to take John A.'s meeting by force. Instead of listening to John A.'s speech, his supporters hurriedly wedged desks against the windows to protect themselves from flying glass and tried to barricade the top of the staircase from the marauding mob. Eventually Mowat's crew departed, but John A.'s confidence had been shattered, and his grief over his one-time friend's actions was profound.

For the first time, John A. had to struggle to win Kingston. To show his level of sacrifice, on July 23, he attended a meeting of Kingston's Temperance Society and publicly swore off the evils of alcohol. The *Montreal Star* reported that he delivered a short address at the meeting, explaining his miraculous conversion to sobriety. It all seemed too good to be true. It was. As soon as John A. returned to the privacy of his apartments, he toasted his own hubris. To no one's surprise, he never became a member in good standing of the society.

Though some Conservative Party members supported Rep by Pop, John A. held firmly against it in favour of a federal union of the British North American provinces. Even Kingston's local papers criticized John A.'s aversion to the Rep by Pop scheme. Despite the schisms in his party, however, John A. miraculously pulled victory from the jaws of defeat. When counted, the vote was 758 for Macdonald, 474 for Mowat. John A. was elated. His mood improved even more when he learned that George Brown had lost Toronto, taking his tattered Rep by Pop with him.

For the first time in his professional career, John A.'s much vaunted public magnetism had almost failed to save him from defeat. In the future, he would have to reinvent himself to suit the temper of the times. For now, however, he could afford to celebrate. The night of his election victory, he rode a carriage through the streets of Kingston, toward Hazeldell. As her son's carriage approached, eighty-four-year-old Helen rose from a chair and stood unsteadily in front of the Hazeldell house to greet him. John A. embraced his mother warmly, as other family members stood in line to congratulate him. Afterwards, the family gathered around a picnic table and ate a meal Helen had helped to prepare, as the sun set on the horizon.

The same month John A. celebrated his victory, America's Civil War commenced, with Britain taking the Confederate side. Personally, John A. favoured neither North nor South to win,

George-Étienne Cartier. *(LAC C002162)*

but he knew Britain feared that, should the North win the war, it might try to invade Canada and claim it as its own territory. Britain wished Canada to arm itself accordingly in the event of such a calamity. In response, John A. and George-Étienne Cartier introduced the Militia Bill and tried to pass it in the House. The bill called for a force of fifty thousand men to defend the border, if necessary. The Opposition thought the bill was too expensive – and alarmist. For weeks, the bill languished in the House, with the French expressing particular resistance to its introduction.

On May 20, 1862, by a vote of 61 to 54, the Militia Bill was defeated. Shortly afterwards, the Conservative Party fell, and John A. and Cartier immediately submitted their resignations. For John A., after eight years as Attorney General, three as Opposition Leader for Canada West, and eighteen years in government, leaving was a relief.

"You will have seen that I am out of office. I am at last free thank God and can now feel as a free man. I have longed for this hour & only a sense of honour has kept me chained to my post," he wrote to his sister Margaret.

At last, John A. was on his way home to Kingston, his mother, his sisters, Williamson, and his son. His first objective was to resume working full-time at his law office to pay off bills.

By the time he arrived in Kingston, the family was discussing another move to a farm named Heathcliffe, which Williamson planned to buy. John A. worried about uprooting Helen once again in her fragile condition. However, the issue became moot when, on October 24, Helen died peacefully at Hazeldell. John A. had been by her side exactly when he needed to be, filling him with much solace. Out of respect for Helen's death, Williamson delayed his plans to move for a year.

Macdonald had little faith that the new government, with John Sandfield Macdonald leading the Liberals, would survive a year. Though he may not have known it himself, rather than retiring, John A. was simply taking a breather. He was only forty-seven-years old, and he understood better than anyone that absence makes the heart grow fonder. It was inevitable that he would be called back, and equally inevitable that, if he were, he could not refuse.

Despite promising to settle down in Kingston, John A. soon got itchy feet. Shortly after his mother's death, he travelled to England, where he remained until February 1863. Ostensibly, he was conducting some Trust and Loan Company business for his law office. In truth, he was testing the political water to see if he retained favour among British officials.

It didn't take long for him to find the answer. Members of the highest levels of society feted him like royalty. Invitations to attend private functions flowed in. Several dignitaries tried to convince John A. to return to Canada to lead the Conservatives. He mulled over the possibility of running for office once again but was only prepared to make a definitive move when the pear was "ripe," as he told a friend.

Meanwhile he enjoyed his stay in England, and travelled to Scotland to tie up lose ends in his family's personal affairs. By reconnecting with his past, he was obtaining a new perspective on himself. He met never-before-seen relatives. In fact, the trip rejuvenated his spirits as little before had done. He wrote to friends that he felt "sound in wind and limb."

Sound enough it seems to steer his course right back to Quebec and the halls of power. In May 1863, Sandfield Macdonald's Liberal government was dissolved, and though it was re-elected in the fall of that year, the ineffectual government was deadlocked with the Reformers. In December of 1863, Sandfield Macdonald appointed Albert Richards, a Reform MP for South Leeds, as Solicitor General. According to parliamentary rules, Richards was obligated to run for re-election in his constituency. With Richards seeking re-election, the Reformers temporarily lacked the required majority to lead the government. As a result, Macdonald made his move, determined to win South Leeds from Richards, and thus permanently disrupt the balance of seats in the House. As he raced from one town to another throughout South Leeds, John A. attracted a strange ally in the form of former Reform Party member Thomas D'Arcy McGee. Fortunately for John A., Sandfield Macdonald had dismissed McGee from his party during the 1863 Cabinet shuffled. McGee never forgot the slight.

A former Fenian from Ireland, later from the United States, McGee now championed the cause of national unity in Canada. He had supported the Militia Bill, viewing the Union Army as an elephant in Canada's tent, or at least right outside the tent. Should the North win the Civil War, they might be happy to join the Fenians and attack Canada, he thought. An excellent speaker, McGee could summon considerable support among the Irish Catholics in Canada West as well as Canada East, which could ultimately only enhance John A.'s chances of leading the country.

In January 1864, John A. and McGee embarked on a public-relations spree to "fight the union battle," in McGee's words, in Western and Eastern Canada. McGee told Macdonald that he promised to fight the battle anywhere he might be of use, with advantages "to the vast public interests at stake." The two new friends also shared another objective, this one far less lofty: namely, to get as drunk as they could along the way. In the evenings, they ate supper, drank wine, then led singsongs, one of their favourite ditties being "A drunken man is a terrible curse / But a drunken woman is twice as worse." During their whistle-stop tour of the Province of Canada, when critics complained about the degree of alcoholism prevalent in the Conservative Party, John A. jocularly warned McGee, "This Government can't afford two drunkards – and you've got to stop."

John A. easily beat Albert Richards in South Leeds, the win sweetened by the fact that Richards had also been Solicitor

General. With Richard's defeat, John Sandfield Macdonald lost his majority in the House. He gamely tried to hold on to power but finally, by March 1864, resigned his seat under pressure.

From the affairs of state to the domestic politics, early in 1864, James Williamson reluctantly asked John A. to visit Hazeldell to discuss the thorny question of tensions between him and Louisa. Without Helen as her closest ally, Louisa struggled to retain dominion over even the smallest things in the house. When she wasn't trying to assert her authority, Louisa spent long hours alone in her room, eschewing the company of even her own sister.

John A. told an exasperated Williamson he would try to resolve the ongoing friction arising between Louisa and her brother-in-law after the parliamentary session ended. With Parliament in such disarray, however, he never got a chance.

In March 1864, Sandfield Macdonald had recognized his party lacked enough seats to exercise control over the House, so he resigned. That left the government in a quandary. Were they condemned to re-electing the same individuals, just to see their administrations fall before they achieved any of their objectives? As author Donald Swainson points out, some members of the House discussed the possibility of building a common coalition. Macdonald himself offered to step aside should a new leader be willing to form an effective government. Finally, as a temporary solution, another Conservative Party was formed, headed by Dr. Étienne Taché as its titular leader. The Quebec-born Taché was elected to the legislative assembly of the Province of Canada in 1841 as a member from Canada East (Quebec); however, he held a series of posts in back-to-back administrations. His administration became known as the Taché-Macdonald government, but less than three months later (by June), it, too, had collapsed.

As summer approached, all eyes in the House turned in the direction of John A. The man, who would ultimately list himself in the parliamentary registry as a "cabinet maker," could stubbornly reject other people's ideas. When the word *Confederation* rose from a whisper to a roar in the House among his colleagues, however, Macdonald began to see its merits as a way of permanently solving the tensions between Canada West and Canada East. In order to draft a plan to achieve this Confederation, he would soon receive help from new allies.

At the same time, John A. had other unions on his mind. Unbeknownst to most of his friends, except his private secretary, since his 1860 valentine party in Quebec, John A. had set his romantic sights upon a woman who matched him in brains, wit, and humour, a woman who was destined to turn Ottawa upside down. Even as slow courtships go, this one broke all records, but John A. was now in a mood to make a move. He had fallen in serious like.

VII

PLAYING THE MARRIAGE CARD

As she dined with her brother Richard at the Rossin House Hotel in Toronto in December 1856, twenty-three-year-old Agnes Bernard had been unaware of a secret, albeit married, admirer. His name was John A. Macdonald, and he was dining with a colleague at the same hotel. As Agnes rose to leave, John A. ran his eyes up and down her tall, slender frame, across her taut and tawny skin, to her sun-burnished cheeks, and finally to her "fine eyes," jet black, the same colour as her hair. When he asked, his colleague informed him they were "an English family settled on Lake Simcoe. I do not know their names." From that moment on, John A. had consciously filed Agnes's attributes away in his memory bank to collect interest, while his colleague collected information about her family's identity.

Within six months, John A. had offered Agnes's brother Richard a job as his private secretary. When Richard declined, John A. asked Richard's elder brother, Hewitt, who quickly accepted the offer. Hewitt had established a high, if not entirely highly popular, public profile in Barrie, Ontario, through his work as a lawyer with the firm of Patton, Bernard & Ardagh. He was also an insurance agent for the Colonial Life Assurance Company, as well as a municipal councillor. He regularly wrote editorial opinion pieces for the local papers, the *Northern Advance* and the *Herald*, urging citizens to show a higher degree of social responsibility by volunteering, as he did, to join the local Rifle Brigade, as well as be volunteer firefighters. He vigorously lobbied against the construction of manufacturing plants within the town limits, because of the noxious odours these plants emitted. In letters to local newspapers, businessmen dismissed Hewitt as a "toffee nosed snob." One even questioned Hewitt's manhood. "Bernard would not allow a soap and candle manufactory, but would drive manufacturers without the limits of the town for fear of offence to his aristocratic nostrils; however the public know his predilections, so let it be," wrote one critic cryptically.

On February 26, 1858, the *Northern Advance* officially announced Hewitt's "retirement" from Patton, Bernard & Ardagh. He didn't just have himself to move to Toronto, but also his sister, Agnes, and mother, Theodora, who had moved from England to Barrie to live with him in 1857. This scenario played right into John A.'s hands for, as much as he admired Hewitt, he admired his sister even more.

If Agnes failed to reciprocate John A.'s glances at the Rossin House Hotel in 1856, she certainly showed more willingness in 1858, when she accompanied Hewitt to the opera at Shaftesbury Hall in Toronto. As was his habit following Isabella's death, John A. sat in the front gallery, surrounded by a bevy of beautiful women. Hewitt and Agnes meanwhile sat down below in the orchestra pit. As Agnes raised her head, she met John A.'s gaze for the first time. Even from a distance, she felt drawn to what she called his "forcible, yet changeful face, with such a mixture of strength and vivacity, and his bushy, dark, peculiar hair as he leaned on his elbows and looked down."

Still, it wasn't until Agnes attended John A.'s rococo Valentine's Day party in Quebec City in 1860 on Hewitt's arm (Agnes and Theodora following Hewitt to any city to which his business took him) that she seriously set her romantic sights on John A., and he on her. Agnes and her mother had moved from Toronto to Quebec City to live at Mrs. Steele's boarding house, when John A. began calling on her under the pretext that he wanted to get to know Hewitt's mother a little better. Before long, he and Agnes were courting, attending musical shows, dining at restaurants, and strolling through the city's parks. He was soon besotted by Agnes's wit, erudition, and intelligence, resembling so much that of his mother, Helen's. Agnes's Huguenot background also proved alluring, since she both spoke and read French with ease, and possessed a passion for politics.

As their courtship evolved, they discovered yet more characteristics in common. For one thing, they both loved power. "My love of power is strong, so strong that sometimes I dread; it influences me when I imagine I am influenced by a sense of right," Agnes admitted in her diary. John A. confessed to possessing much the same vice. "I don't care for office for the sake of money, but for the sake of power; for the sake of carrying out my own views of what's best for the country," he said. It was therefore easy to understand what drew the two together, and what might conceivably drive them apart.

Hewitt and John A., meanwhile, shared similar business habits, many of them bad. Both failed to pay taxes on investment properties. In 1860, B. W. Smith, sheriff of Barrie, seized and sold lands and tenements belonging to Hewitt Bernard, due to his failure to pay taxes. Similarly, in 1867, John A. received from the Ottawa Collector's Office a notice to pay taxes on his law-office property. The notice contained a stern warning from the city councillor: "If the said taxes be not paid a Warrant will be issued according to law." John A. hardly shrivelled in fear. Fully a year passed before he finally advised his staff to pay the fee.

Agnes instinctively knew the nature of John A.'s faults. She had heard stories of his dissipated habits, especially from Hewitt, who had seen his employer carried from late-night dinners feet first more than once, yet she felt certain she could change him and transform him into the settled, sober family man she secretly believed he always longed to be. She would soon discover her naiveté.

Agnes's family background was as exotic as John A.'s was conformist, yet financial reversals marred both childhoods. Agnes's father, Thomas Bernard, and his wife, Theodora, had moved from England to the British colony of Jamaica in 1826. There they had four boys in rapid succession: Hewitt, Richard Barrett, Philip Hewitt, and Walter Stewart. Two infant daughters died within days of each other in early 1834, victims of one of the island's numerous epidemics caused by its dirty drainage system.

Thomas Bernard, a lawyer, developed an impressive reputation on the island. He entered politics as a member of the assembly for St. Catharines and as a justice of the peace for various

Agnes Macdonald loved power as much as her new husband. *(LAC PA026681)*

counties, joined the volunteer militia, and served as a firewarden for St. James' Anglican Cathedral. In addition to serving in a political capacity, Thomas owned a five-hundred-acre sugar-cane plantation named "Dirty Pit," located on a clifftop several miles south of Spanish Town. The plantation's profits kept the family financially comfortable enough that they could acquire additional properties. To retain his wealth, however, Thomas knowingly circumvented the law by hiring black slave labour in contravention to the Abolition Bill passed by the British Parliament in 1808. In retaliation, in 1832, slaves burned down several of Thomas's properties. Fearing for his family's safety, Thomas reluctantly freed his slaves, the government reimbursing him for the loss of his livelihood. When a government subsidy proved insufficient to support his family, Thomas went bankrupt. It was into this embittered atmosphere that Agnes was born on August 24, 1836.

Rather than leave the island, in 1840 Thomas moved to Spanish Town to practise law. By this time, his elder sons, Richard and Hewitt, were in England studying law, while Philip, Walter, and Agnes lived in "the confines of the hot, dirty city life" of Spanish Town. During the summer, the family rented a house in the Blue Mountains, where, as she grew older, Agnes learned to garden. While Thomas supervised his sons' educations, Theodora educated Agnes in literature and religious studies, but like her future husband John A., Agnes grew easily bored and turned to poetry to relieve her frustration. At nine she wrote in her schoolbook, "I do not strive to please / You dearest Mother, in the least / But, for the future, I'll be good / I'll not be naughty or be rude / But let my better conduct prove / My sure affection & how deep my love."

Agnes's eldest brother, Hewitt, returned to Jamaica in the mid-1840s and established a law partnership with friends on the island. Shortly afterwards, as sales of sugar and coffee bottomed out, the economy of the island plunged into a recession, which showed no signs of abating. Then, in March 1850, Asiatic cholera struck the island, killing thirty-two thousand inhabitants in all, Thomas Bernard among them. The family laid his body to rest at Claremount Chapel in the parish of St. Ann's.

As Thomas's eldest son, Hewitt assumed responsibility for the female members of the Bernard family. The year after the cholera epidemic struck, he convinced fifteen-year-old Agnes and her mother, Theodora, to move to England and stay with family members while he investigated business opportunities in Canada. His brother Richard accompanied him, but Philip, twenty, and Walter, eighteen, declined to leave Jamaica. Agnes never saw Philip or Walter again. Though they all planned to meet eventually in Canada, Philip chose instead to pursue business opportunities in Mexico, where he died of undisclosed causes, while Walter remained in Jamaica and bought a sugar plantation. He died on the island in 1861.

Agnes and Theodora settled in the small village of Lacock, just outside Bath, England, for three years and waited for Hewitt to invite them to Canada. Agnes made good use of her time in England, studying French and painting with local tutors. She enjoyed reading classic literature, but wasn't afraid to voice her opinions, even if they were negative. For instance, she developed a visceral distaste for Nathaniel Hawthorne, American author of such daring literary fare as *The Scarlet Letter* and *The House of the Seven Gables*, whom she dismissed in her diary as a snob. "Hawthorne's English notes [sic] which I am reading, annoy me a great deal. It is an amusing book to me, I suppose, in some way, or I should not read it, but he is sneering and prejudiced. In the bottom of his heart I can see he, in spite of himself, admires Oxford and our beloved Cathedrals, but in a grudging and reluctant manner. It makes my mouth water to think how much the beggar saw and my eyes water to see how little he appreciated!"

Agnes had matured into a woman of strong opinions and adventurous tastes. When Hewitt summoned her and Theodora to join him in Barrie, Ontario, Agnes viewed it as simply another great adventure. After docking in Quebec City, they travelled by ship to Montreal, then again by ship to Toronto. Hewitt met them in Toronto, and rode with them on the Huron and Simcoe Railway to Barrie. Before a fortnight passed, the two women had thrown themselves into social activities organized by the local Trinity Anglican Church, where Hewitt was churchwarden. Agnes also taught Sunday school, and copied out the morning sermons for the minister, Rev. S. B. Ardagh, who also happened to be one of Hewitt's law-firm partners.

For a young woman of Agnes's sophistication, Barrie's social entertainments lacked excitement. There was Barrie's Philharmonic Society and the Lake Simcoe Boat Club, for which Hewitt acted as commandant, but Agnes sought edgier excitement. In the winter months, she enjoyed ice fishing for cod and tobogganing at top speed down the region's hillsides at midnight on "coasters" made of wood, slowing down and finally stopping on the surface of a "frozen pine-fringed lake." Like her future husband, she also had expensive tastes, which she liked to satisfy by embarking on regular shopping trips to Toronto.

John A. and Agnes's courtship experienced several starts and stops, invariably initiated by the king of cold feet, John A. Some accounts suggest that John A. proposed to Agnes as early as 1860, and she refused. If she did refuse, it was almost certainly because she believed rumours about his more dissipated habits when out of her sight. Much to her dismay, he persisted in reading trashy French novels, and there were rumours that he continued to visit other women, especially rough-and-tumble tavern owners like Eliza Grimason. A series of personal tragedies further slowed the romance's momentum. In 1861, when Agnes's brother Richard died, he left behind a pregnant widow, who subsequently gave birth to a daughter. Meanwhile, Helen Macdonald's death drove John A. into a spiral of depression and heavy drinking. Money problems may have also played a part in keeping the couple apart. On March 27, 1864, John A.'s law partner, Archibald Macdonnell, suddenly died. His death greatly diminished the amount of income John A.'s law firm raised. As a result, nearing fifty years old, John A. suddenly realized that he was again deeply in debt, so deeply in debt that he despaired of raising himself out of it. As a consequence, rather than admit the truth to Agnes, he allowed the romance to cool, content to monitor her movements through Hewitt.

The last and most persuasive reason why the romance cooled was that John A. had embarked, along with his colleagues, on the challenge of his life: namely, to attempt to draft virtually the entire Constitution for the federal union of British North America in Quebec in the summer of 1864. Ironic as it seemed, the idea had originally come from George Brown, former leader of the Clear Grits and owner of the *Globe* newspaper. Brown sought to devise a system of government that would work to solve constitutional problems in the Province of Canada. The group, known as The Great Coalition, included Étienne Taché, George-Étienne Cartier, George Brown, D'Arcy McGee, and Alexander Galt, a former inspector of finance in the Macdonald-Cartier government.

John A. personally drafted virtually the entire Constitution for the federal union of British North America in two weeks. It was a monumental task. Hewitt Bernard was present to record the proceedings. Already appointed chief clerk in the office of the Attorney General, Canada West, by the conference's second day, Bernard was its executive secretary.

In his book *MacDonald: His Life and World*, Professor Peter Waite reveals that, after completing this almost-miraculous amount of administrative work in Quebec, John A. fell off the wagon, showing up for meetings three hours late and half drunk. At one lunch, his eyelids drooping, he initiated an old argument with George Brown over contracts for the Parliament Buildings in Ottawa. At last, Alexander Galt gently steered John A. to a more private place.

On September 1, 1864, John A. joined his fellow Confederation delegates on board the steamer the *Queen Victoria*, in the journey to Charlottetown. The conference there was to be the first of three designed to project Confederation as a reality to the public.

Upon seeing the *Queen Victoria* steam into the harbour, W. H. Pope, the provincial secretary of Prince Edward Island, borrowed an oyster boat from a local fisherman and rowed out to where the *Queen Victoria* was moored. There, he officially welcomed the group to the Charlottetown Conference.

A revived John A. was superb at the social aspects of the event. He schmoozed the Maritimers by hosting balls and cocktail parties, punctuated with political talk. Soon the conference members travelled on to Halifax, Saint John, and Fredericton.

On October 10, the Confederation Conference proceeded to Quebec City. Delegates from Newfoundland, Prince Edward Island, Nova Scotia, and New Brunswick held discussions in the makeshift Parliament Buildings on the hills above the St. Lawrence River. John A. also dominated this conference. He moved the first resolution, consisting of a plan for British North America to be promoted by a federal union under the Crown of Great Britain. The conviviality that had dominated the Charlottetown Conference soon dissipated, however. Newfoundland was unimpressed with the notion of a federal union. Prince Edward Island similarly disliked the draft constitution, fearing it would lose its identity unless it obtained special privileges. For a few days, it appeared as if the federalist scheme might unravel.

In public, John A. played the part of a consummate conciliator and conference leader. He charmed the Maritime delegates and their wives at parties, yet in private buckled under the strain, sometimes to a shocking extent. On October 20, Governor General Francis Monck's sister-in-law wrote him, "John A. Macdonald is always drunk now, I am sorry to say, and when someone went to his room the other night, they found him in his night shirt, with a railway rug thrown over him, practicing Hamlet before a looking-glass."

No matter how bizarre his private behaviour might have become, however, John A.'s restorative powers never failed him. During the conference, he had been practically a one-man band. His social itinerary was dizzying. He introduced Maritime leaders to Quebec leaders, toasted each at special dinners and celebrations, danced, delivered speeches extemporaneously, and told jokes, all the while selling the Confederation scheme to a reluctant audience. As a measure of his success as the host of the event, even after the conference officially broke up, several delegates from the East remained to enjoy the hospitality of the French Canadians.

As productive as the work was, each provincial legislature still had to accept the Confederation scheme. The Colonial Office in London also had to approve it. The process, which had started out so promisingly, threatened to drag out indefinitely if the Maritimers continued to react coolly.

John A. frenetically stoked the Maritime delegates' interest, even accompanying them up the Ottawa River to the site of the new permanent Parliament Buildings, which were still under construction. In the middle of his umpteenth speech, however, he suddenly seized up, fell back in his chair, and nearly passed out. As the rest of the roving delegates journeyed toward Toronto, John A. disembarked in Kingston to seek respite within the hornet's nest that now constituted his family at Hazeldell.

As John A. attempted to rest, Louisa and Margaret buzzed about him plumping pillows and cooking healthful meals made from vegetables from their own gardens. Then James Williamson reintroduced his plans for the family to move to a new and more spacious home as soon as possible.

This was just the kind of domestic complication John A. didn't feel he needed right now. In fact, he greeted conversations like these with mild resentment. While it was true that Hugh John could not have flourished without the paternal intervention of Williamson, it was also true that Williamson received many employment opportunities for his friends after obtaining references from John A. In return, he tended to take for granted the status he enjoyed from his association with John A. And the fact was, at this time, John A. was sick, his colic gnawing his intestines like a clawhammer. Sometimes, he grew so jaundiced that the whites of his eyes appeared yellow.

John A. spent six days in Kingston trying to regain his health. During his stay, he examined Heathfield, a property located a mile and a quarter outside of town, which Williamson had already leased as the family's next house. One of its previous owners, a druggist named Charles Heath, had named the house. The two-storey Ontario cottage-style house featured a spacious kitchen on the main floor and two servants' bedrooms in the rear wing, a generous-sized drawing room, a dining room, a slightly smaller parlour, and four bedrooms. There was also a large cellar and a nearby well filled with fresh water. The first floor included a water closet, and a single stove heated the two water closets on the second floor. As added features, the house also included a coachhouse, a woodshed, and a summer kitchen. Best of all, it was surrounded by five acres of arable land, more than enough to help the occupants avoid arguing over the size of their respective gardens. Just in case, however, Louisa bought an acre from Williamson, in which she planned to plant vegetables. Margaret, on the other hand, intended to plant her vegetables in her husband's garden.

Finally, to satisfy Louisa's desire to live in a house owned by her brother, John A. assumed the lease specifically for her. Much to Louisa's satisfaction, Margaret and James were now her tenants. Whenever John A. was in town, he would sit at the head of the table, with Louisa facing him at the opposite end. Over the ten years he was to rent the house, John A. sent gifts to improve the property, including a set of brown and white tiles with scenes from Shakespeare's plays to be set around the fireplace and packets of special seeds for Louisa to plant in the garden. He even contributed £400 to help Williamson pay for necessary repairs to the structure.

Negotiations over the pecking order at Heathfield proved almost as tough as the Confederation talks, and John A. left Kingston more exhausted than when he arrived. He headed back to Quebec by train to address the Canadian Cabinet about Confederation, and to secure the approval of the Colonial Office.

Expanding the country westward was also high on John A.'s list of priorities. John A. knew that the Hudson's Bay Company would have to sell its property in the prairies, with the Imperial government picking up the tab. This was necessary if a railway was to be built to traverse the country. Meanwhile, the civil war was concluding in the south, reawakening fears of the Union Army invading Canada, with the Fenians not far behind.

In February 1865, the Confederation debates began in the House, which was located in Quebec, since construction on Ottawa's buildings was not yet complete. John A., leader of the assembly, compellingly convinced his colleagues that, without Confederation, Canada would descend into anarchy, with no stable government to unify it. He stressed that a stronger Canada meant a stronger defence against American aggression. It was a powerful tactic in light of the tensions of the time. He envisioned a federal state, run by a centralized government located in Ottawa, rather than by each province, yet he emphasized the importance of providing each province with its own autonomy when it came to cultural interests, a scheme that did much to pacify the French Canadians. Parliament, meanwhile, was to have a House of Commons, with members elected by voters, and a Senate, whose appointed members would represent each region.

The present Province of Canada was to be divided into the provinces of Ontario and Quebec. To John A.'s credit and relief, the Parliament approved the Constitution he helped draft by a vote of 91 to 33.

John A. wanted to acclimatize himself early to the city that would become the country's capital. For several long months, he chose to struggle with the Confederation scheme in his unheated East Block office in Ottawa, while living in a house on Daly Street in nearby Sandy Hill with Hewitt, Alexander Galt, and Charles John Brydges, an executive of the Grand Trunk Railway.

Rev. Thomas Bedford-Jones, rector of St. Alban's Anglican Church in Ottawa, was one the house's most frequent visitors. He and Hewitt had struck up a friendship after meeting at a dinner party. Bedford Jones approved of Hewitt's social self-constraint. To him, Hewitt was a "zealous churchman," who "at the end of his business day, was glad of what the Scotch would call a friendly crack, or a little music, if he did not play Patience as he smoked a quiet pipe."

Agnes decided to remain living in Quebec City during the beginning of 1865, where she ventured into the countryside to paint, watercolours being her specialty. Painting became her escape from the torment of reading Hewitt's letters from home, which he filled with tales of John A.'s high spirits and popularity, especially among the women. Hewitt had good reason to torture his sister in this way. He'd seen John A.'s moral weaknesses up close, and didn't wish to see his sister to be drawn into his dangerous vortex. Hewitt may have underestimated his sister's own love of power, however. Rather than turn away from John A., she pursued him even more ardently, moving out of Canada altogether for England, thereby forcing John A. to stop taking her presence near Hewitt for granted.

Agnes had another reason for moving abroad, instead of following John A. and her brother: Ottawa's drainage systems. Governor General Monck's sister Elizabeth warned them that the city's drainage systems were so "atrocious" that "residents had to pay a fifteenpence to have a boy bring water to them." Agnes and

Theodora knew that Jamaica's 1832 cholera epidemic had almost certainly travelled through Jamaica's poor drainage systems, and they feared suffering a similar devastation. Rather than wait for construction on the Parliament Buildings to be completed, Agnes and Theodora took Frances Monck's advice to "keep out" rather than move to what Monck dismissed as a "squalid city" of "dirt roads."

By the late spring of 1865, Agnes and her mother were busily unpacking moving boxes in a handsome house on Grosvenor Square, financed by Hewitt. "England is a delicious country for the rich, but I should hate it for the poor, and there is no denying, at least, I think not, that the middle class toady and fawn," Agnes later recorded in her diary, clearly considering herself a member of the former rather than the latter class. Agnes's confidence was probably more misplaced than she might have imagined. After all, Hewitt handled his finances as badly as his employer did.

In good times, John A. enjoyed his independence. In bad, he sought a women's touch. These were good times, and he was making the most of them, keeping Agnes at arm's length in the process.

In April 1865, Macdonald, accompanied by McGee, Galt, and Brown (whom John A. kept referring to patronizingly as "Sonny" during their voyage, his antipathy toward his one-time nemesis having returned), sailed for England. Upon arrival, the men checked into the swanky Westminster Palace Hotel, located on Victoria Street near Westminster Abbey and government offices. The hotel, which visitors described as realizing "expectations even of the luxurious commercial classes," contained two hundred rooms, thirteen sitting rooms, gentlemen's and ladies' coffee rooms, and several committee and dining rooms. Most conveniently, it also featured telegraph communications between it and the Houses of Parliament. The hotel was also the first of its kind to have elevators and was well situated within walking distance to parks, as well as to Belgravia, Pimlico, and Knightsbridge.

An omnibus could carry visitors into the centre of town in less than ten minutes.

On May 30, John A. and his colleagues were formally presented to Queen Victoria at Buckingham Palace. This was heady stuff. Rather than being viewed as mere colonials, the men were treated like ambassadors. According to the *Illustrated London News*, Queen Victoria, still in mourning for Prince Albert, nevertheless greeted the men warmly, wearing a black silk dress, with a train trimmed with crepe and jet and a Mary Queen of Scots cap with a long veil ornamented with large pearls.

Happy to prick conventionality when it suited him, within days John A. and his esteemed colleagues attended Epsom Downs, where, like naughty schoolchildren, they blew peas through peashooters, at unsuspecting victims, collapsing in laughter with every direct hit.

Following the meetings, John A. remained in London for a week. While there, he received an honorary degree of Doctor of Civil Law from Oxford University. "This is the greatest honour they can confer, and is much sought after by the first men," he excitedly wrote Louisa.

By the spring of 1866, the Confederation ship had sprung a leak. Some members of the coalition of Confederation delegates, particularly delegates from the Maritimes, were squirming anew about the concept and what they might lose when it became law.

In April 1866, New Brunswick faced a new election when the anti-Confederation government collapsed. In an effort to ensure a favourable vote, John A. and his colleagues virtually financed the successful campaign of Leonard Tilley of New Brunswick. Shortly after Tilley's victory, Charles Tupper rushed a pro-Confederation resolution through the Nova Scotia assembly.

There was a mixture of bad and good news to come. On June 2, 1866, Fenians killed nine Canadians and wounded thirty others near Niagara Falls. The attack fuelled enthusiasm for Confederation as a defence against American invaders. Newspapers warned of further and even more ferocious attacks to come, but, after some time passed, it became apparent that no sustained offensive was in the offing. Yet John A. remained apprehensive. The attack brought on bad memories of his defence of Nils von Schoultz and, as usual, reflectiveness sent John A. into a drunken tailspin. The *Globe* accused him of being so drunk that he had had to "cling to his desk in the House to prevent himself from falling," when addressing the House as the minister of militia. As was his habit at such times, John A. took to his bed and made his critics wait until he felt strong enough to resume his duties.

All the Confederation delegates, including the Maritimers, knew that London had to host one more constitutional conference to "work out the details" of the new Constitution, including the country's new name. Just when fortune needed him the most badly, John A. lay in a depressive state in his bed at the Daly Street house in Ottawa, either unwilling or unable to board a vessel to England.

Exasperated and enraged, the Maritime delegation sailed for Britain in July without John A., hoping their actions would force him to get up. John A. did not budge. The rest of the delegates wouldn't follow the Maritime delegates without John A., and John A. had no intention of leaving until he was good and ready. Finally, on November 14, 1867, he was steady enough on his feet, and calm enough in his mind, to sail from New York to London.

As he set off, John A. appeared to worry less about losing the Maritime delegates than he did about losing Hewitt Bernard as his private secretary and friend once the conference ended. The two men had grown close during their time living together in Ottawa and working on the new Constitution. On a previous trip to London, however, Hewitt had romanced Georgina Mayne, the daughter of Sir Richard Mayne, chief commissioner of the Metropolitan Police in London and one-time member of Parliament.

The two became engaged sometime in 1865. No wedding date had yet been set, but with Agnes and Theodora now settled in London, Hewitt weighed the advantages of remaining close to his blood relatives. John A. used their voyage to England to convince Hewitt to move his new bride to Canada. At this point, John A. no doubt sweetened the pot by promising Hewitt a chance for unlimited advancement if he remained in his employ.

It didn't take much imagination to realize that John A. had ulterior motives in persuading Hewitt to remain in Canada. John A. missed Agnes. Just as he had been a less-than-ardent husband to Isabella when his political career was on the ascendency, so he was an insensitive suitor as he faced his canonization as Canada's saviour. Now, however, realism set in. His rapidly advancing age and diminishing health preyed on his mind, and there were periods when he felt intensely lonely. He had neglected his family for his career, and now he held the laurels and not much else. His son, Hugh, was no longer a child, but a nineteen-year-old student at the University of Toronto, having completed prep school at Queen's College. John A. accepted that James Williamson was more of a father figure to Hugh John than was he. However, Williamson's religious intolerance and strict adherence to the Orange Order made him John A.'s political opponent as often as his ally. It would soon become apparent just how much of Williamson's protégé Hugh John really was.

With the British North America Bill approaching passage in the British Parliament, John A. became a celebrity. The British papers praised his adroit chairmanship of what they termed the London Conference, which officially opened on December 4. Citizens recognized him on the street. In a few short weeks, he had become a star of international repute, yet he retired alone each night to his hotel room. Faced with this stifling emotional future, he set out to woo Agnes once again. There had been many women in John A.'s life, but only Agnes had the "keen wit, quick perception, a liberal mind, and a certain unselfishness of heart" to merit her place beside him. Had Agnes been a conventional woman, she would have walked right past the neglectful John A. as he approached her on Bond Street on December 8, his coattails flapping behind him and his familiar rabbit-fur hat tilted jauntily on his head. Instead, she boldly walked toward him, her excitement swelling with each step. By now, Agnes was no longer a girl, but a thirty-one-year-old woman, who knew what she wanted and what she'd sacrifice to get it. By Christmas, the two were engaged.

During his free days and evenings in London, John A. relaxed at Agnes and Theodora's home in Grosvenor Square. Over tea and crumpets, he convinced them that, poor drainage or not, Ottawa was about to become the shining city on the hill and the centre of a brand-new bustling country stretching from sea to sea. The two women listened to his praise of Ottawa with rapt attention. Perhaps their fears about the city were misplaced after all, and Ottawa could become the cultural centre of Canada. Certainly, Agnes was determined to do her best to establish herself as an example of sophisticated womanhood. Up to this point, life had dealt her a bad hand, but now she was about to achieve prominence as the wife of a celebrity politician.

Not everyone looked forward to the upcoming nuptials. Hewitt, for one, feared Agnes would regret marrying such a mercurial and deeply troubled man as John A. Ottawa bureaucrat Edmund Meredith witnessed Hewitt's misgivings. "Hewitt did everything to dissuade his sister from the marriage," he wrote in his diary.

Undeterred by the challenges that lay ahead for her, Agnes immersed herself in planning the details of the wedding, which was to take place on February 16, 1867, at St. George's Hanover Square Anglican Church. John A. insisted upon marrying her as soon as possible, so she would be by his side during the post-Confederation celebrations. As Agnes packed up her and her mother's belongings in advance of their return to Canada, John A. continued chairing the London Conference, at which the delegates tried to agree on a name for the country, finally settling for the Dominion of Canada.

John A. was content but blindingly weary from work. One night in January 1867, he climbed into his bed at the Westminster Palace Hotel, with the daily newspapers spread around him. Even at the best of times, reading the political news was taxing, but this night John A. was particularly tired, and before he had time to clear the bed of papers, he drifted off to sleep. Unwittingly, he had neglected to blow out the candle on the bedside table next to him, and before long it tipped off the table onto the horsehair-filled mattress, quickly turning the sheets, pillows, blankets, as well as the curtains that encircled the bed, into a blazing inferno.

The stench of his own burning flesh awakened John A. even faster than did the heat from the fire. With as much vigour as he could muster in his arthritic fifty-two-year-old legs, John A. leapt up, pulled the flaming pillow out from beneath his head, yanked the curtains down, and dragged the bedclothes onto the carpeted floor, where he soaked them with water he poured from a jug that sat on his bedside table. In describing the accident to Louisa, he revealed that, as a final safeguard, he tore open his pillows and "poured an avalanch [sic] of feathers on the blazing mass & then stamped out the fire with my hands & feet." With no Jane Eyre to tend to his Mr. Rochester, John A. settled for enlisting George-Étienne Cartier and Alexander Galt to help him pour water on any fabric that might have remained smouldering in the horsehair mattress.

In the midst of his frenzied exertions, John A. failed to notice that his right shoulder blade "was much scorched." Days later, he wrote to Louisa, "My shirt was burnt on my back & my hair, forehead & hands scorched. Had I not worn a very thick flannel shirt under my nightshirt, I would have burnt to death."

The following morning, a doctor dressed John A.'s right shoulder, and John A. returned to the conference. Two days later, he discovered that the wound was infected. He returned to his hotel, where a doctor ordered him to bed. There he stayed for eight days. "I had a Merry Xmas alone in my own room and my dinner of tea & toast & drank all your healths in bohea though you didn't deserve it," he joked to Louisa. In order to rest, he had to cancel a planned trip with Agnes to the home of his cousin Evan Macpherson's for dinner, and a separate trip to William Clark's house, probably to inform his former brother-in-law of his upcoming wedding to Agnes.

Black clouds streaked across the sky above St. George's Hanover Square Church in the heart of Mayfair as Agnes and John A. exchanged vows before the Right Rev. Bishop Francis Fulford, the Metropolitan bishop of Canada. Behind Fulford stretched to the ceiling a magnificent stained-glass window of Flemish glass depicting the Last Supper.

England's *Leader* newspaper described the wedding as "a splendid affair." John A. wore his diplomatic uniform, complete with sword (which he didn't get stuck between his legs), while Agnes wore "traditional white satin" with a veil of "Brussels lace with a wreath of orange blossoms." George Tupper's wife, Emma, acted as one of the bridesmaids, as well as Georgina Mayne, Hewitt Bernard's fiancée. The other bridesmaids were Jessie McDougall and Joanna Archibald, friends of the bride. Two of the four bridesmaids wore blue silk dresses, matched with blue crepe bonnets, the other two wore "purplish pink" dresses, with pink crepe bonnets.

Following the wedding, Hewitt hosted a breakfast for the ninety wedding attendees in the ballroom of the Westminster Palace Hotel. The Ottawa *Daily Citizen* newspaper of March 8, 1867, described the event as a "brilliant reception." The paper revealed, "the tables were spread with every delicacy by a most artistic chef de cuisine and a profusion of the choicest plants in endless variety of full blossom and perfume. On the plate of every guest was a bunch of violets and snow-drops." John A. arose to toast the bride. Alluding to the Confederation plan in which the provinces united under the government of a female Sovereign, he proclaimed that as a "conscientious man," he felt bound to put his own theory into practice.

News of the wedding took even John A.'s former law partner Alexander Campbell by surprise. "And so you are going to subside into matrimony?" he wrote. "I am delighted to hear it and offer my best wishes to Miss Bernard. I didn't think you'd a done it."

After a brief honeymoon in Oxford, England, John A. and Agnes returned to London, where the British North America bill received its first reading in the House of Lords. Following this event, Queen Victoria invited John A. to a special court. "Now you must understand that this was not a general levee or drawing Room where everyone goes, but a special court at which only those specially summoned appear," John A. was at pains to inform Louisa by letter. Upon entering the room, the Queen extended her hand for John A. to kneel and kiss. When he rose, she said, "I am very glad to see you on this mission," whereupon John A. bowed and responded, "I hope all things are going well with you." Near the conclusion of the audience, John A. emphatically declared his intention to place Canada under the Queen's sovereignty "forever." The Queen then informed John A. that she was entrusting him with the formation of the first government as prime minister. Lord Carnarvon, the colonial secretary, was in attendance, as was Princess Louise, the wife of the Marquess of Lorne, who would eventually serve as Canada's Governor General. Princess Louise would hate Ottawa as much as Agnes did; however, in time she would hate Agnes even more.

Agnes vowed that her place was to be perpetually, even obsessively, by her husband's side, regardless of the nature of the occasion. "I have found something worth living for – living in – my husband's heart and love," she confessed in her diary. In the beginning, John A. found her wish to share in all of his accomplishments endearing. There is no question, too, that they shared a passionate physical relationship. Yet sooner than anyone, except perhaps Hewitt, could have anticipated, John A. would start to chafe at her ubiquitous presence in all aspects of his life. Agnes refused to become a decoration on her husband's arm but rather wished to be his confidante and adviser. John A. introduced her to some of his fellow Confederation delegates, whom she evaluated with a shocking degree of sanctimony. As Sandra Gwyn notes in her book *The Private Capital: Ambition and Love in the Age of Macdonald and Laurier*, Agnes disliked George-Étienne Cartier on sight, not because he was "exceedingly egotistical," in her words, but because he had brought his mistress with him to London, a woman named Luce Cuvillier, a dazzling and "brilliant sophisticate" who was said to "wear trousers in the privacy of her country home and to stomp around smoking cheroots in the style of George Sand." Indeed, despite her own French ancestry, Agnes sniffed at French pretensions altogether. "The French seem always wanting everything, and they get everything," she wrote with disdain in her diary.

When the BNA Act finally passed in the British Parliament, Agnes snuggled contentedly against her husband in the gallery. Without knowing it, she was already at the top of her game. From here, it would all be downhill.

Agnes and her mother, Theodora, spent their first few days in Ottawa unpacking possessions in John A.'s Daly Street home. The experience proved a strain. The stone-terraced house had been roomy enough for John A. and Hewitt, but proved much too cramped for Agnes and her mother. Worse, the sewage pipes leading to the street stank of rotted human waste that seeped into the family's clothing, hair, and even skin. What had started out as an intermittent olfactory annoyance for Hewitt and John A. quickly became such an overpowering problem that John A. was forced to move his papers up to Theodora's room, once Hewitt's room, located on the house's top floor. To make room for his mother, Hewitt, who had recently broken off his engagement to Georgina Mayne, moved into the garret. With her memory of her father's death from cholera spread by dirty drains still fresh in her memory, Agnes complained bitterly to John A. about their accommodations. He could do little, however. Housing in Ottawa was at a premium. Then, too, because of the recent death of his law partner, Archibald Macdonnell, John A. was grievously in debt yet again. For the time being, at least, the family would just have to make do where they were.

On May 6, 1867, John A. returned to his office in the Parliament Buildings. On this most joyous of days when he was to inaugurate Confederation, he was in a foul mood and stomped past bureaucrats lining the hallways to buttonhole him for a job. Once inside his office, he poured himself a stiff drink and lay back on a large red-leather chesterfield. The drink did not improve his humour, but plunged him into an even-more-brooding funk. He even failed to join some of his fellow delegates celebrating their achievements at the Rideau Club. George-Étienne Cartier's charming banter usually saved endlessly self-congratulatory meetings like this one, but he was still in London. As the clock clicked loudly in the background, it even looked as though John A. might skip a luncheon of cold beef and mutton served in the dining room. At last, at about two-thirty, John A. wobbled into the room and began eating and drinking, the Cabinet members eyeing him nervously. As celebrations to inaugurate Confederation go, this one was a flop. Bureaucrat Edmund Meredith, who attended the meal, described in his diary the inglorious manner of John A.'s departure. "John A. carried out of the lunchroom, hopelessly drunk. What a prospect Mrs. John A. has before her!"

By July 1, the day of the country's official celebration, John A.'s mood had improved appreciably. He and Agnes awakened just after midnight to a 101-gun salute but were too excited to go back to sleep. As the sun rose over Ottawa, citizens poured into the streets to celebrate Canada's official birthday. Church bells pealed from every direction. Three hundred visitors boarded the steamer *America* to cross Lake Ontario from St. Catharines to join in the cheering. In every city, town, and hamlet in Canada, celebrations broke out. "This new Dominion of ours came noisily into existence," Agnes recorded in her diary. With little pomp or ceremony, Governor General Monck drove up to the Parliament Buildings, strode into the East Block, and proceeded to John A.'s office, where he bestowed on him a knighthood.

As impressed as John A. was with his title, Agnes's excitement bordered on the hysterical. Now that she was Lady Macdonald, even their house had lost its stench. On July 5, she wrote in her diary, "I was an insignificant young spinster & what I might write did not matter, now I am a great Premier's wife & Lady Macdonald & 'Cabinet Secrets & Mysteries' might drop or slip off unwittingly from the nib of my pen."

Friends and even parliamentary foes stopped by John A.'s house to congratulate him, one of them John Sandfield Macdonald, whom Agnes dismissed as "very boring." During the evenings, John A. held meetings with potential ministers, while Agnes eavesdropped from an adjoining room. "Here in this house the atmosphere is so awfully political that sometimes I think the very flies hold Parliament on the kitchen Tablecloth," she wrote. She simply held her husband "in awe," though that feeling didn't stop her from trying to deflate his self-importance by teasing him. "Today he rebelled, poor man, & ordered me out of the room," she wrote. "I went at once but he relented, the good old Boy & after he called me back – he got the worst of it!"

For the next few months, harmony reigned throughout the house on Daly Street. "On the whole, I think he likes me near him," Agnes wrote of her husband. Indeed, never again in their lives would they live together as harmoniously as they did during the remainder of 1867 and into 1868.

Agnes particularly enjoyed those few evenings when John A. sat quietly at home in the second-floor parlour, playing Patience, his favourite card game, or read aloud excerpts from books such as *Lockesley Hall*, as she rested her head on his shoulder. She found his "soft Scottish brogue" the "sweetest music to [her] ears." Hewitt, whom John A. had promoted to deputy minister of justice, as well as Theodora, often joined them. As for her own reading habits, Agnes chose only those books John A. deemed "acceptable," usually clunkers such as *Jesuits in America* or *The Last Chronicle of Bartlett*, which even Agnes dismissed as "tedious." As passionate as Agnes was, she was squeamish about reading books containing sexual content. Whenever she breached the rules and read novels, she flagellated herself for her weakness. On Sunday mornings, she faithfully attended St. Alban's Church, usually alone. Upon her return home, she often found her husband still dozing or, much to her distress, meeting with Cabinet members in their parlour.

As a husband, John A. proved as unpredictable as he was impulsive. Providing her with only a single day's notice, John A. swept Agnes off to Toronto by train during their first summer as a married couple. Visitors crammed into their compartment all the way to Prescott, offering their congratulations. Once in Prescott, the group left by steamer for Kingston, where they visited briefly with John A.'s family. The steamer then continued to Toronto, where its weary occupants disembarked for the Queen's Hotel, located just north of Front Street. The hotel was among John's A.'s favourite watering holes, and one of the places where he had hammered out the terms of Confederation with George Brown. John A. particularly enjoyed receiving guests in the hotel's Red Parlour, with its large marble fireplace, luxurious crimson sofas, and velvet curtains. The room also featured a fully stocked bar, which John A. refilled on a regular basis with the finest in wines and liquors. Agnes enjoyed strolling in the large garden on the east side of the hotel when she and John A. weren't being "overwhelmed," in her words, with visitors, engagements, and parties. There was a separate parlour for women, as well as a games and billiards room. Each bedroom, meanwhile, featured running water, baths, and business telephones.

Back in Ottawa, Parliament officially convened on November 7, and Agnes sat in the gallery. When he thought no one was looking, John A. glanced up and winked at her or communicated information to her via sign language. When Agnes wasn't in the gallery, she could often be found perched on the steps of the parliamentary library, reading intently. Some parliamentarians resented her presence in this male domain. In an insulting jab at her sharp, angular features, one referred to her as John A.'s "mole catcher of a wife." At the end of each day, the couple rode a sleigh home down Sparks Street, the snow licking their foreheads as they nestled together to keep warm. "I tell him, his good heart and amiable temper are the great secrets of his success," she later wrote in her diary.

Agnes was both overly confident and brutally self-critical, especially in pleasing her husband. In January 1868, "dear, good, solid" Hugh visited from Toronto, where he was still studying at the University of Toronto. "One cannot help respecting & loving him – John is both fond & proud of him but the boy has been brought up necessarily much away from his father who is almost always in the seat of government & immersed in political affairs and never remains long at his, that is Hugh's home with his Aunts." To celebrate Hugh's visit, Agnes hosted a small tea party for him, but she was so nervous she spilled tea over her fingers and into his saucer. Even worse, she felt she failed to entertain him sufficiently. "Tea and games and supper, but it was very stupid, I could do nothing to promote gaiety." John A.'s natural vivacity saved the evening, but didn't bolster Agnes's self-confidence. "He was charming, and we could never have done without him," she confessed, with a faint note of inferiority.

When she tried to host official dinners, the results were worse. Her menu choices tended to be stolid, consisting of such standbys as mock-turtle soup, mutton, and apple pudding. Though guests never complained, her husband filled the breach. "John says the dinner last night was a failure," she wrote sadly. "Perhaps my having ordered it to be ready an hour too soon might have had something to do with it."

No matter how hard Agnes tried, her husband upstaged her at his own parties. "He can throw off a weight of business in a wonderfully short span of time; oftentimes he comes in with a very moody brow, tired & oppressed – his voice weak, his step slow & ten minutes after he is making clever jokes & laughing like any School Boy, with his hands in his pockets & his head thrown back."

The very sociability she adored in John A., she abhorred in women, most particularly her next-door neighbour Charlotte Rose, wife of John A.'s great drinking buddy, John Rose, who was now minister of finance. She was full of charm, flattery, and syco-phancy toward her social superiors, though Agnes feared her "cosy yet cunning smile." Agnes couldn't compete with Charlotte, and she knew it. As her jealousy deepened, there became a kind of flamboyant vulgarity to Agnes's self-restraint. She withdrew into herself, deciding that "a repressed life" was the only honourable kind. "The longer I live & the more I see, the more strong is my conviction that a gay, unthinking life is not only wrong & per-verted but most unsatisfactory . . . and that a humble thriving self-recollecting, self-denying life is not only the safest & best but the happiest beyond all compare."

Agnes also disliked women who wasted their time on "Modern Novels." "Of all things, I hate the fashionable delin-eation of passion in novels à la mode. The scenes in Cometh Up [as a Flower], especially Nellie's last interview with her lover when, herself a wife, she tells him how dearly she loves him may be pow-erful, but in my humble opinion only coarse." She tried to create reading parties for her few women friends, but their popularity soon petered out because of Agnes's militant intellectualism.

She also disliked the type of women, usually American, who visited Canada with myriad "dainty toilettes . . . [attired] in most effect harmonies" . . . and "so blazing with diamonds that only strong eyes could gaze on their glitter unprotected." Each year, women of this type attended balls throughout the capital, and Agnes noted that "clasping not only slender throats, rounded arms and glossy hair, but also draperies of rich lace, and 'combinations' of colour delicately mysterious, these flashing jewels conveyed an effect of 'cash down' that was positively exasperating."

To compensate for her lack of personal diversion, Agnes frequently voiced her opinion concerning party politics, even recommending individuals for political appointments. She noted in her diary that whenever she "pressed on him an appointment Sir John looked very benign, very gracious, very pleasant – but – answered not one word! He never does!"

On top of all else, she was insecure about her plainness. Her teeth bothered her. In fact, as probably few knew, she had false teeth. Her dental bill on July 6, 1868, included the "repair of new tooth on old plate," gum treatments, and having teeth set in a rubber base, for a total cost of $49.

To compensate for her lack of friends, Agnes's life revolved around her husband ever more closely. She liked to keep him near her, alone. "I wish there was a law outlawing work on Sundays," she wrote. Through much coaxing, she eventually persuaded him to give up his Sunday-morning political powwows.

John A. chafed at Agnes's fussy ministrations. He loved parties and dashed off to them, leaving Agnes at home nursing her disapproval. When he wasn't attending parties, he was taking refuge in his office in the East Block. The office was roomy and comfortable, complete with deep carpeting and a large fireplace.

When Louisa wanted to visit with John A. and Agnes, he had to turn her away because of the stench from his house's drainage system. As she was prone to do, Louisa lapsed into periods of "intense melancholy." She no longer had Hugh John to care for, and, despite being John A.'s surrogate, she felt more and more like a third wheel in the Williamson home. Agnes sympathized with Louisa's plight and wrote her often.

Then there were the professional pressures. John A. had to entice the Maritime provinces to join in the Confederation scheme, but several provinces continued to hold out, including Nova Scotia and Prince Edward Island. Meanwhile, British Columbia refused to join the scheme unless they received a government promise that the land extending to British Columbia had been annexed from the Hudson's Bay Company, opening the way for construction of a cross-country railway. On top of it all, John A. continued to suffer economic problems, exacerbated by the devastating news that the Commercial Bank of the Midland District was teetering on the brink of bankruptcy. If the bank failed, John A., who was a director and shareholder, would lose his greatest source of income. Before this happened, a greater tragedy soon occurred, blocks from John A.'s own doorstep.

For weeks, D'Arcy McGee had been ill, plagued by portentous nightmares about his death, which he tried to slough off with his usual droll insouciance. John A. warned him about the dangers of insurgents in Canada, who did not appreciate his attacks against fellow Irish Catholics. McGee shrugged his warning off. In March, he told a colleague, "There is no danger of my being converted into a political martyr. If ever I were murdered, it would be by some wretch who would shoot me from behind."

On the night of April 6, 1868, McGee rose in Parliament to voice

D'Arcy McGee. *(William Notman/LAC C016749)*

his confidence in Charles Tupper's ability to persuade Nova Scotia to continue to support Confederation, in defiance of Joseph Howe's determination to repeal union attempts. His speech was impassioned and showed much of his distinctive fire. He reasserted his renunciation of Fenianism and his determination to support a united Canada as a prophylactic against those he now condemned as a roving band of murderous rogues, intent of invading Canada and trying to annex it to the United States.

John A. listened to the speech with one ear shut. He felt sick from the fumes from his home, as well as from overwork. Shortly after the debate concluded, McGee and John A. walked down to the bar of the House and purchased two cigars, each lighting one up. His spirits revived, John A. walked out the main door of the Parliament Buildings to catch his carriage. McGee chatted about Nova Scotia with Dr. J. F. Forbes, the member for Queens County, and joined Robert Macfarlane, a young member from Perth, Ontario, as he ordered a whisky and water. McGee and Macfarlane later proceeded to the cloakroom in the west lobby and then toward the main exit through which John A. had just departed. McGee was cheery as he and Macfarlane stood briefly to admire the full moon. The air outside was crisp, and smelled of freshly fallen snow, which lay in high drifts along the wet roadways.

Enjoying the fine weather, McGee and Macfarlane chose to walk home down Metcalf Street, moving slowly to accommodate McGee's bad right knee, which pained him but did not prevent him from walking. When the two men reached Sparks Street, they parted ways, as McGee proceeded along Sparks Street to Mrs. Trotter's boarding house. He made a jaunty spectacle in his black cashmere overcoat, black gloves, and new white top hat, leaning lightly on a bamboo cane topped with a silver handle.

Back at John A.'s home, Agnes had sat up waiting for him, as she did most nights when he worked late. She felt a queer sense of foreboding but couldn't explain to herself why. She stood up, and sat down, tried to read her Bible, then stood up again and peered out of the house to see if her husband was approaching. Finally, at approximately two-fifteen in the morning, she entered her mother's room and sought refuge on her bed. Theodora scolded her for sitting up for so long. Just then, Agnes heard carriage wheels outside her front door and "flew down" the stairs to welcome John A. home.

"We were cozy after that," she wrote. "He coming in so cheery – with news of the debate, I sitting by my dressing room fire, with his supper." In a curious tableau, as John A. ate, Agnes knelt on the floor, thanking God for their many blessings. Soon after, she went to bed, leaving John to digest his meal.

Mrs. Trotter's boarding house had three entrances. McGee took his key out of his coat pocket and inserted it into the latch keyhole of the middle entrance. Thinking she heard tapping, Mrs. Trotter opened the door. Just as she did so, she heard a shot fired behind McGee. According to the court proceedings, she testified, "a flash came in the door, appeared not more than half a yard from my face." She then reflexively ducked behind the door. It was lucky she did so, as the spent bullet embedded itself in the door frame of the entrance. Mortally wounded, McGee stumbled and fell flat on his back as blood streamed from his upturned head onto the road. His legs were in a spread-eagle position. Both of his arms stretched backwards, the left one extended at a right angle, the cane beneath it. His left glove remained on his hand, while the right glove lay beside his body. Despite the velocity of the bullet, it had failed to knock McGee's top hat from his head. His half-smoked cigar lay by the doorstep.

At John A.'s house, Agnes had just drifted off to sleep while John A. remained relaxing in her dressing room. In the early-morning hours, they heard an "insistent knock" at the front door. Agnes recorded the rest of the events in her diary. "I threw on a wrapper and ran into my dressing-room, just in time to see John throw up the window & to hear him call out, 'Is there anything the matter!!' The answer came up fearfully clear and hard thro' the cold moonlit morning. 'McGee is murdered – lying in the street – shot thro' the head.'"

Within minutes, Hewitt, still dressed, joined John A., as both men, reeling with disbelief, boarded a carriage that raced them across Sapper's Bridge to Mrs. Trotter's. There they found McGee still lying on the street, his lower face clotted with blood. The .32-calibre bullet had entered the back of his neck and exited through his mouth, propelling his false teeth into the hallway of the boarding house. John A. cradled McGee's head in his lap and pressed his fingers against his neck, checking for vital signs. Soon after, Dr. McGillivray arrived and confirmed the death. As John A. supported McGee's head, and McGillivray his feet, they carried the body inside, placing it on a coach. As a touching gesture of tenderness, they removed McGee's shoes, beneath which he wore woollen socks, and replaced them with carpet slippers.

After listening to the witnesses excitedly blurt out their accounts of the murder, John A. proceeded to the *Times* office at four o'clock in the morning and telegraphed the news to the police. A few hours later, all the major newspapers in the country would carry a headline announcing McGee's death. George Brown in the *Globe* spoke reasonably kindly of his former colleague but added somewhat uncharitably, "Mr. McGee was intensely disliked by a faction of his countrymen here. [Of] late he has been most temperate and abstemious, but he always had on him the shadow of coming disaster."

Agnes anxiously waited for John A. and Hewitt to return home, trembling with fear, "for one could not tell how many more assassins might be lurking in the graylit streets," as she noted. Finally, at five o'clock, both men came home. Hewitt proceeded upstairs silently as John A. walked into the parlour, his overcoat stained with McGee's blood. There, he collapsed into a chair. "He was much agitated, for him, whose self command is so wonderful," Agnes wrote. "'McGee is murdered, it's true,' he said, his face a ghostly white."

PRIVATE DEMONS

Before the sun had risen, John A. was back in his office making all the funeral arrangements and initiating a search for the killer. With his face ashen from "fatigue, sleeplessness & regret," as Agnes noted in her diary, he announced McGee's death to the members of Parliament and recommended that his widow and two daughters receive monetary settlements. Agnes stayed home, lying on the sofa, "half paralyzed." Only three days before, McGee had dined at the Macdonald home, and Agnes had trouble aligning her recollections of McGee's vivacity of that night with the ignominious image of him lying lifeless on the street.

Under the circumstances, Agnes wanted to cling as closely as possible to John A. On April 25, she learned that John A.'s livery stablekeeper, a man named Patrick Buckley, might be "deeply implicated" in McGee's murder. She feared John A. had been "exposed" by driving with him. On Sunday, April 26, she proudly noted in her diary that she had used her feminine wiles to successfully coax John A. into accompanying her to church, which left her overjoyed. "John was so dear and good about going to church. He said he was weary and would not but when I looked ever so little sad, he got up at once and dressed in a hurry."

McGee's death renewed John A.'s commitment to settling down to a quiet life at home. He and Agnes now united in a common cause, finding McGee's killer. Agnes accompanied her husband to and from Parliament, to try to rid herself of fears about his safety. In all, a sense of mutual protectiveness enveloped them, renewing their love and passion for each other. Agnes was considerably relieved when a twenty-eight-year-old Irish tailor named Patrick Whelan was charged with McGee's murder after police found a fully loaded .32-calibre Smith & Wesson revolver in his pocket. John A.'s cabman, Patrick Buckley, was briefly jailed but released for lack of evidence. Despite this exculpation, the Macdonalds, as well as the Desbarats, who owned a printing company located on the right side of McGee's door, refused to

190

employ Buckley again as their driver, believing he was among those involved in the conspiracy to kill McGee.

Even by the standards of the day, where a type of brutal frontier justice still reigned, the trial of Patrick Whelan, in September of 1868, was bizarre. Agnes and John A. attended, but John A. wasn't content merely to view the proceedings from the spectators' seats. In a totally improper gesture, he actually sat beside the judge, Chief Justice William Buell Richards, whom Agnes dismissed as "ponderous." In a stroke of irony, one of John A.'s former schoolmates at the Kingston Grammar School, Orangeman John Hillyard Cameron, defended Whelan, while the Catholic James O'Reilly acted as prosecutor.

Agnes didn't sit idle in the spectators' gallery but wrote perceptively about the proceedings. She noted that Whelan sat opposite the judge with "folded arms, within the wooden dock listening intently hour after hour into [sic] the deliberate unfolding of his doom!" Few of Whelan's features escaped her scrutiny. "He is a small, mean-looking yet determined man of some eight and twenty with a largish head and brownish hair brushed back, a low-wrinkled fore-head, blue, intent, cunning eyes, coarse Irish features and a long reddish beard. [I] think that there is but little doubt that he is one of that unfortunate, misguided fraternity, the Fenians," she wrote. It seemed to her that "as each witness stepped out of the box, the impression of the prisoner's guilt seemed to increase and deepen," yet she couldn't deny possessing a tincture of sympathy for the defendant, and noted perceptively,

All day long this went on – for many long day – and still sat the Prisoner wonderfully collected with all eyes generally fixed on him, and with the narrow margin of hope – he must have had at first growing narrower as the sun went down. Once or twice when one of the principal witnesses for the defence palpably exaggerated or by clever cross-questioning showed that some statement was incorrect I saw a sort of shade pass over his face – and a tremor of the lines below his mouth. Occasionally, too, he bit at his moustache, and stroked it roughly with nervous fingers. But he munched apples too, at intervals, and watched the flies creep on the ceiling and laughed when the Constable's foot slipped as he was about to lead him forth for his dinner.

On the day of the verdict, Whelan arrived in court dressed entirely in black, except for a bright green cravat. After closing arguments, most of the spectators left for dinner, already convinced Whelan would be found guilty. Agnes and John A. also left, since they were to entertain guests for dinner. However, at the last moment, they cancelled their dinner plans and re-entered the courthouse. As soon as they did, they noted with disgust that it was almost entirely empty, in Agnes's words, "the excitement over." She elaborated: "Nothing ever struck us more painfully than the aspect of things at that hour in contrast to what had been going on all day." She added with true distress that most spectators had left the court to "eat, drink and make merry, to walk, to gossip, to lounge," [while] those that remained were "half-asleep," and "doubled up on the wooden benches of the gallery leaving the wretched human thing they had so long gazed at to its lovely misery."

Whelan, meanwhile, sat in the prisoner's dock under a "pale light." Agnes observed his "wide-opened unwinking eyes, a set face, the lines hardened by intense restraint, motionless, yet fearfully active, silent, yet passionately speaking," as the judge sentenced him to hang. Agnes wrote, "They tell me he cannot feel!! Cannot feel!! Perhaps not in the refined sense of our word, not perhaps with the details of cultivated suffering but can a living healthy man, young and active, in whose veins the blood bounds quick and strong, can he know he shall be sentenced to hang by the neck until his body be dead and not feel!" Agnes ultimately concluded, "If men then do not feel, then capital punishment is useless murder."

Whelan maintained his innocence. "Now I am held to be a black assassin. And my blood runs cold. But I am innocent. I never took that man's blood."

Whelan would remain in custody for five months. A fresh snow had fallen on the morning of February 11, 1869, when he was led to the gallows, his last words, "God save Ireland and God save my soul."

The trial had been traumatic for both John A. and Agnes. As soon as they returned home from the trial's final day, Agnes rested on a sofa, sick and weak. She was glad to have her entire family around her, including John A., Hewitt, and her "darling mother." Her illness, however, resulted from more than just the trauma of the trial. The fact was, Agnes was four months' pregnant, and she excitedly hoped all her dreams of womanly fulfillment were finally about to be realized.

VIII

FEELING THE SQUEEZE

A gnes Macdonald's New Year's Day party of 1869 was among the happiest she could remember. She was now eight months' pregnant, so heavily pregnant she feared the seams of her velveteen dress might burst as she manoeuvred around the bouquets of MPs and social doyennes pressed into the parlour of the Daly Street house, chatting between sips of champagne and nibbling on a variety of hot and cold canapés. Later in the afternoon, John A.'s Cabinet colleagues, including Charles Tupper and George-Étienne Cartier, feasted on a lunch of mutton cutlets rolled in a potato paste, clinking crystal glasses as they traded as many compliments as they did good-natured barbs. This was Agnes's element. With easily as prodigious a memory as her husband, she soaked up every word her guests uttered, for future reference.

Agnes would have preferred her official duties for the winter to end with this event. Instead, she had one last duty to fulfill before giving birth. Days after the New Year's party, she called on Lady Young, the wife of the new Governor General, at Stadacona Hall, the Governor General's official residence. What she saw – and smelled – impressed her little. Appearing more like a gypsy fortuneteller than a diplomat's wife, Lady Young received Agnes into her presence reclining languidly on a chintz sofa, "arrayed in a rich robe of violet satin, thickly quilted and trimmed with Swansdown," the sickening scent of hyacinths overpowering even the acrid aroma of burning wood from the room's fireplace. Agnes, as round as Humpty Dumpty, teetered on a small hassock, growing dizzier by the minute. After twenty excruciating minutes, she excused herself and rode home in her carriage, gulping in the winter's fresh, clean air. Writing later in her journal, she described the scene in Lady Young's parlour as "floridly fictive," crammed with "too much luxury," and "though wonderfully pretty to look at is not healthy or wise."

Agnes's pregnancy had not progressed without its rough patches. During her first trimester, she felt "headachy" and "languid." To distract herself, she lay on a settee in her drawing room, embroidering more pillowcases than she could ever use or even give away, as she oversaw the servants' house cleaning. Her intellectual curiosity, however, remained acute. She scoured every newspaper delivered to the house, including the *Globe*, the *Leader*, the *Kingston Herald*, and the *Montreal Gazette*. And, of course, she read books voraciously in both French and English. She favoured biographies, including the *Life of Elizabeth Fry*, or books about statesmen, "because of my husband's tastes and career." She also enjoyed *Paul the Pope and Paul the Friar*, by Anthony Trollope, long one of John A.'s favourite authors.

In her second and third trimesters, she walked daily to the Parliament Buildings to watch John A. from the gallery, then strolled home with him arm in arm at dusk, discussing politics along the way, leaning her head on his shoulder for comfort. Being pregnant did not stop her from occasionally making a scene in the House, however. On one occasion, disgusted by the choice of a new Speaker, she rose, stamped her foot loudly, and shouted from the gallery, "Did ever any person see such tactics?"

John A. was also experiencing a lull in the electrical storm that was his life. For one thing, he was no longer "on the bust." On January 30, he convinced Joseph Howe and his fellow Nova

Scotians to remain in Confederation. Agnes took much of the credit. Breaking open her favourite recipe book, she had organized a dinner in Howe's honour. As the wine flowed and the roast duck filled their stomachs, John A. and Howe discussed the advantages of Nova Scotia continuing to support Confederation. John A. was even more charming than usual, and the evening was a great success. "I have never seen my husband in such cheery moods," Agnes wrote afterwards. "I feel gloriously proud and thankful at his having 'won' in Nova Scotia – hardly a year ago one of the leading men from there told me in seriousness and some dismay that the 'country,' meaning Nova Scotia, was in a state of complete rebellion, that it needed but one false or nasty move to kindle a flame that might lead to a very important and very disastrous consequences."

Agnes's roast duck may have gone some distance in seducing Howe to remain in Confederation, but, practically speaking, John A. made Nova Scotia's entry far more attractive when he threw in some lucrative federal subsidies to place Nova Scotia on a par economically with its neighbour New Brunswick. It was a brilliantly timed bribe, as was John A.'s bonus of appointing Howe as a member of his Cabinet. With Nova Scotia's support in Parliament, John A.'s Conservative Party was about to reach its zenith of power.

Always politically astute, Agnes was ecstatic. She laughingly reminded John A. about the time shortly after their marriage when they had bumped into Joseph Howe on a street in London. John A. had said to Howe, "Some day soon you will be one of us," to which Howe replied jocularly, "Never! Never! You shall hang me first." Now, he had been brought into the fold, all due to her and her husband's ingenuity. She noted in her diary: "Mr. Howe is elected and is coming up. The members have mustered strong and the House is in excellent temper. Sir John's government has now such a large majority. I hope and believe it will make good use of its power and that all clouds which darken it may pass away."

If John A. felt ripe with power, Agnes felt even more so. Her pregnancy filled her with a sense of invincibility. She may have acted like a tomboy in her youth, and relished the relative emancipation she enjoyed living with her mother in London while being supported by Hewitt, but she was no suffragist. The only freedom she ever sought was within the confines of a marriage. In her mind, her pregnancy not only established a divine purpose for her life, but elevated her above less fortunate single women. "I often think what an unsatisfactory existence women must have who, passing girlhood & having no particular vocation, never realize the joys of wife & mother & spend their lives in trying to fill the void which nature has decreed they should experience."

Her ecstasy didn't last long. Her "suffering," as she referred to it, began at 4 a.m. on February 7, 1869. She quietly climbed out of bed, and read, then prayed to God for the stoicism she would need to endure her pain. When she finally climbed back into bed, John A. wrapped his arms around her comfortingly. "[My] darling held me in his arms, until first now, when I feared I'd disturb his precious sleep," she wrote. She was scarcely back in bed an hour when she was forced to rise again, the pains more regular and strong. She held out until early afternoon, when John A. called for a doctor. By evening, the baby seemed no closer to being born than it had been at midday. Agnes pushed and pushed, the effort leaving her delirious with exhaustion. Chloroform, the preferred soporific of the day, failed to relieve Agnes's suffering. The baby's head was large, possibly too large to fit through the birth canal. As John A. held her hand and the doctor positioned his forceps on each side of the baby's head, Agnes pushed one last time. Finally, at 3:15 p.m. of February 8, Mary Theodora Macdonald entered the world with a kittenish cry.

Nine weeks elapsed before Agnes felt well enough to resume her diary entries. Her euphoria over her daughter's birth was as palpable as it was touching. "She is lying asleep in her blankets, my own darling baby – my little daughter, the sweet gift from

Heaven, my Mary – dark-eyed, soft thing. What word can tell how my heart swells with love and pride – she is truly dear."

Agnes's effusions slowly dissipated, however, as over time she visited her daughter's nursery and was forced to examine her closely. She was dear, yes. She was sweet, undoubtedly. She smiled. She cooed. Yet, something was wrong. Her head, unnaturally large at birth, continued to swell, while her legs dangled from her torso like shrivelled pipe cleaners. She failed to squirm and kick as a normal child would do, but instead lay prostrate on her pillows. With each day, her infirmities grew as impossible to ignore.

At first Agnes defiantly denied the evidence she and John A. observed concerning their daughter's health. She invented explanations, bargained with God, but finally her subconscious fears bobbed to the surface. On April 25, she wrote, "My baby is sweet and bright and well. My dear little child. I have read nothing today. My heart has been cold and dull, my frame weak. I seem to be waiting for something. Perhaps it is for light!"

On May 1, doctors at last provided the light. Mary, they announced, had hydrocephalus. "The day has been stamped with the world's great seal, it is graven I think with the word disappointment," Agnes wrote. The clouds that Agnes had feared might "darken" her husband's majority government instead hovered above their own house, bringing with them a heavy downpour of pain and sharp regret.

By contrast, John A. never publicly declared his private pain over Mary's condition, but there are signs that her birth forced him to mature emotionally. In the beginning, few of his political associates were even aware that Mary possessed a serious physical problem until they visited the Macdonald's home. Those invited to the house for dinner must have been moved by what they saw. For half an hour before the meal started, John A. sat gently massaging his daughter's thin legs, or in his soft Scottish brogue spinning fairy tales he concocted out of his own

> May. 1st 1869.
> Saturday.
>
> The day has been stamped with the world's
> great seal - it is graven, I think - with the word
> "Disappointment." Perhaps yesterday was one of the
> saddest times in my life - let it pass - let it die - only
> teach me - Heavenly Father, to see the lesson it was
> destined to teach, and while I learn it, to do so
> cheerfully - Busy as usual on Saturdays - drove
> early - went to market - & came home for visitors.
> The Chancellor, Speaker, and many members came -
> with his cousin & some ladies. Old Potts had to leave
> One suddenly, and Baby will miss her sorely -
> At 7.30 - we sat down 12 to dinner - 3 selves, Mrs Bayard,
> Mr & Mrs Bolton. Mr. Lewin,

Agnes's diary entry describing shock over discovering Mary had hydrocephalus. "Only teach me, Heavenly Father," she writes, "to see the lesson it was destined to teach, and while I learn it, to do so cheerfully."
(Family Papers, Baroness Macdonald, Vol. 559A)

imagination. Determined to maintain a jaunty air of optimism in front of the child, he nicknamed her "Baboo" and bought her small gifts to help her exercise her finger muscles, including rattles and dolls. With Mary, he was demonstrably affectionate, loving, and tender in a way that he had been unable to be even with his own sisters when he was a boy.

As an infant, Mary experienced periods of fussiness, fever, and ill temper. Her cries kept her parents up all night. "Last night, dear baby was so wakeful that I had no real rest. It is wearing," Agnes wrote. During the day, she bundled her up in hand-crotchet blankets and took her for buggy rides in the sunshine, past the city's shops and the sympathetic gazes of onlookers. Their solicitousness was almost more than she could bear. Perhaps there was still a chance, a slim one, that the baby would start to move her legs, might, in fact, even walk alongside her mother and father one day. It's clear that, for years, both John A. and Agnes held out this hope, buying back braces for the girl, as well as carriages that they strapped to a pony's back, so Mary could go riding. But for now, she and John A. watched and waited. "I took my darling out early in the fresh, fine air, trying hard to get some colour into her cheeks, and strength to her limbs. She lies, in spite of her thirteen and one half months still on the pillow of her little carriage, smiling when she sees me, and cooing softly to herself," Agnes wrote.

Temporarily lost in denial over Mary's condition, Agnes passed Mary's care onto a nurse but soon grew jealous of Mary's transfer of affection to her. "I had charge of darling baby all the afternoon and she fretted for her nurse, and I felt, as I always do, how wrong this state of things really is, when a child loves so much more dearly a stranger than its own mother," adding, "so many occupations keep me from the nursery."

Agnes had no more occupations than she'd ever had. Instead, she invented diversions. She haunted the corridors of the Parliament Buildings like a wraith, dressed in black, a large cross at her neck, waiting until her husband could accompany her home. At three dollars a carriage ride, these trips deeply gouged into the family's pockets, but John A. did not complain.

Medical specialists predicted that Mary would probably be unable to walk without assistance, feed herself, or reason beyond the age of ten – if she lived that long. Both parents refused the controversial treatment of the day, the Quinke puncture, in which a doctor literally punctured the spine with a sharp instrument to release the intercranial fluids. Mary could die of the infection it might cause.

How severe was Mary's hydrocephalus? Doctors practising in her day obviously considered all forms of hydrocephalus equal. Had they not, Mary might have become a more highly functioning adult. In 2005, Dr. James Drake, a neurosurgeon with the Hospital for Sick Children in Toronto, examined several photos of Mary as a young woman and suggested that she probably suffered from a "mild form of hydrocephalus" that could be treated today by inserting a shunt at the base of her brain to release the brain fluid. Had this treatment been available in Mary's era, she would have been far more alert, ambulatory, and independent.

Addressing the curvature of Mary's spine, and her atrophied legs, Dr. Drake offered the even-more-intriguing theory that, in addition to hydrocephalus, Mary may have suffered from cerebral palsy, which, if true, ultimately allowed her limited mobility, including the ability to type.

Nursing a disabled child was expensive, and financial insolvency was the most persistent anxiety John A. and Agnes shared. There was more bad financial news to come. In late 1869, the Merchant's Bank of Canada had assumed the assets – and even larger liabilities of the grand old Commercial Bank, whose first director, George Mackenzie, had been John A.'s legal mentor. Just when John A. most desperately needed some financial security to pass on to his family, he wondered where to get it. No one from the Merchant's Bank felt brave enough to tell him exactly how much he owed and how he might finesse paying the debts of his late law partner, Archibald Macdonnell. Unable to bear the uncertainty any longer, John A. finally wrote a personal letter to Hugh Allan, the president of the Merchant's Bank, seeking clarification. Within a week, Allan broke the shocking news. In total, John A. owed more than $79,000, not only for his own debts, but for those his late law partner owed to lending companies.

After some serious fiddling, John A. devised a repayment strategy using all the cash he could raise, plus profits from the sale of a tract of land located in Guelph, which he had purchased in 1842. The property was his most lucrative asset, since Guelph's population had quadrupled as a town, and sales of property skyrocketed to match the demand for housing developments. Hugh Allan promised to submit John A.'s proposal to the bank's board of directors.

Seeking the restorative power of sea air, John A. vacationed briefly in Portland, Oregon. Upon his return, he discovered the bank had still not responded to his repayment proposal. Unable to bear the suspense any longer, after an extended dry spell, John A. returned to the bottle.

At fifty-four years old, John A. had no appreciable assets to draw on to support his family except a public servant's salary of $5,000 a year, with approximately $1,700 coming from his crippled Kingston law office. By the time the Merchant's Bank finally accepted his repayment strategy, John A. was prostrate with stress.

By the end of 1869, Agnes stopped trying to reform her husband. She had given up wine "as an example" to him, but to no avail. She had prayed, but felt her prayers had been unanswered. Instead, she plunged into a self-flagellating despair. "What has changed with me since this day last year, when I sat writing, as I write now, in my big diary?" she wrote. "Wonderfully little – and yet wonderfully much. Outwardly all is nearly the same, except that my darling child's smile brightens my home but in my heart I feel that much is wholly different. I ought to be wiser, for I have suffered keenly in mind. [Only] One, who knows all our hearts, can tell how keenly and painfully or how for long weeks and months all was gloom and disappointment. I was over confident, vain and presumptuous in my sense of power. I fancied I could do too much and I failed signally. [I] am more humble now."

On the political front, in 1870 John A. received disquieting dispatches concerning the activities of Louis Riel, the Métis crusader for the inhabitants of the Red River Colony, located smack in the middle of Rupert's Land, the very land that the Hudson's Bay Company had recently sold to the federal government for $300,000.

Riel was no intellectual lightweight, but a Montreal lawyer, educated by the Jesuits, and firmly convinced that the inhabitants of the colony had as much right as inhabitants of the country's other colonies to decide whether they wished to join in Confederation. On December 8, 1869, he had established a provisional government in Rupert's Land. Indeed, he was prepared to fight to the death to ensure that the rights of the region's inhabitants were upheld.

John A. considered Riel a curiosity, then a fascination, then an enemy. Yet, even John A. recognized the cleverness of his opponent. Although John A. felt that American writers had trumped-up stories of insurrections in the Red River Colony to incite Anglo-Canadians, he could not slough off Riel's logic so easily. In the winter of 1869, he had approached Riel through an advance party, headed by Lieutenant William McDougall, his designated lieutenant-governor of the North-West Territories. To McDougall's shock, Riel blocked his entry to the Red River Colony. In response, McDougall belligerently boasted to Riel that Queen Victoria had already officially approved the transfer of the northwest to Canada on December 1. McDougall had lied. In truth, the Queen had refused to finalize the deal until the insurrection had been contained, which John A. convinced her had been done by the middle of December. Nevertheless, in John A.'s opinion, McDougall's "criminal stupidities" derailed any hope of healthy negotiations with Riel. Upon John A.'s instructions, McDougall retreated to Ontario, in humiliation.

McDougall's ignominious treatment at the hands of Riel inflamed the tempers of Orangemen throughout Ontario, who prevailed upon John A. to attack Riel and his fellow insurrectionists by force. Instead, John A. sent a second emissary named Donald Smith to the territory. Smith had some early successes. He conducted a series of meetings with representatives of the French- and English-speaking parishes to discuss settlement terms. Together, the parish members drew up a "list of rights," which stipulated the terms under which they would consider sending representatives to Ottawa to discuss Confederation.

Upon learning of Smith's progress, Riel's supporters elected him president of a provincial government that had no real legal status. Fed up, two military leaders, Captain Schultz and Captain Boulton, tried but failed to kill Riel, only elevating him and his authority in the process.

On March 4, 1870, John A. discovered that Riel had crossed the line between being a crafty negotiator and a murderer. After conducting a military tribunal that lasted less than twenty-four hours, Riel condemned a young soldier named Thomas Scott to death after finding him guilty of taking up arms against his provisional government. Scott was wrestled into the street, yelling, "This is horrible! This is cold-bloodied murder!" before the bullets silenced him.

As quickly as Ontario Protestants rose up against Riel, the French Catholics in Quebec sided with him. This included John A.'s long-time friend, colleague, and fellow Father of Confederation, George-Étienne Cartier. John A. was wedged among these warring parties. He had also to consider the possibility that the Fenians in the United States might take advantage of the unrest in the western settlement.

Together with Cartier, John A. met with Father Richot, Alfred Scott, and Judge Black, all three delegates of Riel's "government," to hammer out the terms of achieving provincial status for what would become Manitoba. John A. kept the discussions informal, because he did not wish to negotiate with the men as official delegates of a legitimate government, but merely as representatives. Nevertheless, he ceded on establishing separate schools for Roman Catholic children and protecting the distinctive French culture from a certain onslaught of Anglo-Saxon settlers. With this, Assiniboia was poised to become the new Province of Manitoba.

The strain from trying to appease everyone but himself proved too much for John A. On a perpetual drunk now, he wove between the Russell House tavern and the parliamentary bar. Colleagues noted that he had trouble balancing himself on two feet. He was sick. Sick of worrying about money, about the opinions of others, sick with grief over his daughter, and just plain physically sick. As the weeks passed, Agnes noted his pallor, perpetual exhaustion, and the excruciating muscle spasms he suffered in his back. Finally, John A. took to his bed. Sir Stafford Northcote informed former British prime minister Benjamin Disraeli of John A.'s condition. "His habit is to retire to bed, to exclude everybody, and to drink bottle after bottle of port. All the papers are sent to him, and he reads them, but he is conscious of his inability to do any important business and he does none."

Within a week, John A. rose from his dead drunk and returned to Parliament to pass the Manitoba Act. Following this victory, he authorized Col. G. J. Wolseley to lead a militia force supported by British regulars to ensure that the transfer of power in Manitoba would pass without violence and that Riel should receive amnesty. Did he hope revenge would be part of the purpose of the trip? Probably yes, and probably no. Like most other English Canadians, he was conflicted. Not so his son.

Twenty-year-old Hugh John, who had recently graduated with a Bachelor of Arts from the University of Toronto, was beside himself over his father's negotiations with Riel's representatives. He had been in the midst of starting his legal studies when news of Riel's insurrection and murder of Thomas Scott reached him. With more bravado than good sense, he raced to see John A. in Ottawa and, over his father's protestations, informed him he would be joining Wolseley's regiment when it set out for Manitoba. It was an improbable vision: Hugh John, as wispy as a blade of straw and plagued with asthma, resolutely trudging through mud toward an uncertain confrontation. On May 2, 1870, the *Leader* newspaper reported that Ensign Hugh John Macdonald of the 16th company, 1st Ontario Rifles, could "hardly contain his delight at his good fortune." Whether John A. knew it or not, appeasement was the last thing on Hugh John's mind.

Upon his return to Toronto from Ottawa on May 3, a celebratory-spirited Hugh John took some buddies to Soyer's soda shop on University Avenue, where they all drank to his health, as well as to the annihilation of Riel. Hugh John left the restaurant on a high and sprinted along King Street with the same cocky confidence with which his father had done so many years before. Along each block, friends and acquaintances stopped to congratulate him on his honour. Only the *Telegraph* newspaper poured rain on Hugh John's parade by referring to him as a "beardless youth."

Serious, bordering on the sanctimonious, Hugh John lacked his father's disarming humour and charm, describing "halfbreeds" as "neither good looking, nor strictly virtuous." Still, to the relief of his fellow militiamen, some of his father's bawdy humour managed to slip through the cracks. Tellingly, one of his favourite poems contained the stanza "Mary mother, we believe / That without sin you did conceive / Teach, we pray thee, us believing / How to sin without conceiving."

John A. must have realized the folly he had brought upon his son by abandoning him to the ministrations of Williamson and of Louisa, who lived in a state of perpetual distemper due to her position as a third wheel in Williamson's homes. Put simply, he had forfeited the heart and soul of his own son for political ambition. Now he could never reverse the damage.

As evidence of the gulf between Hugh John and his father, the number of collected letters exchanged between Hugh John and Williamson are three times greater in number than those exchanged between Hugh John and his father. Then, too, the tone between the two sets of letters is also markedly different. Hugh John referred to Williamson as his "dearest friend and advisor," while he addressed his father as "my dear old papa." The subjects contained in the letters also differed greatly. Hugh John wrote Williamson concerning primarily family gossip. By contrast, his letters to his father resemble military dispatches, most containing brief descriptions of political or military successes.

On May 6, as Hugh John performed field exercises and target practice at the Crystal Palace near the lakeshore in Toronto, John A. left the council chambers and entered his office. An aide brought him lunch, but just as he began to eat, an indescribable pain gripped the upper-right side of his stomach. He wobbled to his feet, knocking his chair to the floor, and as he gripped the sides of the lunch table, several pieces of china tumbled onto the carpet. The pain was nowhere and everywhere, constant and rhythmic, unbearable and unstoppable. The bell-tower clock outside his window struck two, as his body sank to the floor.

Having heard John A.'s muffled cries in his adjoining office in the East Block, Hewitt rushed into the room and saw the prime minister, pale as paste, lying on his rose-coloured rug, beads of sweat plopping off the grey ringlets of his hair onto his tartan suit. Hewitt called Dr. James Grant, who diagnosed John A. as having passed a large gallstone. The stone had passed, but John A. remained senseless. He did not even recognize Agnes as she rushed into the office, determined to camp out with her husband for as long as it took him to recover.

Back at the Crystal Palace, Hugh John received a telegram informing him that his father had collapsed and was near death. The *Globe* newspaper described John A. as very "low" and losing ground fast.

When Hugh John arrived in Ottawa on May 10, he saw his father, moaning and swallowing spoonfuls of liquid that Agnes fed him. When he began to revive, Agnes rubbed some whisky onto his face and chest. "Oh do that again," John A. whispered. Seeing his father in this state frightened Hugh John and reminded him of how finite his father's life truly was. Hugh John remained until May 15, though his father had not recovered fully enough yet to acknowledge his presence. Hugh John's battalion was marching into the maelstrom on May 29. Had John A. been in better health, he almost certainly would have physically restrained his son from going.

Hugh John returned to Toronto on May 12. He wrote copious notes during Wolseley's briefing sessions. On Sunday, May 29, he ate lunch with a fellow soldier named Coyne and another named Bell at the Crystal Palace. A third soldier named Biggar joined the two men. In a letter home, Coyne described a "disgusting faux pas" Biggar had committed at a temperance sermon, where he alluded to "John Smith getting drunk and being sent to gaol whilst John Somebody-else got drunk and received high government appointments, in consequence and notwithstanding. Hugh John looked strange, but managed to appear not to notice the allusion to his father."

On instructions from Wolseley, Hugh John filled his knapsack with biscuits, soft bread, salt pork, beans, potatoes, and meat for the excursion. While some of the other soldiers and officers bolstered their courage with swigs of rum, Hugh John demurred. Unlike his father, he was a teetotaller, and settled for packing only tea or plain water.

From the start, the volunteer militia that marched westward resembled the gang that couldn't shoot straight. The English-speaking members of the militia – all 285 of them and all from Ontario – wished to nail Riel's head to a spike as retribution for Scott's death; the 77 French-speaking militiamen considered the trip pacifistic in nature and harboured sympathy, if not admiration, for Riel.

Louis Riel, 1865.
(LAC C006688D)

Fuelled by do-goodness, Hugh John marched resolutely through pouring rain and searing sunshine, arriving in Port Arthur on June 26. Nothing too exciting had occurred during the initial leg of the trip, aside from six-oared boat races and fishing. "I don't know when I will leave here and can't say that I am particularly anxious to do so," Hugh John wrote to Coyne. The fact was, he was uncomfortable around the rough men alongside him who kept jokingly referring to him as a "mere stripling." Their constant drunkenness and ensuing hangovers disgusted him. "I can assure you that it is no easy work to look after a lot of fellows who do not know how to do anything for themselves. This work fell particularly heavy on me as my Captain was on the sicklist and the Lieutenant on detachment, your humble servant being in charge of the company," he wrote.

Hugh John not long after his first attempt to bring Louis Riel to justice. *(LAC PA025364)*

Despite feeling nothing but disgust toward some of his fellow soldiers, Hugh John marched with them through ankle-deep mud, mosquitoes, black flies, and "small game" crawling over them day and night. "I really believe the devil got up this expedition for the purpose of getting hold of my immortal soul, as I am already beginning to swear a little," Hugh John confessed in a letter to Coyne, who had remained in Toronto to study law.

After braving rapids, portages, strong head winds, and storms, Hugh John and his fellow militiamen arrived at Fort Garry on August 27, only to find that Riel had "run like the coward he is," in Hugh John's words. "On arriving here, we were all very much disgusted to hear that Riel and his gang had been allowed to escape when they could have easily been caught and that no one was to suffer death for the murder of poor Scott."

As his son, in John A.'s words, was "playing soldier," John A., along with Agnes, Mary, and Dr. Grant, sailed to Charlottetown, where they rested at a friend's house named Falconwood. They stayed until September 15, when they returned to Ottawa. Dozens of well-wishers, recognizing the potential catastrophe of losing John A. as their leader, met the couple at the train station. James Williamson and Margaret had sent a basket of grapes to mark their return. In thanks, John A. later posted Williamson copies of the often sardonic British political magazine *Pall Mall Gazettes* that admirers supplied him in Prince Edward Island, "if his tastes run that way," he wrote Margaret.

John A. and Agnes greatly benefited from their vacation, but Mary, whom John A. called "a great source of anxiety," suffered intermittent bouts of illness. "Poor little Baby . . . has had a hard time of it, but if we get her home here safely, I have more hopes of her than I ever have had," he told Margaret, adding the stern postscript: "I shall have Hugh summoned home at once – He has had his 'Outing' & must now go to work."

Hugh John was happy enough to obey his father's order to return now that "Satan," as he called Riel, had "escaped." In contrast to his expedition west, on his return trip Hugh John suffered neither a blister nor a mosquito bite. He rode in a buggy all the way back to Ottawa, halting to shoot ducks and prairie hens and cooking them over an open campfire. He reached Ottawa in early November, just in time to help the family move to a new, more spacious home named Earnscliffe on the outskirts of the city. John A. had leased Earnscliffe from a friend named Thomas Reynolds, who temporarily moved abroad in late 1870.

As soon as he arrived home, Hugh John entered into a "violent debate" with his father concerning "the manner in which the loyal inhabitants have been and are still being treated" in the Red River Colony. In his letters to Coyne, Hugh John accused John A. of being too lenient toward Riel, which he called "repugnant to his

Tory notions of justice." Hugh John's harangue against his father didn't end there. "I pitched into the whole policy of the government on the Red River matter and I don't doubt that if they (that is the government) [sic] only knew it they would feel distressed not to say alarmed. My father did not say much after I finished but his looks were downcast and his spirits low for several days," he admitted to Coyne. Hugh had extracted his pound of flesh, oblivious to the danger that his letters might get "lost" or "stolen" and their contents be published in a news-paper, much to his father's embarrassment.

Despite his braggadocio, Hugh John suffered crippling self-doubt. He was unsure of which course he should follow in his future: law or business. Either way, he would have to compete with his father, a colossus in the imagination of most Canadians. His father prevailed upon him to resume his law studies; he even arranged for an articling position in the law office of Alexander Harrison in Toronto, but Hugh hedged and grumbled. Though he did return to law school, he spent his examination study periods back at Earnscliffe. Not that Hugh liked Earnscliffe much. Winters were the worst, when the property's lush green lawns grew slick with ice, and the flowing river at the base of the cliff on which the house stood tensed with frost, transforming it from a picturesque blue to a slate grey. Hugh complained that John A. and Agnes were not treating him as the adult he assumed himself to be. He complained in a letter to a friend:

I am working like the very devil now trying to be ready for my first Intermediate examination on the 8th of next month. I read all my spare time in the office, at four o'clock go for a walk, and then from 7 till 12 p.m. I read and smoke at home. I had a great battle about smoking downstairs, but I told them [Agnes and John] that if I could not smoke downstairs I would take my books up to my own room and smoke and read there. This they did not consider wholesome so they at last gave in and now I puff away in the dining room.

Then there were the social indignities. He couldn't invite his buddies over for dinner, "route off anyone," or "set off any squibs" (firecrackers). "Good Lord, wouldn't my mother raise a row if I routed her out and squibbed her," he complained. Hugh John's complaints didn't stop there. "I can't flourish about with red pokers, shy water over people, rub chairs on the wall or go in for a regular good scuff for five minutes by the clock. No sir, my mind is made up that this the last experience I shall have of living at home and that when I go up to Toronto again to study I will start fresh on my own hook and remain so."

Next to the pressures his father suffered at his age, Hugh's complaints seemed trivial. At twenty, John A. already represented an established law firm and significantly contributed to his family's support. Yet father and son did share two things in common – a propensity for mischief and a love of grandiosity. If John A. could place a horse's body in a house of worship, then Hugh John could "squib" people, smoke in his father's house, or march off to Manitoba to avenge Riel's murder of Thomas Scott, audaciously remonstrating with his father for what he considered his incompetence.

Preoccupied by post-adolescent reveries, Hugh John barely noticed his father's physical, emotional, and financial sufferings. Nevertheless, John A.'s friends and colleagues, including Hewitt Bernard and old friend David Macpherson, frightened by his brush with death earlier in the year, set the wheels in motion to establish a Testimonial Trust in John A.'s name so he would have some money to leave to his family. In all, John A.'s colleagues eventually deposited a total of $69,062.52 in two Ontario banks. Until that time, John A. knew nothing about the plans that had been afoot.

As if he didn't have enough pressures to deal with, while John A. lay ill in June 1870, George-Étienne Cartier travelled to

British Columbia, then a thriving mining centre, to hammer out the terms of its entry into Confederation. He made the staggering promise that the government would cross the wilderness and blast through rock to create a cross-country railway within ten years. Six representatives from the province were appointed members of Parliament, and eight months later British Columbia became Canada's sixth province.

Back at Earnscliffe, more than 130 guests arrived to enjoy "hot oyster soup" and "sips of sherry" on New Year's Day. Agnes could almost imagine her life as normal but for one thing: John A. wasn't there to assist her. Instead, just when she needed him most, he had "ordered a Council!" as she recorded in her diary. "I had set my heart on having him with me. He only came in at dinner time." Before John A. had a chance to relax, however, Governor General Young called him to Rideau Hall to discuss the international fishing-grounds issue and which delegates he should send to Washington in February. After the meeting, he returned home, white with exhaustion, leading Agnes to note, "I think this American fishery question bothers Sir John. I suppose it is ticklish business as Brother Sam may show fight." That was an understatement.

In February 1871, as part of a five-man British delegation, John A. travelled to Washington to negotiate several issues, most predominately the fisheries question. The Americans were fishing within a three-mile limit off Nova Scotia, New Brunswick, and Prince Edward Island gratis, refusing to purchase licences to do so. Despite the presence of marine cruisers, the Americans fished on, pugnaciously daring the Canadians to show force. The Colonial Office assured John A. that, in order to fish within the three-mile limit, Americans would have to pay "adequate compensation."

John A. also wanted to balance the scales by obtaining tariff concessions from the Americans, but he had to battle not only the Americans, but the British, who wanted to reconcile with the United States at almost any cost – and the Americans knew it.

John A. was good at card games, but this time his cards were dealt from a bad deck. All these factors made John A. feel insecure. He wrote to John Rose. "I contemplate my visit to Washington with a good deal of anxiety. If things go well, my share of the kudos will be but small, and if anything goes wrong, I will be made the scapegoat at all events so far as Canada is concerned."

Agnes had no doubt whatsoever that she and Hewitt would accompany John on the trip, offering companionship and support. She fumed when, upon arrival in Washington, no American official thought it important enough to greet the prime minister of Canada. In consequence, the trio rode a bus to the Arlington Hotel. The first few days in town were consumed with dinners, receptions, and visits to officials of the State Department, House of Representatives, and Senate. Wedged between his British colleagues and American statesmen, John A. felt like a colonial hick. It didn't take long to realize that the Americans were willing to humour the Canadian contingent but had no intention of acceding to their demands, which in addition to the fisheries question and reciprocal trade included restitution for Fenian attacks on Canada. Even the British treated John A. as a third wheel. They considered giving away the fishing rights for a payoff from the United States, but John A. held out for a reciprocal trade agreement. It was a humiliating excursion, certain to end in political disaster.

By March, John A. was sick of Washington, sick of negotiations, and especially sick of the endless late-night partying. "We are overwhelmed with hospitalities which we cannot refuse," he wrote. A British delegate named Lord de Grey agreed. "Our life here is rendered very intolerable by the endless feasts," he said. "We work all day and dine all night. And some wag in the newspapers says we are not a Joint High Commission, but a High Commission on Joints – the joke greatly delights the Washingtonians." Agnes, meanwhile, worried about Mary, alone with her nurse now for more than a month. Still, another month of tedium and frustration yawned before them.

Finally, Lord de Grey offered to sell the inshore fishing rights to the Americans, along with free fish. In protest, John A. considered resigning as commissioner of the delegation, but seeing no other way out ultimately yielded to de Grey's deal. The Americans offered absolutely no restitution for their Fenian raids and laughed out of hand at any thoughts of reciprocal trade agreements. "Never in the whole course of my public life have I been in so disagreeable a position and had such an unpleasant duty to perform as the one upon which I am now engaged here," John A. wrote to a friend. Only by reminding himself that he was representing the British government could John A. finally sign what began known as the Treaty of Washington. As he did, he half-whispered to a colleague, "Here go the fisheries."

John A. returned to Ottawa with his tail between his legs. In the House of Commons, he tried to put a shiny gloss on Lord de Grey's capitulation but without success. "[We] ask the people of Canada through their representatives to accept this treaty, to accept it with all its imperfections, to accept it for the sake of peace, and for the sake of the great Empire of which we form a part," he announced to the House, tongue firmly planted in his cheek.

In the late spring of 1871, John A., Agnes, and Mary retreated from the pressures of the world to a sprawling house they purchased named Les Rochers, just outside of Rivière-du-Loup, near Quebec City. Poised on a cliff, the house featured a panoramic view of the St. Lawrence. From a second-floor balcony, Mary sat in her wheelchair watching ships pass by. Once settled in, Agnes painted several watercolour landscapes with names such as "A Wet Day at Rivière du Loup" or "The Water Lily at Anchor at Sunset," as well a self-portrait of herself wrapped in hand-crotched shawls, relaxing before a fireplace.

During their summer in Rivière-du-Loup, Agnes had left instructions for servants to pack up the Macdonald family's

Agnes's self-portrait was painted before the fireplace at Earnscliffe.
(LAC E003525167)

belongings at Earnscliffe so they could move to a new home shortly after their return to Ottawa in August. Earnscliffe's owner, Thomas Reynolds, had written to the Macdonalds in the spring telling them of his plans to reinhabit the home upon his return from England in the fall.

A local realtor found a charming home for Agnes and John on 194 Chapel Street in Sandy Hill, luckily without the oppressive stench from leaky drainage pipes. Agnes soon set about refurbishing and redecorating the house, throwing money about with the same financial abandon that characterized her husband's spending habits. On January 6, she hired employees of the A.K. Mills Company to replace the marble in the fireplace, and to install an iron grate for the price of $19. Two days later, she hired Harris and Campbell cabinetmakers and upholsterers to construct a black-walnut London stool, place a twenty-five-pound horsehair mattress on her bed, and set up a black-walnut Spanish couch and a centre ottoman for a total cost of $96.45. In March, she ordered an antique mahogany table for $42. In April and May, she ordered workmen to install a large cupboard in the basement. She also ordered two new keys for the front door, two enamelled door fasteners, one large sliding bolt for the dining-room window, two silver-plated knobs for the drawing room, and sixty-six feet of fencing for the property, at a total cost of $98.37. The more she altered the house, the better she could come to terms with living in it, especially after leaving the splendour of Earnscliffe. For her, its main attraction was its proximity to St. Alban's Church. Even at St. Alban's, Agnes succeeded at leaving her mark on the congregation, not all of it positive.

Soon after her move to the Chapel Street house, Agnes butted heads with St. Alban's rector, Rev. Thomas Bedford-Jones. The church was badly in need of reconstruction. It was already $5,000 in debt, with interest collecting daily. Agnes suggested that Bedford-Jones should rent pews, and sell hand-knitted clothing and homemade baked goods to church parishioners at bazaars, just as she and Theodora had done at their church in Barrie. Bedford-Jones was horrified. He equated renting pews with graft, and bazaars as akin to carnival shows. If nothing else, Agnes was a woman who could bide her time. Bedford-Jones had no more stepped on board a vessel sailing to Ireland for a vacation than Agnes and Theodora raised the $5,000 through a bazaar and by squeezing money out of the most affluent members of the congregation.

Back in Kingston, meanwhile, John A.'s sister Margaret suffered serious bouts of illness. Her lungs burned, and she felt unable to inhale deeply without suffering intense pain. On good days, she worked in the garden. On bad days, she lay on a settee, weak and drained of energy. Doctors were at a loss to explain the nature of her illness. John A. sent Margaret medicinal reinforcements, probably morphine tablets, via Louisa. "Send some of those pills [Margaret] takes delight in at home in your next letter," Louisa wrote. "They are marked on the top, one to be taken every

night, if there is none left [Robert] will mix them at once as he has
the perscription [sic]; do not forget them if you please as they will
come nicely in a letter."

Around this time, Louisa Macdonald came in for criticism
from a most unexpected source: none other than James
Williamson's son, James, who was acutely aware of his position as
eventual heir to his father's estate. On April 22, 1872, James wrote
to his father from Scotland:

> I am glad to hear you have the prospect of soon being able
> to relieve your property [Heathfield] of its present burden,
> with the exception of a portion of land which you mention
> belongs to Miss Macdonald during her lifetime. I do not
> know the circumstances under which you made the pur-
> chase, but it certainly appears to me, with my imperfect
> knowledge of the facts, that this latter arrangement is by no
> means advantageous to you and still less so to your heirs.
> Why eh? Miss Macdonald's debt be left a burden on the
> property until her death, and not wiped off as soon as pos-
> sible! I do not see the advantage of postponing the redemp-
> tion of a certain part of the land in the manner indicated.
> Indeed, I fear it will only land you into the hands of the
> lawyers, whose company, officially, should I think, be
> avoided as much as possible under any circumstances!

John A. was unaware of Williamson's frustrations with the
Heathfield property ownership. The property was in John A.'s
name, after all. If he was deleterious in paying Louisa's rent, then
he considered it a matter Williamson could have brought up with
him, rather than with his son.

By the summer of 1872, John A. prepared himself for another gruelling election campaign. He knew Riel's uprising had seriously

eroded his popularity in Ontario, a region that held eighty-eight seats, which thought John A. had been too lenient, meanwhile the French thought he had dealt too severely with Riel. In addition, though Parliament passed the Treaty of Washington, Ontarians and Maritimers considered it a sellout.

Poised for the political fight of his life, John A. entered a campaign that featured bribery on a scale heretofore unimaginable. Although all candidates indulged in the practice, none did so with more gusto than John A. In fact, he spent significant amounts of his testimonial funds buying off voters. He raised the rest of the money from businessmen such as Hugh Allan. Cynics joked that even the dead were pressed to vote.

In advance of the election, John A., Agnes, and Hewitt moved to the Queen's Hotel in Toronto, where John A. ran up his usual high bar bill entertaining potential financial contributors to his campaign. As important as it was to court the wealthy, it was equally important for John A. to depict himself as a common working man. On July 11, he and Agnes accepted an invitation to the Toronto Music Hall for a Toronto Trades Assembly meeting. There, representatives of the trades unions presented Agnes with a gold bejewelled casket "as a slight token of our appreciation of your timely efforts in the interest of the operatives of this Dominion."

"I ought to have a special interest in this subject," John A. said, accepting the box on his wife's behalf. "Because I am a working man myself, I know that I work more than nine hours every day myself; and then I think I am a practical mechanic. If you look at the Confederation Act, in the framing of which I had some hand, you will admit that I am a pretty good joiner; and, as for cabinet-making, I have had as much experience as Jacques and Hay themselves."

In the midst of the election, John A. also had to deal with George-Étienne Cartier's promise to British Columbia to build a cross-country railway within ten years. He needed funds – fast.

Sir Hugh Allan, of the Merchant's Bank in Montreal, and David Macpherson of Toronto, who had acted as the brainchild behind John A.'s Testimonial Fund, each wished to provide capital for the railway, but, as financial competitors, neither was inclined to jump at John A.'s suggestion to merge their talents into one company. Finally, Macpherson buried his pride and met Allan on Allan's Montreal turf to try to work out a deal. In mid-July, however, Allan raised the ante by insisting that he would contribute money only if the government appointed directors favourable to him as president, and that allowed him to own the majority of the stock. John A. refused Allan's terms. In response, Allan withdrew his demand but not his influence in John A.'s political campaign. As a businessman, he was always in search of political leverage, so Allan continued to supply Macdonald and his party with campaign funds.

Meanwhile, Opposition leaders in the House thought the idea of ploughing through dry prairie and blasting through rock to build a railway was a fool's game. In Agnes's words, they considered it "an entirely ridiculous project which pretended to carry engines, carriages, baggage cars and traffic across inaccessible mountains blocked by snow for half the year, through terrible gorges, dense with gigantic timber and impassable scrub, and through rocks miles in extent which dynamite itself would have little effect on."

John A. wanted to get the job done on George-Étienne Cartier's schedule, partly because by now there was an emotional factor to consider. George-Étienne was ill with Bright's disease, a condition that made his hands and feet swell grotesquely. Like Macdonald, Cartier distrusted Hugh Allan because of his connection to American bankers. Nevertheless, Cartier, too, had an election to win. In political desperation, both Cartier and John A. accepted money from Allan to finance their campaigns. In all, Allan contributed a total of $350,000 to Conservative candidates, with $45,000 of it going to Macdonald and $85,000 to Cartier.

Even though John A. refused to make Allan the president of the Canadian Pacific Railway (CPR), he still wired him a request for an additional $10,000 in campaign contributions. When the election ended, John A. had hung on to office, but his friend Cartier suffered a bitter defeat in Montreal East.

Once the pressures of the election were over, John A. reconsidered installing Allan as president of the Canadian Pacific Railroad until he became aware Allan had promised American investors a stake in the charter, then, much to their fury, reneged. Then, in December 1872, George McMullen, the proprietor of the *Chicago Post* and an associate of Allan, dropped in at John A.'s office. McMullen did not bring with him greetings of the season but a threat. He would expose the financial relationship between Macdonald's Conservative Party and Hugh Allan, unless John A. appointed Hugh Allan as president. Initially, John A. reacted dispassionately. Threats were one thing. Actions were another. Perhaps McMullen was bluffing. Perhaps the whole mess might simple "fizzle." A month later, McMullen and John A. met for a second time. This time, McMullen produced telegrams John A. had sent to Allan, as well as to Allan's lawyer, J. C. C. Abbott, the most infamous telegram stating, "Immediate. Private. I must have another ten thousand. Will be the last time of calling. Do not fail me. Answer today."

Once John A. realized that McMullen could prove he had accepted bribes from Hugh Allan, Reform member Richard Cartwright noted that he looked like a "hunted animal driven absolutely to bay." He was drunk most of the time now and unable to face the spectre of political ruin. He established a Royal Commission of Inquiry into the affair, explaining that he had accepted funds only to save Confederation, but before the courts could hear his case, he received another blow. On April 2, before a full House, a Liberal MP named Huntington accused the Conservative Party, and John A. in particular, of selling the CPR charter to Hugh Allan as repayment for his monetary contributions during the 1872 election campaign. Though John A. did not yet know it, the Liberals also possessed the incriminating telegram he had sent to Allan's lawyer, J. C. C. Abbott, begging for an additional $10,000. The Liberals had obtained it by paying a clerk $5,000 to lift it from Abbott's files. Before long, the letter was quoted in the *Montreal Herald*, *L'Evenement*, and in George Brown's *Globe*, which gleefully printed the headline, "THE STORY OF THE PACIFIC SCANDAL! A TEN-COLUMN BROADSHEET."

The only paper harder on John A. than the *Globe* was the satirical paper *Grip*, but at least *Grip* had a sense of humour. Its owner and primary cartoonist, John Wilson Bengough, exulted in the railway debacle, depicting John A. alternatively as a fox, a naughty schoolboy, a flying insect, and even as Sherlock Holmes. Under more benign circumstances, no one enjoyed these caricatures more than John A. himself, who said of Bengough, "There is one Canadian artist who draws me with power and graphic skill. [My] friend Bengough possesses . . . artistic skill and perfect accuracy in portraying my countenance."

Unfortunately, several members of John A.'s government didn't share his sense of humour. Some jumped ship, fearing their reputations would suffer in the fallout from the scandal. With each defection, John A.'s confidence crumbled further. Even his ally George-Étienne Cartier was too ill to rise in his defence.

Following the fall election, Cartier had sailed to London to seek treatment for his Bright's disease, still hopeful of making a full recovery. It wasn't to be. On May 20, 1873, he died abroad. Newly appointed Governor General Lord Frederick Dufferin immediately informed John A. by letter. Shattered, John A. collapsed in his office chair, with his head buried in his hands. He was alone now; his friend, "bold as a lion," was dead, and the future of his railway was in the hands of newspaper columnists and Opposition critics. On the orders of Queen Victoria, Cartier's casket was loaded onto the royal vessel *Druid*. Five days later, the ship arrived in Montreal harbour, where hundreds of people greeted it, clutching handkerchiefs.

Even Agnes had softened toward Cartier, despite his lust for mistresses, bawdy songs, and alcoholic spirits. When John A. arranged a posthumous knighthood for Cartier, Agnes, who was sitting as usual in the gallery of the House, wrote in her diary of Cartier, "He has been, and is, a useful man, and an honest one which is saying a good deal."

John A. was so visibly distraught he could barely attend Cartier's funeral, which was held on June 13 in Montreal. Mourners watched him half-stumble and half-shuffle down the road behind the funeral cortège as it proceeded past Place d'Armes and St. James Street. More than one observer feared he might faint before the journey ended. How many dear friends had he buried in his relatively young life? Why had he been spared? Lord Dufferin, who travelled to Canada for the funeral, observed in a letter written during this period, "As a consequence [of Cartier's death] for this last few days, [John A.] has broken through his usual abstemious habits, and been compelled to resort to more stimulants than suit his peculiar temperament. It is really tragical to see so superior a man subject to such a purely physical infirmity against which he struggles with desperate courage, until fairly prostrated and broken down."

Days later, John and Agnes attended the christening of Lord Dufferin's newborn daughter, Victoria. Here before them was a healthy baby, lustily crying as cold water dribbled across her forehead. Meanwhile, back at home, Mary, sweet and dear as she was, remained propped up against cushions like a rag doll, bright, alive, but condemned to suffer a lifelong infirmity without any brothers or sisters to care for her. John A.'s grief was indescribable. Had it not been for Agnes's steadying arm, it was unlikely he would have made it through the ceremony. Once again, Lord Dufferin recognized John A.'s despair, noting, "Cartier's funeral was too much for him, and he was in a very bad way – not at all himself – indeed quite prostrate, but he contrived to pull himself together on the morning of the day he was to appear in church in a most marvellous manner."

With the Parliament in summer recess, John A. searched for the nearest bolt-hole. He chose Rivière-du-Loup. A man's pride was as priceless as gold, and now John A. faced a type of emotional bankruptcy heretofore unknown to him. He dreaded returning to Parliament on August 13 to do the unthinkable: defend his honour, and that of his party members.

One of John A.'s favourite poems was "The Dream of Gerontius." Cardinal John Henry Newman's poem describes in dream form the thoughts, feelings, and sensations of a man dying, and whose soul is ultimately escorted by an angel to Purgatory, where all the mysteries of the world are explained.

Possibly, John A. was remembering this poem when he vanished from his cottage in Rivière-du-Loup early on August 3, leaving Agnes and Mary behind. Day turned into night, and he failed to return. Instead, on the morning of August 5, a messenger knocked on the front door, bearing a telegram to the distraught Agnes from a "friend" asking about the "state of her husband's health." A few minutes later a second messenger arrived, bearing yet another telegram, hinting that some calamity had befallen Agnes's husband.

Had she read the August 4 *Montreal Witness* newspaper, Agnes would have collapsed in shock. Under the heading "SAD [SIC] OF THE PREMIER," it read, "A telegram was shown to several gentlemen in the city this forenoon anent the doings of Sir John A. Macdonald, at Rivière-du-Loup. It stated that yesterday afternoon Sir John attempted to commit suicide by jumping from the wharf into the water. He was rescued, but now lies, it is asserted, in a precarious condition."

The August 5 issue of the *Globe* repeated the same story; however, the following day, in the form of a "correction," insinuated that "something had happened to the Premier, which his

This painting of Agnes's depicts boats moored at Rivière-du-Loup, where John A. purportedly attempted suicide. *(LAC E003525168)*

friends were endeavouring to hush up." On August 6, the *Globe* added, "The sensation concerning the Premier is rapidly dying out under the influence of repeated assurances that the rumour was without foundation."

What was the truth? The stories converged like river rapids. In response to the rumours, John A. and his handlers flew into overdrive to control the damage, insisting that Opposition members had completely fabricated the story in order to "feed the excitement which the publication of the McMullen correspondence, a few days before, had produced." They wrote that Agnes had taken the telegrams announcing John A.'s suicide to her husband, who was as mystified by their contents as anyone else, and that in response he despatched numerous telegrams to friends, colleagues, and relatives, assuring them he was well, one of the telegrams reading, "It is an infamous falsehood. I never was better in my life."

He never was better in his life? Hardly. The reality was that, for at least two agonizing days, John A. was indeed missing, probably on a drunken bender precipitated by the disgrace in which he found himself.

In his biography of John A., historian Donald Creighton had his own theory concerning John A.'s disappearance. According to Creighton, when John A. "could bear it no longer, he stole away from his modest farm cottage and took the Grand Trunk Railway train west to Levis." Nobody knew where he was. Even the frantic Agnes was ignorant of his condition and his whereabouts. For a few days at least he lay, as Dufferin later said, "perdu with a friend in the neighbourhood of Quebec." Creighton does not rule out a suicide attempt. All reports of the incident agree that Lord Dufferin felt the situation was serious enough that he reported John A.'s condition to the Colonial Office in London.

On August 14, John A. returned to Ottawa to prepare for the next day's assault. Agnes accompanied him, leaving Mary and Theodora to try to enjoy the remainder of the summer at Rivière-du-Loup. John A. was going to turn the tables, accusing the Liberal MP Huntington and the Liberal Party in general of stealing the incriminating letters from the office of Allan's lawyers. He was going to blame Allan. He was going to blame everyone but himself, and he was also going to save his Party, or so he thought. "[All] I want is a full and fair opportunity of proving the facts just as they are. I am content to abide by the result," he wrote Dufferin on August 4, though the letter was not sent until August 7.

On August 15, Lord Dufferin prorogued Parliament until October 23. John A. struggled to avoid unduly alarming Mary, then four years old, and Theodora by concentrating on the minutia of domestic affairs. He wrote Mary on August 25: "My dearest Mary, You must know that your kind Mamma and I are very anxious to see you and Granny again. We have put a new carpet in your room and got everything ready for you. The garden looks lovely just now. It is full of beautiful flowers and I hope you will see them before they are withered. There are some fine melons in the garden. You must pick them for dinner and feed the chickens with the rind. You remember that Mamma cut my hair and made me look like a cropped donkey. It has grown quite long again. When you come home, you must not pull it too hard. I intend to have some new stories for you when you come in the morning into Papa's bed and cuddle him up. Give my love to dear good Grand Mama and give her a kiss for me . . . and so goodbye my pet and come home soon to your loving papa."

As much as Dufferin respected John A., on October 16 he wrote him a letter, clarifying that he held him and his colleagues to blame for extorting money from Hugh Allan in exchange for considering him for a position as president of the railway. Dufferin's letter ended with an ominous declaration. "[As] Minister of Justice and the official guardian and protector of the laws, your responsibilities are exceptional and your personal connection with what has passed cannot but fatally affect your position as minister."

Dufferin had hoped John A. would take the hint and resign. John A. soon discovered that Dufferin wasn't the only person who thought it advisable for him to go. Some members among John A.'s more virulent critics threatened to remove him physically if he didn't see the light and remove himself politically. On September 13, one Montreal resident, using the pseudonym "Joseph," wrote John A. the following ominous letter:

Sometime before Mr. McGee was assassinated, I warned him that if he did not resign his seat he would be killed some way. He took no notice of my warning, and you know what happened to him. Well sir, I give you the same warning. If you do not resign your seat in the Cabinet, not only yourself but your colleagues alas, that is the whole Cabinet, you shall be the victim, you will be killed likewise in some way or other. I shall not myself assassinate you, as I did not assassinate McGee, but I am the cause l'auteur (believe me) you shall not see the first of January 1874. You are a traitor and you shall perish, I tell you . . .

Ask Mrs McGee if her husband had not good warning. Let her show you the letter I addressed to him at the time. The country will get rid of you some way or other. It is done with you. Reflect well upon what I am telling you.

Another member of the public wrote: "I take the opportunity of advising thee, I have been thinking of thee this long time and principally about thy soul, Dear Sir John; does not thy soul trouble thee or the sins of this world . . . meet me in heaven and I will tell thee my name."

Rather than being intimidated, John A. fought on. On the night of October 31, he and Agnes rode to the Parliament Buildings together. He was suffering what she referred to as one of his "headaches." He was unsteady on his feet, and his face was pinched and blotchy. Together they entered the House. At a crucial moment, Agnes released his arm and ascended the stairs to the gallery, where, alongside Lady Dufferin, she leaned over the railing, listening to every syllable John A. uttered.

At 9 p.m., John A. rose and began to speak, at first awkwardly, then with more assurance. Within an hour, Liberal-Conservative Party members were pounding their desks with approval. Five hours later, party members on both sides of the aisle greeted his wry witticisms with applause. Lady Dufferin's and Agnes's eyes swam with tears. There was no denying the tragic truth, however. John A.'s career as prime minister was over.

On November 3, he submitted his official resignation to Lord Dufferin and later that night announced his resignation to a hushed House. Agnes, who could not bear to see her husband capitulate, avoided the session altogether. When next she saw her husband, he was sitting in his drawing room wearing his favourite silk dressing gown and leather slippers, reading. As she entered the room, he looked up briefly and stated, "Well, that's got along with."

"What do you mean?" Agnes asked.

Grip cartoon commenting on the Pacific Scandal.
(Metropolitan Toronto Reference Library)

"Why the government has resigned," John A. replied. "It's a relief to be out of it." Sensing he preferred to be alone, Agnes quietly left the room, returned to her parlour, and wept.

Few except John A. were aware of the ironic postscript that accompanied this tragic tableau. During the Pacific Scandal, subscriptions to *Grip*, the tabloid that had so mercilessly caricatured John A. during the crisis, rose by an astounding 25 per cent, good news for those who owned shares. Fortunately, John A. had quietly scooped up three hundred shares shortly after the paper's debut in 1873. As a result, financially speaking, John A.'s political downfall became his financial gain.

IX

A MATTER OF HONOUR

John A. might have been finished with the Liberal-Conservative Party, but the party wasn't finished with him. Less than twenty-four hours after he resigned in November 1873, his caucus members declared him their leader again.

Two months later, in January 1874, Liberal leader Alexander Mackenzie won election as prime minister, while John A. clung to power in Kingston by a mere thirty-seven votes over his opponent. Suspicious of John A.'s slim victory, Liberal Party member Dr. John Stewart, known as "the most cantankerous and testy character who ever strode the streets of Kingston" and the first professor dismissed from the medical faculty of Queen's University, filed a formal petition, charging John A. with bribing voters. Bribing voters was hardly a practice confined to Conservative Party members but seemed a useful accusation to rid the House of John A. altogether.

"I should be sorry to think that his public career was over [as] he is certainly the best statesman in Canada," Lord Dufferin said, in response to John A.'s predicament.

On September 17, a political cockfight erupted in an Ottawa courtroom. All that was missing were the open kegs of brew. Conservative Party sympathizers, "wearing a sort of hysterical smile on their lips, and looking at the circumstances as children and grown-up simpletons do evil fortune," wrote a *Globe* reporter, sat on one side of the courtroom, while "cool in their communications, confident and inflexible in their determination to see the thing through," Liberal Party members sat on the opposite side.

A corpulent bailiff recited the charges against John A. with a buffoonish solemnity that only reinforced the carnival-like atmosphere before him. John A. stood accused of "bribing, treating, and unduly influencing electors," "impersonating voters," "keeping houses of entertainment," "threatening voters with loss of employment," "hiring cabs and purchasing railway tickets to get voters to the polls," and "hiring many 'canvassers' to bribe voters."

Dr. Stewart entered the courtroom first, his tiny, purposeful steps precipitating "a torrent of hisses and groans," from Conservative spectators. By contrast, John A.'s jaunty jog to the defendant's table unleashed "a hurricane of cheers." It took a full half-hour for Chief Justice William Buell Richards to quell the noisy spectators enough to start the proceedings.

No sooner had the court convened, however, than John A.'s counsel, Richard Walkem, dropped a bombshell. John A., he announced, would vacate his seat in Parliament, conceding that his party members had committed some indiscretions on the campaign trail. He would deny altogether, however, all charges against him of bribery, and he warned Stewart that, should he continue prosecuting the case, he would have to pay the court costs.

Dr. Stewart's lawyer, James Bethune, sat dumbfounded. Was this a stunt? Then he asked the court for a few minutes to consult with his client. When Bethune resumed, he announced hesitantly that his client would continue to press the charges "to some extent," "at least till they could see what the result would be."

Sensing that no legal blood would flow that day, spectators left the courtroom in droves. Bethune battled on, trying to prove that the Conservatives had committed serious instances of bribery, but his witnesses were less than stellar. Even those who admitted to taking money from the Conservative Party developed amnesia when tracing it back directly to John A.

James Shannon, the owner and editor of the *Kingston Daily News*, testified that he received "$1,000 from various parties" and "$500" from John A. personally but grew fuzzy about exactly how he spent the money, recalling that he spent some of it on election "expenses" and probably forwarded the remainder to Alexander Campbell, the general manager of John A.'s campaign. Campbell had conveniently escaped to New York during this period to avoid subpoena. Meanwhile, a witness named Issac Noble admitted the Conservatives paid him $40 in rent for a ward meeting at his home, but insisted he only took the money because by comparison the Grits' bribe came up short.

John A.'s lawyer argued that his canvassers and agents knew the difference between what was legal and what was illegal, and that in all elections monies were spent by both sides contrary to statutes, whether it be "treating" voters to drinks, tipping cab drivers, or any other expenses incurred during elections.

The verdict was a draw. After three days, Judge Buell declared John A.'s seat vacated but cleared him of personal bribery charges, though he concluded his party was guilty of "corrupt practices." The *Globe* labelled John A.'s victory a "narrow escape." John A. probably agreed but took solace in the fact that he would live to run another day.

In December, John A. did just that via a by-election. This time there were no open votes, and the law promised to prosecute anyone suspected of bribing voters. The good news was that John

A. won Kingston yet again. The bad news was that he beat his opponent by only seventeen votes.

John A.'s air of jaunty detachment was a facade. The truth was, he felt his career was over. Author Peter Waite in his book *John A. Macdonald* recounts that in February, while walking down Sparks Street, brooding about his fate, John A. decided to visit the *Citizen* newspaper offices. "Boys," he said, "publish an editorial paragraph in today's *Citizen* announcing my resignation of the leadership of the Conservative Party." The editor slammed down his pen and replied, "Sir John, my pen will write no such announcement, nor will it be published in the *Citizen*."

John A. was still drinking up to two bottles of brandy a day. He missed his old colleagues, like George-Étienne Cartier, but he especially missed his favourite drug, power. When his law firm's biggest client, the Trust and Loan Company of Canada, moved its headquarters to Toronto late in 1874, John A. wasted no time opening a law firm on 25 Toronto Street in the same city. Consequently, he became a long-distance commuter, spending as much time in Toronto as he did in Ottawa. His law partners were now James Patton, Robert Fleming, and Hugh John, who had graduated that year from the University of Toronto. In fact, whenever he was in town, John A. lodged with Hugh John on King Street West.

Agnes remained in Ottawa, caring for Mary, hosting book-club meetings and other small social events to compensate for her husband's absence, as well as to distract her from the oppressive reality that, at an age when he should have been able to afford retirement, John A. still had to scramble to make ends meet. For a time it seemed she was the Chapel Hill house's only healthy inhabitant. Hewitt suffered from chronic spells of unexplained muscular weakness, while Theodora's health was visibly deteriorating.

For the next months, John A. decided against participating in House debates, since Prime Minister Alexander Mackenzie's dry, pedantic speaking style lulled him to sleep. Finally, he could avoid speaking no longer. On the afternoon of February 10, while Agnes was visiting friends in the Niagara region, John A. began drinking brandy in the Senate bar, fortifying himself for his first major speech as the Leader of the Opposition. By 3 p.m., he was so drunk he could barely place one foot in front of the other. He spoke with impressive clarity, though everyone present knew he was "sprung." When Alexander Mackenzie responded to the speech, John A. grew fractious, interrupting him constantly. Embarrassed, Conservative Party ministers tried in vain to steer him out of the House, but John A. petulantly refused to budge. In reviewing John A.'s behaviour, Charles Belford of the *Mail* remarked, "John A. is helpless as a baby."

The Macdonalds had more than merely political trials to overcome, but personal ones as well. On February 28, 1875, Theodora Bernard died while Agnes and John A. were in Toronto on business. Hewitt had come into Agnes's drawing room to pay his evening visit to Theodora, and, as they sat talking by the fire-place, she suddenly clutched her chest and said, "I feel a sudden pain here, a strange sensation," and pitched forward in her chair. By the time Hewitt reached his mother's side, she was dead.

As soon as Agnes saw the messenger enter the house she was visiting in Toronto, a "chill" passed through her heart and her head began to "swim." As the only girl in a family of boys, Agnes viewed her mother as her most trusted friend, ally, adviser, and teacher. Then, throughout all the arduous years of moving from country to country, from Jamaica to England, waiting for Hewitt's call to join him in Canada, she and Theodora had turned to each other for companionship and support.

Theodora's "long dark coffin" stood in the drawing room of the Chapel Street house, and Agnes rarely left its side. In "wild and desperate pain," she knelt by the coffin and prayed, imagining that if she stared at her mother's pale face long enough, she could almost see her lips moving "in voiceless welcome."

Reverend Bedford-Jones of St. Alban's Church officiated at Theodora's funeral on the evening of March 1. The following day, he conducted a memorial service at the Chapel Street house, at which Agnes and Hewitt clung to each other for support. For several minutes, Bedford-Jones fussed and fidgeted, delaying the beginning of the service. Finally, a frustrated Hewitt turned to Agnes and whispered, "What are we waiting for?"

"Sir John," she replied as Hewitt looked on in shock, unaware that in an effort to please his grief-stricken wife, John A. had converted to Anglicanism from Presbyterianism just the day before. Two or three minutes later, John A. sprinted into the room, knelt beside Agnes, clutching a small Altar Manual in his hands. Bedford-Jones recalled that John A. could "scarcely speak the words" as he delivered the eucharist to him. Following the service, Bedford Jones joined the family for breakfast.

Agnes settled into a leaden state of grief mixed with disbelief. Eleven days after the funeral, she wrote in her journal, "Oh, my mother, my mother, gone from me, gone to your sainted rest, can you see your desolate child now? – can you hear within and do you forgive? So much that might have been different – that is what makes my pain so very, very, very keen, that fearful thing regret!"

James Williamson extended his sympathy to John A., Lady Macdonald, and Colonel Bernard by letter but immediately switched gears, reminding John A. that he had still not officially accepted an invitation to a "non-political" gathering at Queen's to take place on April 28. Oblivious to the waves of grief that enveloped the entire Macdonald household, Williamson wrote, "Do send a favorable reply as soon as possible. We have stood staunchly by you." Bad timing was the least of Williamson's sins, however. In closing, he asked John A. to endeavour to get the Reports of Geology, Surveys & Public Works, and Marine & Fisheries for the present Session forwarded to him "as soon as possible."

A week later, John A. told Williamson that he had written to Dr. Snodgrass, the president of Queen's, informing him that he would "endeavour to be at the Banquet, but could not yet say so positively." He also promised to secure the reports Williamson requested.

John A. obviously made allowances for Williamson's insensitivity, for he knew his brother-in-law was suffering under his own pressures. For one thing, Margaret's health had taken a turn for the worse. Her breathing was so laboured that she was virtually incapable of leaving her bed. Doctors held out no hope for a cure, ludicrous in light of the fact that they could not even determine the exact nature of her illness.

The critical state of Margaret's health plunged John A. into fears for his own mortality. He was sixty years old now, not old, but no longer capable of bouncing back physically or emotionally as quickly as he had once done. He had converted to Anglicanism to make Agnes happy. He had humoured James Williamson to keep Louisa happy. He lavished love and attention on Mary. He had, it seemed, kept everyone happy but himself. Perhaps a change of address was the answer.

Together, he and Agnes travelled to Toronto in late March to scout out houses. One of those they considered subletting belonged to Thomas Charles Patteson, an editor with the *Toronto Mail* newspaper. Patteson was travelling to Europe for a year in the fall, and agreed to rent his house to John A. while he was gone. John A. and Agnes were invited to visit. Over dinner, the group discussed life in Toronto. The city's population had quadrupled since John A. had lived there with Isabella in 1856. Pedestrians hurried to board clanging horse-drawn streetcars, and budget retail stores such as Eaton's and Woolworth's dominated the city's core.

Sir Charles Tupper, who had already moved to Toronto himself, joined the group for what should have been a pleasant evening. Despite everyone's best efforts to be gay, however, a drunken John A. inexplicably began insulting Tupper, afterwards stumbling upstairs to bed. Tupper merely shrugged the incident off and left for home. Shortly after Tupper's departure, Patteson also retired to bed. Not long after he did so, he saw Agnes walk out the front door and sit forlornly on an iron bench near the front gate. Shivering, she wrapped a shawl around her shoulders, as a damp veil of humidity enveloped her. When Patteson looked out his window again at 6 a.m., she was still sitting on the bench, lost in thought.

John A. and Agnes returned to Ottawa to prepare for their move. Shortly after, on April 26, 1875, Rowe & Ebrant Company auctioned off the contents of their Chapel Street house. Among the items on the block was a crimson wool hearth rug; a black-and-white sideboard, with a marble top and rich carved back; cheese plates; teapots; fruit dishes; feather beds; a sewing machine; an iron crib; a child's bath; and most poignant of all, one Sleepy Hollow Arm Chair, with poles for an invalid's use.

In July, John, Agnes, and Mary again sought refuge at Rivière-du-Loup. Agnes contemplated the daunting task of starting over again in a new city, her entire life already disrupted by constantly being on the move. Now she was moving again, this time with a disabled child. Though she was only forty, deep lines encircled her mouth. The light no longer shone from her eyes, and her hair had turned white virtually overnight. Statuesque as a young woman, she now neared rotundness, her closets filled with dowdy wool shawls and heavy linen frocks. Increasingly, she eschewed jewellery of any kind, except religious symbols.

An aging Agnes. *(Topley Studio Fonds/LAC PA025534)*

John A. was 5 feet 11 inches, and his weight had increased to 180 pounds. He was not fat, but thickened, in part from the high-calorie drinks he so enjoyed. He still suffered "catarrh of the stomach," as doctors called it, and tried to stick to a bland diet of white bleached fish and milk. Agnes's unhappiness oppressed him, as did Mary's disability. Then, too, his sister Margaret's declining health preyed on his mind. He informed Louisa by letter that for the benefit of all, it might be best if the entire family moved away from the Heathfield house and into a boarding house closer to the centre of Kingston, where they would be near medical doctors and services. With Margaret's age, he feared her recovery would be slow, "and unless carefully husbanded, may never return."

With their summer sojourn ended, in September, John A., Agnes, Mary, and Hewitt packed up and moved to Patteson's house in Toronto. The house was strictly utilitarian in appearance and possessed none of the gingerbread-house charm of their homes in Ottawa. The building was long and flat-fronted, and constructed out of grey stock brick; its most attractive feature the rolling grass that surrounded it. Within a year of settling in, however, John A. located a more elegant house at 63 St. George Street, close to the University of Toronto, where Hugh John had studied law with an indifference bordering on the comatose.

John A. tried to devote more time to his Toronto law firm, and to forming a closer bond with Hugh John, but both attempts failed to go as smoothly as he would have liked. For more than a year, James Patton, Fleming, and Hugh John had run John A.'s law office in Toronto, as John A. travelled back and forth to Ottawa. There had been plenty of work, in fact, more than they could handle by themselves, and frustration soon set in. John A. was needed in the Toronto office on a regular basis, and, more often than not, he was off plotting a political comeback. In March, Fleming had even drafted a letter of resignation to John A. In his letter, Fleming blamed his departure on Hugh John. He complained that Hugh John had not "fulfilled his promise" in the firm and had not helped the other partners "secure business," as he thought he might, or "procure the agency of some of his more senior legal friends throughout the country." Instead, he had lazed around the office, evincing an "indifference to the practice of law altogether."

John A. refused to accept Fleming's resignation and enticed him to stay by offering him an additional cut of the profits. At the same time, he wrote a confidential letter to Patton explaining that "after much persuasion," he had convinced Fleming to stay. Losing him, he said, would "cripple" the law firm, and that "Hugh and you could not set on without his assistance." "All this is strictly confidential," John A. added, "and must not be mentioned to Hugh – but you should know it nonetheless."

Even when Hugh John escaped the eye of a storm, he was blown in strange directions by its winds. In 1876, he announced to John A. his intention to marry a woman named Jean King, six years his senior, a widow, and a Catholic! John A., whose first marriage was to a woman who was his elder, predicted his son's act of rebellion would end in disaster and categorically refused to grant Hugh permission to wed King.

With his penchant for nurturing hurt feelings, Hugh promptly drafted a letter resigning from his father's law firm, effective in January 1876.

> [I] am grieved that we should part from any disagreement, I dare say it will be all for the best, for I can quite understand that it will be as much pleasanter for you not to have me in the office and as far as I myself am concerned I feel confident that by attending carefully to business and making the best use of such talent as I have I will manage to get on in the world and keep my head above water. [I] hope too that you know that wherever I may pitch my tent I will always be both ready and willing to do your bidding and will always hold myself in readiness to

advance your interests in any way in my power, for although I think you are acting in an unnecessarily harsh manner towards me respecting my engagement I have no doubt that looking at this matter from your standpoint you are justified in the course you are taking, and I certainly can never forget the numbers of kindnesses done to and favours conferred upon me in times past. Your obstinate but affectionate son, Hugh J. Macdonald.

From John A.'s perspective, he had intervened to save Hugh John's legal career with his firm, yet here was Hugh John returning the favour by submitting his resignation over a woman, and the wrong woman at that! If John A. suffered guilt over abandoning Hugh John during childhood, he recovered from it sufficiently to accept Hugh John's resignation with chilling alacrity. "Dear Hugh," he wrote, "I have your note of the 30 ult. I have today as you wish mentioned to Mr. Patton your intention to leave the firm of Macdonald & Patton & strike out a house for yourself. He agrees with you that the end of the year will be a convenient time for you to leave, so that you may consider that as settled."

Despite his father's renunciation, in July Hugh John travelled back to Kingston, where he married King, his father being conspicuously absent from the ceremony. Following the wedding, Hugh John opened his own law firm and "pitched his tent" on King Street. Together, he and Jean visited with James Williamson and Margaret on frequent occasions, but each time came away even more depressed. By now, Margaret was near death, and Hugh John wrote to his father on March 11, preparing him for the worst. Finally, on April 18, Margaret, whom John A. described as his "oldest and sincerest friend," died in bed at Heathfield with John A. and the rest of her family by her side.

Moll's death marked a turning point in Louisa and Williamson's living arrangements. Louisa had never got along with Williamson particularly well, though each had learned to tolerate the other's idiosyncrasies. Now, left rattling around in their large farmhouse, their power struggles seemed senseless and unnecessary. Within a month of Margaret's death, Williamson wrote to John A., informing him that they would be taking up his earlier advice to move from Heathfield to Kingston to be closer to vital amenities.

In August, the two rented Mrs. Waddington's boarding house on Wellington Street. The house was in John A.'s name, and Williamson was again Louisa's tenant. It was far smaller than Heathfield, and soon Louisa began writing to John A. complaining about the number of books Williamson scattered about the house. As usual, John A. tried to mollify Louisa, explaining that she would be receiving $1,100 for the four acres of property she'd owned on the Heathfield property, a considerable appreciation over what she'd paid for it. He then asked if he might send Mary and her maids to visit, an event Louisa always relished.

Politically, things were looking up for John A. Alexander Mackenzie's momentum was beginning to stall, and his party started to lose popularity. *Grip* joked that it would have been better for Mackenzie had he worked less hard and done a little more wining and dining, or "poking bartenders in the ribs, jovially, like John A., but he could never be taught these little arts."

In addition to his dour and pinched political style, Mackenzie's problems were basically twofold. There was a worldwide Depression and Canada's income from custom duties had dried up due to slower trade. Then, Mackenzie alienated British Columbians by reneging on John A.'s promise to build a railway to the West Coast, explaining that insufficient funds would forestall construction indefinitely. In response, the B.C. government threatened to secede from Canada, a threat Mackenzie failed to take seriously.

To combat Mackenzie's apparent apathy toward building a prosperous united country, John A., along with Charles Tupper, drafted a National Policy, which would introduce high tariffs to protect Canada's industries from foreign competitors. The plan called for an increase in the price of imports, which in turn would enable Canadian manufacturers to compete with goods imported from other countries. With the money they made, businesses could then build manufacturing plants and thereby increase production of goods to satisfy the home market. "Canada for Canadians" became Macdonald and Tupper's catchphrase. To complete the country's independence, Macdonald promised to oversee the completion of the national railway to transport goods from one section of the country to the other, further benefiting its economy.

Slowly but surely, John A.'s party began to rise again, winning a series of by-elections in 1875 and 1876, and reducing Mackenzie's majority of seats from 70 to 42. Beginning in the fall of 1876, sixty-one-year-old John A. was back on the hustings, attending a series of political picnics hosted by the Conservative Party. Always a master of stagecraft, he delivered stirring speeches atop picnic tables, as mothers and fathers lounged on the grass, their children gobbling fried chicken, corn on the cob, cold cuts, jams, cakes, and candies. If John A. couldn't campaign in taverns, he'd bring the taverns to him, courtesy of Eliza Grimason, who delivered kegs of whisky to each event and even personally drove John A. from engagement to engagement in her fine horse and buggy.

In his speeches, John A. blamed everything from potato bugs to weevils ravaging the country's crops on Mackenzie's Liberal government. "Be sure, my friends that, the weevil will come again with the Grits," he declared. He reminded audiences that under the Conservative government, land had been fertile and the crops plentiful. Once he'd blamed Mackenzie personally for the country's ills, John A. unfurled his National Policy, which he promised would save the country from economic ruin.

Fully returned to the campaign trail, John A. devoted little time to his Toronto law practice, driving Patton into a fury. The breaking point occurred when in an attempt to repair relations between the two of them John A. invited Hugh John to rejoin the firm – not only to rejoin it, but to take control of the business altogether, paying his father money for the use of his "name and influence." This was manna from heaven for Hugh John, who had struggled, unsuccessfully, to keep his Kingston law office afloat. In fact, by the time John A. reconciled with him, Hugh John couldn't even afford to pay the fifteen-dollar train fare to Toronto. Upon Hugh John's return, Patton submitted a formal request to dissolve his partnership with John A. With Hugh John back in the picture, the new name of the firm became Macdonald and Macdonald.

All through 1877 and the first part of 1878, Hugh John managed the office with a friendly, man-about-town air. This professional affiliation with his father was the making of him. He felt a sense of purpose to his endeavours. Jean King provided him with a happy private life, which impressed John A. As a result, John A.'s feeling toward Jean softened. Hugh John and Jean's daughter, Isabella, whom they nicknamed "Daisy," was born in June 1877.

John A. was on the road for much of the fall of 1877, stumping with a renewed vitality and purpose and staying at the houses of friends, such as that of his stalwart friend Eliza Grimason. Back in Toronto, Agnes set about redecorating the ground floor of the St. George Street house by applying fresh coats of paint and wall-paper. She also installed new copper plumbing throughout the building, as well as overseeing the installation of a black iron fence around the front lawn. Once spring came, she planted a new garden at the rear of the house, next to a chicken coop, where Mary's pet hen, Sarah, squawked noisily.

Despite her love for her, Agnes was not above using Mary as a pawn, coaching her to write her father a series of plaintive letters, begging him to come home. On October 12, 1877, Mary wrote, "Your wife Agnes sends her love. She did not tell me to say so, but I am sure she would if she knew it. I have a little dog that my Uncle gave me. Dear Father, when are you coming back? I hope you will be back soon for Agnes misses you very much and says often to me 'how I wish my husband was back.' The house seems so dull and lonely without you and I miss my evening stories very much."

By October 21, John A. was back in Toronto, where a letter of complaint from Louisa awaited him. With characteristic impulsiveness, she decided she did not wish to continue sharing the Kingston boarding house with Williamson, but instead wanted a house of her own. John A. soon changed her mind about living apart from Williamson. With utmost patience, he also explained that she had just entered into the second year of the house's lease, so would have to keep it until September 1878.

Louisa listened to her elder brother's advice, then, as usual, did the exact opposite. In early 1878, she paid an extended visit to John A.'s home in Toronto. From there, she wrote a letter to Williamson asking him to give Mrs. Waddington formal notice of their intention to leave the Kingston boarding house. Even in victory, however, she couldn't resist levelling a barb against her brother-in-law. "Will you be sure and speak of our going to Mrs. Waddington when you pay her on the 20th. When I spoke to her in October I said it was from no fault we had with the house, only there was no room for your books."

Louisa told Williamson that she had picked out the perfect alternative, a three-storey stone house located at the southeast corner of Earl and Sydenham Streets, near Queen's University and St. Andrew's Church. John A. would list himself as the official tenant, and pay all the rent and taxes, while Williamson could rent space from him.

For the remainder of 1878, Agnes kept tabs on her husband by accompanying him on the last leg of his election campaign. She climbed on board and alighted from dozens of dusty trains that trundled to as many vote-rich whistlestops as possible. Back home in Toronto, Hugh John and Jean cared for Mary, with the assistance of two nurses. Everywhere John and Agnes went, female spectators complimented Agnes on her outfits, while male critics shouted insulting comments about her husband's drinking. Agnes had matured into a political veteran, pouring lemonade and laughing at the rude jokes of the rough-hewn farmers who wanted to shake her hand, their own hands often caked with dirt and manure. Curiously, however, she failed to recognize the duality in her own character, disapproving of women who meddled too much in politics, arguing that doing so made them "too violent a partisan" and "apt to ride [their] hobby to death."

On the night of September 17, 1878, John A. won re-election to office. The extent of his victory stunned the Liberals. However, for the first time, Kingston did not support its Conservative candidate. Eliza Grimason, who had done all she could to raise support in Kingston, was crushed. "I went around town the next day crying till I hadn't an eye in me head," she told John A. "Never mind," a sanguine John A. informed her. "They're all below me yet." Eliza derived some comfort from the fact that the electors of "British Columby" at least could appreciate him. After his victory, she told him to retaliate by taking the best position he could in the "hull" country, "and tell them all to go to the divil." With this, John A. roared with laughter and said, "The country would go to the dogs if [I] did that."

The paint had barely dried inside the St. George Street house in Toronto when Agnes and John started packing to move back to Ottawa. During the interval following the election, John A. had returned to the house tired but triumphant. He wrote to Louisa, "I am in good health, but have not yet quite regained my strength." Instead of ending their lease on the house, however, they rented it out to Hugh John, Jean, and Daisy.

Upon arriving back in Ottawa, John A. and Agnes moved into Stadacona Hall on Laurier Avenue East, finally a house large enough to entertain friends and dignitaries. The house was the first to provide John A. with a spacious office where he could work in solitude, fresh air filtering through open windows.

Agnes and John A. arrived back in Ottawa just as Lord Dufferin and his wife were leaving. John A. had always considered Dufferin's manner overly "gushy," but Agnes and Lady Dufferin had struck up a warm friendship, especially since Lady Dufferin had shown great kindness to Mary.

Each year, Lady Dufferin and her daughter Nellie invited Mary to sell flowers and fill out raffle papers at church bazaars held at Rideau Hall. Mary also attended annual plays performed by the children of the aides-de-camp. At the age of nine, Mary could now read, and speak, albeit very slowly.

John A. never gave up on Mary, hiring a German woman trained in the "Swedish movement treatment" to rub and pound her shrivelled legs until they became more flexible. He scoured magazines for the latest in back and leg braces. He wrote to Louisa, "She is beginning to stand. I hope to see her walk yet." The older she got, the more optimistic he felt about her physical stamina. Without his realizing it, her pattern of improvement matched the standard pattern of cerebral palsy. According to Dr. Drake of the Hospital for Sick Children, "The most activity among children with cerebral palsy consistently occurs during the early teen years, then drops off."

Mary also attended her contemporaries' birthday parties, and they hers, although she was forced to sit in her wheelchair while the other children enjoyed games such as Pin the Tail on the Donkey and Ring around the Rosy. Rather than being perturbed by the noise and confusion, Mary always seemed content, at least according to her mother. Other observers, including an acquaintance of the family named Lilian Desbarets, however, called Mary "a pathetic sight," adding, "She was just like a large rag doll with

Mary Macdonald, fourteen in this photograph, defied the odds
and lived until she was sixty-three. *(LAC PA025746)*

an oversized head being carried around among gay and active
children. At the conclusion of one event, as the children lined up
to depart, party favours in hand, John A. lured them back by
placing another record on the Victrola. As the children swirled
and danced around Mary's chair, John A. leaned down and whispered, 'You see, Mary they don't want to leave your company.'"

On October 17, 1878, John A. was sworn in as Canada's third
prime minister by Lord Dufferin, and soon after the ceremony,
Dufferin departed for England to join his wife and daughter. His
replacement fulfilled all of Agnes's negative expectations. The
Marquess of Lorne was an amiable sort, but his wife, the tall, lean,
artistic Princess Louise, daughter of Queen Victoria, lorded her
royal pedigree over her supposed inferiors, including Agnes.
Certainly, the two women shared a history. Louise had disliked

Agnes ever since 1867, when, while sitting in the royal box at the Grand Opera House in London, she had risen to accept the applause of the audience and noticed, with obvious disapproval, that Agnes had risen alongside her.

Eleven years later, the two women still detested each other, especially after John A. tactlessly praised Louise's "graceful skating" as well as her technical skill in watercolour painting. The second compliment must have particularly stung Agnes. After all, the childless Louise could avail herself of a special studio in Rideau Hall in which to paint, benefitting as well from the advice of artistic icons such as Lanseer and Millais, whereas the near-penniless Agnes had had to struggle along with second-rate tutors in an airless attic.

The citizens of Ottawa got their first glimpse of the patrician Louise as she and her husband rode a carriage through a snow-storm toward Parliament Hill, where they opened Parliament on February 13, 1879. Just six days later, the couple hosted their first state ball at Rideau Hall. Following protocol, Lorne took Agnes as his partner in the opening set of quadrilles, as Princess Louise danced with John A. Punch was served, along with various liquors, and quite soon John A. was drunk. Word spread that, while inebriated, John A. insulted Princess Louise, and that Lady Macdonald treated her with a lack of respect.

Reform member Richard Cartwright, who observed the "incident," accused John A. of "taking a liberty" with Princess Louise, whom he called "a great lady." Never an admirer of John A.'s in the first place, Cartwright insisted that John A.'s behaviour had been so egregious that Prince Louise "was obliged to request his retirement from her presence."

If the ignominy of the accusation was hard for John A. to shake, it was even more so for Agnes, who vehemently proclaimed her husband's innocence. Agnes was so distraught that she asked John A. to write to Lord Lorne, asking whether John A. should issue a denial. Lorne replied more laconically than Agnes would have liked: "Certainly, if it is worth while to contradict such reports. There is no foundation whatever for the statements made," he responded. From then on, Louise and Agnes engaged in a cold war, which lasted until 1880, when after a tobogganing accident, Louise returned home to England, leaving her husband behind to complete his tenure.

John A. was pleased to return as prime minister. He built a Cabinet of close friends, in particular appointing Charles Tupper the minister of public works, a position from which he could oversee the building of the CPR railway, one of John A.'s great priorities. He appointed Leonard Tilley the minister of finance and made himself minister of the interior so he could manage the settlement of the West.

To raise money for the railway, John A. decided to travel to England, to line up funds from the British government. Agnes wished to attend the latest stage shows and shop for fashions and gifts for Mary. Mary would remain behind with servants at Rivière-du-Loup, relaxing in the nearby saltwater baths.

Agnes sailed on June 21. John A. meant to follow her after he tied up some work; instead, he collapsed from an attack of cholera. Dr. Grant and Tupper raced to his side. He was prostrate with severe abdominal pains, combined with diarrhea. His temperature rose to frightening heights, then levelled off. He was desperate to join Agnes in England, where he had always felt at home.

At last, on July 26, 1880, he sailed for England, arriving on August 4. Agnes had already got a head start on him, at least as far as shopping was concerned. With the interest earned on what remained of their testimonial fund, Agnes invested in a new wardrobe of the finest fabrics, suitable for a prime minister's wife; she also used the time and dollars to buy crystal and china for their home. Like her husband, she had a fondness for fur – in her case, fur-trimmed dresses, fur hats, and muffs. She had booked a suite at Batt's Hotel, on Dover Street, overlooking Piccadilly. She also enjoyed reuniting with "two charming cousins," Annie

Broome and Louisa Scott, who were in London at the same time. "The three are very alike and standing together make a very distingué group," John A. wrote to Louisa after he arrived.

After reuniting with friends, and enjoying a variety of dinner parties, John A. explained to the Colonial Office Canada's need for trade tariffs to keep out American goods and to match the restrictive tariffs already implemented by the United States. As for the railway, he explained that it could only be completed with cold, hard cash, but that its rewards in terms of ease of internal trade would be incalculable.

Britain's Conservative government under Benjamin Disraeli was teetering toward an economic depression, however, so Macdonald decided to wait until a more opportune time presented itself to ask for money. In the meantime, he had the happy distraction of travelling to Osborne, England, where under the watchful eyes of the Duke of Northumberland, the Duke of Richmond, the Lord Chancellor, and the Home Secretary, he was sworn in as a member of the Queen's Privy Council. After the ceremony, the Right Honourable John A. Macdonald and Agnes attended an audience with the Queen. It was fortunate that Agnes had arrived in England before her husband, for her handsome new wardrobe was perfect to wear to all the official engagements they attended, including the opera, the theatre, and dinners with the likes of Lord Carnarvon at his home, Highclere Castle, which John A. boyishly called "one of the swellest places in England." "It would amuse you to see how Agnes swells it," he wrote to Louisa.

John A. returned home unsuccessful in raising British capital to subsidize the building of the railway. However, thanks to the advice of the then minister of finance, Sir Samuel Leonard Tilley, the Lieutenant-Governor of New Brunswick, John A. finally raised three million pounds from the Bank of Montreal.

Shortly after John A.'s return from England, he collapsed one Sunday morning during services at St. Alban's Church. He had felt ill on prior occasions, but he had never fainted without any apparent cause. Frightened about his capacity to continue leading his party, he impulsively submitted his resignation, which his entire Cabinet refused to accept.

Talked back from the brink of retirement once again, John A. made the building of the CPR railway not merely his purpose, but his calling. William Gladstone replaced Disraeli in two successive elections, and the British financing of the railway stalled, but suddenly, in June 1880, with the British economy back on a roll, three offers arrived in a row. The first was made by the Old Canada Company, the second by the Brassey English Railway Contractor, and the third from Lord Dunmore, who was arriving in Ottawa to make his offer in person. Before Dunmore could arrive, however, yet another tender offer arrived, this time from Duncan McIntyre, who already ran the Canada Central Railway that linked Ottawa to Lake Nipissing. Duncan's backers included the directors of the St. Paul Minneapolis and Manitoba Railway, headed by George Stephen, the president of the Bank of Montreal and partner of Donald Smith (Lord Strathcona).

John A. would have to bury a particularly large hatchet in order to work with Strathcona. The Conservative member for Selkirk, Manitoba, during the 1869–70 Red River uprising, Strathcona had eventually withdrawn his support from John A. during the Pacific Scandal and helped force him out of office. John A. had a long memory for those who betrayed him. Even as late as 1878, he had chastised Strathcona publicly in the House for deserting him in 1873, screaming, "That fellow Smith is the biggest liar I ever met!" After the session ended, Macdonald's temper continued to boil. Before anyone could restrain him, he ran toward Smith, screaming, "I can lick you quicker than Hell can scorch a feather."

However, for the sake of the railway, for the sake of posterity, and for the sake of his own ego, John A. met with George Stephen, where they drafted a letter of agreement to build the CPR railway. A month later, they signed the official document:

George Stephen would be the first president of the company, with Duncan McIntyre as its first vice-president.

But as usual, official business made up only a portion of John A.'s concerns. James Williamson, the reliable rock upon which the Macdonalds had sought shelter, was himself breaking up. After subjugating himself to the Macdonald clan, sublimating his despair over losing both his wives, as well as custody of his own son, Williamson was uncharacteristically indulging in habits completely contrary to his character. For one thing, he was staying out late and, when he returned home, walked unsteadily toward his living quarters.

Louisa avoided Williamson by visiting relatives but asked neighbours to keep her posted on his comings and goings. What she heard back displeased her. Williamson, eyewitnesses reported, was "off to the club with a lot of girls," "dining out," and "tea drinking" with such regularity it set Louisa's "hair on end." She finally warned Williamson to shape up before her return. "George Macdonald gives me an idea of your dissipation that is dreadful," she wrote, "so I begin to think it is time to put a stop to that sort of thing and have made up my mind to return home by the end of the week."

Louisa's shock tactics didn't work. Upon returning home, she found Williamson distraught, in part because John A. had once again failed to attend one of the university's functions, as he had promised to do. To try to compensate for his absence, John A. sent Williamson a copy of *Hansard* from the previous session. At the same time, he wrote a note to Louisa, containing his remedy for Williamson's woes: "My dear Louisa, I fear the Professor is breaking up & shall advise him to retire and devote himself to literary pursuits." Fearful that retiring from the university might deprive him of his main reason to live, Williamson stayed on, seeking some middle way out of his despair.

Near the end of the year, John A.'s own health again failed. This time Dr. Grant surmised the culprit was liver disease. When the House resumed in December, John A. was unable to attend, so Agnes, well qualified for the job, attended in his stead, pen poised like a dagger above her journal pages as she stared down from the gallery. Acting as her husband's eyes and ears, she reported on each day's proceedings.

As March neared, and John A.'s health had still not improved appreciably, Agnes became severely alarmed and summoned Hugh John and Louisa to Ottawa to discuss possible plans of action. As soon as Louisa saw John A., she gasped. "I never saw John looking what I call old until this time. His hair is getting quite grey," she wrote to a friend.

Agnes and John A. hastily made plans to seek medical advice on the other side of the Atlantic. For once, John A. did not want to go but had little choice in the face of Agnes's determination. Agnes felt that Dr. Grant, John A.'s Kingston doctor, had a "depressing effect" on her husband, so depressing that, Agnes felt if he told him, "you are too weak," John A. "would give it up." Expectations for John A.'s recovery became so low that, on April 17, Hugh John visited with his father for several hours, "putting things to right," in Louisa's words. Fate's wheel, however, was still in spin. Within five days, a death occurred, but not the one John A.'s loved ones had been expecting. Instead, Jean King, forty-two, dropped dead from a massive coronary. Hugh Macdonald was now a single parent to a child rendered motherless at almost exactly the same age he had been when his mother, Isabella, had died. It must have seemed as if John A.'s initial fears about the marriage were justified after all.

Hugh John reacted to Jean's death with stoic resignation. After all, by now he was a veteran at losing beloved family members. As soon as her funeral in Toronto concluded, Hugh John returned to work at the law firm.

Meanwhile, Agnes and John A., accompanied by Hewitt Bernard, and Agnes's niece May, departed for London, staying again at Batt's Hotel. There, they met with a British doctor named Sullivan, who diagnosed John A. with a stomach ulcer. He prescribed a special diet, with exercise, and John A.'s health soon improved. When the hotel became too conspicuous a place to stay, the group moved to a rented premise called Denmark House, located in Upper Norwood, just outside London, near the Crystal Palace. Before long, the Macdonalds were back in the social swing, attending soirees thrown by Lord Lorne, the Duke of Argyll, and other notable figures.

Euphoric with relief that her husband was on the mend, Agnes visited London's shops with renewed vigour. From Harris and Toms she purchased yards of delicate lace; from Cavendish's, French corsets and a black straw hat trimmed with white lace. For Mary there were bonnets, gloves, purses, and shoes. On the voyage home on board the *Sardinia*, John A. felt gregarious enough to introduce one of the night's entertainments.

Work on the railway proceeded at a lighting pace, despite both physical and political obstacles. George Stephen's stewardship remained adroit under even the most gruelling conditions. Workers were imported from China, Ireland, Scotland, and England to complete the line. These immigrants, seeking a better life, slaved for sixteen hours a day to lay down track, fighting off mosquitoes, black flies, coyotes, and one another. It was said a man died for every mile of track in Western Canada.

John A. painted the railway's completion to the public in broadbrush strokes, and as propaganda it worked magnificently. At a huge Conservative convention in Toronto in November 1881, he announced that, instead of taking ten years, the railway would be completed in five. The crowd roared its approval.

At sixty-seven years of age, John A. had regained his youthful vitality. Agnes felt now was better than never for John A. to buy a permanent home to call his own, one befitting a man of his stature. She knew of only one house that fit the bill: Earnscliffe, the magnificent gabled house they had rented from Thomas Reynolds ten years before. Reynolds had died in 1880, and by 1882, using additional money from his testimonial fund, John A. bought the house for $10,000. "I begged Sir John very hard before he would buy it. He

Earnscliffe, ca. 1870. *(LAC C010371)*

was always thinking of me and a possible future without him and did not want to diminish his savings, by putting it into property," Agnes wrote.

This house rivalled Rideau Hall in stature, which was fine with Agnes. Rideau Hall, after all, reminded Agnes of the imperious Princess Louise. Earnscliffe, by contrast, symbolized the apotheosis of all their political dreams. Prior to moving in, she set about refurbishing it at a cost of $7,000. She punched walls out in

John A.'s jumbled office at Earnscliffe.
(Canadian High Commission [Great Britain]/LAC C050811)

one location and built barriers in another. She commissioned the construction of two false doors in John A.'s study, through which he could escape unwanted visitors. (John A.'s West Block office also contained an escape route.) She also designed an entirely new dining room, and an office for Joseph Pope, who worked as John A.'s private secretary beginning in 1882.

In 1882, Hugh John decided to strike out on his own. He moved to Winnipeg, which was experiencing a real-estate boom thanks to the railway, and opened a law office there. Stewart Tupper, Charles Tupper's son, soon followed, and the two men set up a legal partnership. By the late winter of 1883, Hugh John visited Earnscliffe to announce his engagement to Gertrude (Gertie) Vankoughnet. As it turned out, Gertie and her family knew the Macdonalds well. In 1856, John A. and Isabella had sent Hugh to play at the Vankoughnet's home in Toronto, and Gertrude's uncle Philip Vankoughnet was a long-time friend and colleague of John A. Hugh and Gertie married in April of the same year.

John A. was a man who never forgot his friends, and never let his wife forget them either. Hence, Eliza Grimason became one of the first visitors to Earnscliffe. Widowed in 1867, the same year John A. married Agnes, over the years Eliza had singlehandedly built up her tavern business until she had become quite wealthy, in fact one of the wealthiest women in Kingston. She never forgot John A.'s kindnesses. "There's not a man like him in the livin' earth," she'd say.

If Agnes wondered if there was ever more to John A.'s relationship with Eliza than friendship, she was smart enough not to ask. This took significant powers either of self-control or denial. Once Agnes had pointed out some of the house's beautiful architectural features, and the two women sat down to enjoy some tea, Eliza's eyes zoned in on the one thing she'd been hoping to see.

John A. had a special deck built at Earnscliffe for Mary Macdonald to sit in her wheelchair. *(LAC PA138674)*

"In the fine library there was my picture up beside o' His, just where He sits," she told a friend.

After her visit, Eliza confessed that, though Agnes's looks came up short, her devotion to John A. vindicated her. "She's a very plain woman is Lady Macdonald – not good lookin'," Eliza explained. "But, oh, she's the fine eddication, and that's where she gets the best of thim [sic]. It's her fine eddication that makes her so nice, and she takes such good care o' Him. And if I went back there today she would make as much of me as if I was the richest woman in the country."

Indeed, at Earnscliffe, Agnes could finally be the gracious hostess she'd always yearned to be. She could enjoy some relative peace with her husband. They finally had a few dollars to rub together. He was prime minister again and, though she did not yet know it, he would remain so until he died. Now, the greatest challenge facing him was completing the railway, "before I kiss the angels," as he put it. Agnes planned to be there for the ride.

X

HIS FINAL RACE

For every ten miles of CPR track, disgruntled Native Indians tore up ten miles of track, angry that their buffalo herds had been decimated by the incursion of gun-toting white settlers and struggling to grow enough crops to eat or sell. In July 1884, Louis Riel had slipped back across the American border into Manitoba. At first, John A. greeted his return with detached curiosity, unconvinced that Riel would repeat his earlier efforts. It would be a fatal mistake.

After the rebellion, Riel had fled to the United States to work as a teacher. Despite the danger, he returned to Manitoba because he felt that God, speaking to him in English and French, had imbued him with a mission to protect the rights of the inhabitants of the Red River Settlement. By March 1885, it was clear that he would not settle for restitution for the land lost by the building of the railway, or even accept a bribe to leave the country, but had decided instead to retain the land by force.

With Thomas Scott's murder still fresh in his mind, on March 23, Lt. Hugh John Macdonald, a member of Maj.-Gen. Frederick Middleton's 90th Battalion, again entered the theatre of war, telling his wife he intended to "drive Riel and his friends from their cover if they have not already cleared out." For weeks,

Hugh John again slogged through mud and slush, toward Fort Carlton. Halfway there, he heard that General Middleton had been briefly "captured" by his own men when he failed to remember the secret password necessary to re-enter his camp.

Middleton's "incompetence" depressed Hugh John. As a distraction, he waited for Gertie's hampers of food to arrive to refuel his resolve. Like his father, he discovered "ammunition" in alcohol, which he begged Gertie to include for himself and for the members of his garrison. After several days passed, and the hampers failed to arrive, Hugh John concluded that the Mounted Police had purloined them, "for their own medicinal purposes."

On April 24, he informed Gertie that he had emerged unscathed from some "hot skirmishes" with "half breeds" at Clark's Crossing. Two days later, at Fish Creek, he hastily scribbled a letter in pencil to his father following a battle with the rebels that had lasted for four hours. He had emerged "from the front rank of the skirmish" without a scratch, he bragged, although he had seen nine men killed and forty-three injured. Hoping to jog a few compliments from his father, he added, "I was pleased and rather surprised to find that I was quite cool under fire and perfectly able to handle my men."

Shortly after receiving Hugh John's letter, John A. forwarded it to Louisa for deciphering, since its pencilled contents had smudged during its travels from Manitoba to Ottawa. The letter reassured John A. that Hugh John was safe. As for accolades, Hugh would have to look elsewhere. In his letter to Louisa, John A. damned Hugh John with faint praise. "So far he has – thank God! Escaped & done himself no discredit by his conduct in the field," he wrote.

In Gertie, Hugh found a more receptive cheerleader. "You see, I am not considered completely useless," he wrote, informing her that his superiors had placed two companies of men under his nighttime charge, as they approached "Batochis [sic] Crossing," thirty-five miles from where Riel was stationed with an estimated seven hundred men.

By now, Hugh John's adrenalin was at an all-time high. With dizzying self-importance, he neared battle with Riel at Batoche. He almost didn't make it. By May 11, the right side of his face was so swollen his right eye "was not only closed but quite invisible." Camp doctors diagnosed him as suffering a severe case of erysipelas (a superficial bacterial skin infection usually, caused by group A streptococci). He had waited his whole life to prove himself a man, and now "kicking like a steer," he endured the ignominy of fellow soldiers carrying him by stretcher onboard the steamer *Northcote* to recuperate. After three days, he defied doctors' orders and re-entered the theatre of battle. Or tried to. "Dr. Moore, who was in charge, is only a young chap, so when he wanted me to remain with the invalids, I told him to go to the devil and got up, borrowed a Winchester from Sam Beelson and fell in with 'C. Company,'" he told Gertie. "We steamed down the River slowly and about two miles from Batochis [sic] fell in with the rebels on both banks."

After disembarking from the steamer, Hugh John marched stolidly for eighteen miles, arriving in Prince Albert on May 20. There, he discovered that "three Half breed scouts from Prince Albert" had beaten him to Riel's capture. Trying to pluck up as many threads of his pride as he could, he boasted to Gertie, "Had our fellows taken him he would have been brought in a coffin and all trouble about his trial would have been avoided." More revealing was what he didn't say. The inescapable truth was that, once again, John A. had interceded before Hugh John could administer his avowed "leaden bullet" form of justice.

In the summer of 1885, the 90th Battalion returned to Winnipeg, and Hugh John settled back into his renamed law practice. Two lawyers named MacArthur and Dexter, who had worked for the firm, had left early in the year, replaced by Frank Phippen and William J. Tupper, Stewart Tupper's youngest brother. Meanwhile, to escape the oppressive humidity of Winnipeg, Gertie had taken Daisy and son John Alexander Macdonald, nicknamed Jack, who was born in January of 1885, to Toronto to visit relatives. Both Hugh and Gertie increasingly worried about young Jack's health. He was a delicate child, prone to lung infections, and frequently confined to his crib.

John A. felt Riel's trial couldn't happen fast enough. By August, a jury sentenced him to hang on September 18. For Macdonald, and for English-speaking Canada, the debate about Riel's guilt was over. However, upon returning to the House in September, John A.'s French colleagues demanded a Commission of Inquiry into Riel's mental state, trying to determine whether he could distinguish between right and wrong at the time of the rebellion. John A. indignantly insisted that a man's state of mind during the commission of a crime could not be determined months later. By the end of October, however, he buckled, agreeing to send three doctors to examine Riel – two English speaking, and one French Canadian.

Dr. Michael Lavell, the warden of Kingston Penitentiary, and in John A.'s opinion an "expert" at assessing those lunatics in his charge, concluded that Riel "posed as an inspired leader and Prophet and as such had not much difficulty in impressing a simple and superstitious people." When he asked Riel why he had run around displaying a crucifix before his followers, Riel replied that he had "a superstitious people to deal with and could by such means retain his influence and control over them, and in this manner excite enthusiasm." When he discussed the shame he had brought upon his wife and two young children, Riel crumbled and wept. Though impressed by Riel's obvious intelligence, Lavell nevertheless concluded that he was perfectly aware of right and wrong when he led the rebellion.

Dr. A. Jukes, a surgeon at the Regina prison, and Dr. F. X. Valade of Ottawa also interviewed Riel and cyphered (telegraphed) John A. their separate opinions. Jukes toed the Conservative Party line by agreeing that Riel was sane. But Valade wasn't ready to play along. Instead, he told John A. that Riel may have suffered from insanity during the commission of his crimes.

John A. exploded in rage. He bitterly resented that the entire debacle over Riel had distracted the public's attention from his contribution to the completion of the CPR track. There was worse news to come. On November 9, Cornelius Van Horne, president and chairman of the CPR, informed John A. by telegram that Donald Smith, the very man John A. had accused of being "the biggest liar [he'd] ever met," had driven the last spike into the CPR line two days before, capturing the glory John A. so dearly craved for himself. Instead of being free to celebrate the event, John A. hunkered down in Ottawa, weathering repeated legal onslaughts from Opposition members trying to prevent Riel's execution. Of Riel's fate, he remained adamant: "He shall hang though every dog in Quebec bark in his favour," he said, signing the execution warrant. At last, on the morning of November 16, after reciting the Lord's Prayer, Riel died.

John A. tried to escape the negative public and political reaction following Riel's death by travelling to Rimouski, then leaving for Liverpool on board the liner *Polynesian*. Agnes and Mary accompanied him to Rimouski, then boarded a private CPR car south toward the Maritimes. On December 1, John A. arrived in Liverpool and immediately headed for London and his now-favourite refuge, Batt's Hotel. Invitations from friends poured in. George Stephen insisted John A. stay at his home. Similarly, John Rose invited John A. to join him at his home in London, offering him the services of a brougham that could get him anywhere in "ten minutes." John A. declined, preferring to remain at Batt's. He had much on his mind. Louisa had been ill for some time with stomach complaints, so ill that John had abandoned all hope of her recovery. He had already told James Williamson by letter, "We must now I fear give up hope of her restoration to health and try to make her as comfortable as possible while she lingers with us." Confounding all expectations, however, Louisa rallied.

As it had done so many times before, England restored John A. to health as well, and soon he plunged into London's social scene, dining out almost every night or attending the theatre, Drury Lane being one of his favourites. There he saw the pantomime *Aladdin*. He caught a slight cold while waiting for a train at the station platform in Kent, but soon he was dashing about with such youthful exuberance that friends were forced to remind themselves that he was now approaching his seventy-first birthday.

Back in Ottawa, Mary, now almost a seventeen-year-old woman, typed a child-like letter to her father dated December 22, 1885, filled with disjointed thoughts and feelings. "I suppose you will soon be thinking of coming home. I hope so for I miss you very much, but of course as it is going to do you good I must not grumble," she wrote. "[We] had a lovely trip after we left you we were down at Halifax and St. John. [Mamma] is away just now and how long she is going to stay I do not know. [Have] you seen Her Majesty the Queen? Do you remember what you told me last year about kissing her hand? [What] are you going to do on Christmas day? I will miss you very much. I suppose you will be out in time for your birthday, and then wont [sic] we hug and kiss each other. P. S. If Mamma does not come home for Christmas I am going out with Mrs. Oswald to spend the day at her mothers."

Agnes wasn't home for Christmas. Instead, she was escaping Earnscliffe altogether and not just Earnscliffe, but the political fires she had watched her husband stomp out, the trauma of worrying about money, and the sick realization that Mary would never walk, talk fluently, or see even to her most basic needs without constant supervision. Before Agnes left, she sent out eighty invitations to a birthday ball for John A., which Mary planned to host with the help of the family's servants.

Agnes had developed the same late-in-life wanderlust as her husband, though it led her away from John A. rather than toward him. At Christmas 1885, she travelled west by CPR train, chugging to the top of the Canadian Rockies. The trip brought out Agnes's girlish enthusiasm. For sixteen days and nights, accompanied by friends, a butler, and a maid, she traversed the country by train, admiring the "prairies undulating in soft swelling folds covered with natural hay," stopping off in Winnipeg to visit Hugh John, Gertie, and their children Daisy, or "Dee," and Jack at their "cozy and pretty home." "Every day was a pleasure & a new interest," she wrote. "The CPR were ever so good to me. [Altogether] it was too delightful. [What] astonished me was the comfort & ease of the railway, its strict punctuality, its quiet & prompt management & its little motion. We read, played games, wrote letters, all generally with great ease & this on a line far away in an almost uninhabited country & in depth of Canadian winter." Upon reaching the peak of Mount Stephen, only five hundred miles from the West Coast, the train reversed direction and raced back to Ottawa so Agnes would make it home in time to greet John A.

John A. returned home a new person on January 19, five days after Mary threw him the birthday ball in his absence. At City Hall, a band played "When Johnny Comes Marching Home" as he boarded a cab for a ride along Sussex Street toward Earnscliffe. As his cab clattered by, newspaper reporters standing along the route noted that John A.'s cheeks were "as ruddy as a red apple." Agnes saw the change in her husband as soon as he walked in the door. "He was so tired and worried when he went away that it quite enspirits me to see him so cheery," she wrote.

The joyous idyll didn't last long. None of them ever did. John A. still had to face the groundswell of French opposition that followed Riel's hanging. When the Parliament finally met in February, Riel's ghost paced the floor. Wilfrid Laurier, the new head of the Liberal Party, complained of the Conservative Party, "Had they taken as much pains to do right, as they have taken to punish wrong – the law would never have been violated at all." Yet in spite of the stinging French rebukes, 146 members of Parliament supported Riel's execution, while 52 regretted it.

Though he might have won a vote of confidence in the House, in the court of public opinion, at least the public opinion of French Canadians, John A. had murdered Riel for no better reason than to seek revenge for the murder of Thomas Scott. With sentiments like this sweeping the land, how long could the Conservatives retain their seats? While John A. steeled himself against future political onslaughts, Agnes came to see happiness as anywhere but in Ottawa.

For Agnes, the "brilliantly fine and clear" prairie skies had illuminated the dark corners of her imagination, allowing her to re-evaluate the importance of her life in Ottawa, where she found so much petty social climbing, partisan bickering, and personal heartbreak. As exhilarated as she was upon returning, she also suffered a deep undertow of depression. "Ottawa seems so dull & tame & stupid & *old* after that wonderful new western world with its breadth & clear air & wonderfully exhilarating atmosphere that always seems to lure me on! [I] feel a new person," she wrote to Louisa, oblivious to the effect her words might have on her ailing sister-in-law, herself a virtual shut-in. Then Agnes unintentionally dipped her pen in more acid. "Constantly nursing the sick and housekeeping in Ottawa for a large household & looking after all sorts of things daily for almost two years is fatiguing." If Louisa took Agnes's words personally, she never admitted it. Possibly, she didn't even blame her.

Agnes had dedicated most of her adult life to caring for those much younger or older than herself, beginning with her mother, continuing with Mary, and now with John A., who took an increasing number of "sick" days in bed, his books stacked around him. With age, he caught cold easily, each bout often turning into bronchitis. When he walked, his left leg unleashed a "sleeping demon" of sciatic pain, for which he endured cupping, a cure more painful than the disease. Some days he lay with his head "buzzing with opiates."

Agnes spent increasing amounts of time puttering around the past, reading old letters and examining the unpacked bric-a-brac that government officials had bestowed upon her and John A. to mark celebratory holidays. During one of these forays, she uncovered a box of child's toys containing a broken rattle, a small cart, and some animals. Unable to recognize them, she took them to John A. as he lay on his bed, reading. Initially, he glanced with a lack of interest at the items then, raising himself on one elbow, he took an item in his hand. "Ah!" he said gently. "Those were little John A.'s." Agnes returned the box to where she found it, amazed that, for more than thirty years, the box had mysteriously evaded her detection.

There were, of course, a few happy diversions. Hugh's nine-year-old daughter, Daisy, visited often, introducing a youthful exuberance to the house. Perhaps in Daisy, Agnes found the healthy child she'd failed to have in Mary. "She is one of the gentlest, sweetest children I ever saw, so easily managed," she noted. That winter, Agnes enrolled Daisy in Miss Harmon's boarding school, the girl returning to Earnscliffe on the weekends. Mary, totally lacking in ego, who would never attend school, admired her niece enormously. "She takes great pride with her lessons," she wrote. "Mother received a letter from Miss Harmon the other day in which she praised Daisy for her good qualities and industry at her lessons."

Still, Agnes kicked at this picture of stodgy domestic tranquility, this miasma of monotony that defined her life. The pleasant teas with wives of visiting MPs, the carriage rides into town with Mary that always became an ordeal due to the extraordinary measures necessary to ensure Mary's comfort and safety. Her trip out West had reawakened her restless imagination and her desire to write. Each vista was a stereoscopic picture card come to life, but instead of looking at the country, she wanted to experience it first-hand. The railway was her husband's crowning achievement, and she was determined that he should enjoy it with her. "I shall never rest until he goes too!" she wrote Louisa.

John A. knew a good publicity stunt when he saw one. With another election looming, possibly in the New Year, and his party's popularity with the French in Quebec at an all-time low because of Riel's execution, he decided to make the trip part pleasure and part work.

Prior to the train's departure, however, John A. was running true to form, which meant he was running late, completing paperwork in his office. As nightfall approached, he hurried out of the Parliament Buildings and into a waiting carriage. As soon as he arrived at the station, two servants escorted him up the short flight of iron stairs onto the eight-foot-long train carriage named *Jamaica*, in honour of Agnes's childhood home. Inside was a small group of excited travellers, including Agnes, Joseph Pope, Fred White of the Mounted Police, and two servants. The wine was flowing and coffee brewing, as amidst a chorus of cheers, John A. took his seat opposite Agnes, who was already busily recording her impressions of the day in her diary.

"Off at last! A town clock is striking eleven," she wrote as the train slowly glided, then quickly gained speed westward among the "soft shadows of a summer night." Van Horne had covered the carriage's windows with a fine mesh to keep out dust and mosquitoes, however when passengers pressed their faces against the carriage's narrow windows, all they could see was the full moon wavering between passing clouds and fringes of trees etched against the India-ink-coloured sky. Agnes recorded in meticulous detail the interior of the carriage. Large fixed lamps brightened each little sitting room, providing a "homelike effect." Baskets of flowers stood on narrow tables, "already heaped with books and newspapers." Comfortable sofas lined each side of the car, along with "wide arm-chairs" on each side of the entrance doors. There was a small kitchen in the car, where "a white-aproned cook stood superintending the stowage of sundry useful packages into a neat little cupboard fitted behind two cosy bedrooms placed dos-a-dos in the centre of the car, with a door opening into each parlour." Each apartment contained beds and washing apparatus, including taps issuing hot and cold water. There were also lockers, drawers, mirrors, and lamps.

Though still keyed up with excitement, the passengers reluctantly retired to bed. Lulled by the gentle rocking of the train carriage, John A. fell asleep immediately in his bed located across the aisle from that of his newly hired private secretary, Joseph Pope. Agnes chose to sleep on a "closely curtained sofa," with her maid curled up on a cot beneath a thin sheet on the opposite side of the car. The temperature inside the car hovered near ninety degrees, the humidity making it feel even muggier, but the discomfort didn't deter Agnes from lying awake in a state of exultation. Her husband was realizing "the darling dream of his heart, a railway from ocean to ocean," the dream that had driven him to the depths of despair, culminating in those dark July days back in 1873 at Rivière-du-Loup. How far away that all seemed now.

At dawn, a powerful thunderclap awakened several passengers. Raindrops the circumference of marbles pounded the sides of the car, as lightning flashes briefly illuminated the white clapboard farmhouses dotting the grasslands of southern Ontario. The train continued to rumble across trestles to wind through thick-timbered forests. By noon, it had reached Sudbury. Beyond lay "a wild forbidding land of tumbled rocks, scorched trees, and thickets of scrub," as well as the "abandoned huts used by the navvies during 'construction.'" Agnes noted the presence of "undulating forests" and "cliff ranges, scarred and frowning, rising straight into the sky" and "masses of tumbled rock, shaded red and grey." All at once, an "atom of humanity," in the form of a small child, tottered out to a hilltop, his blond curls blowing across his chubby cheeks, lending a surreal quality to the scene.

The train sped across the prairies, squealing to a stop at the Winnipeg station. Hundreds of excited admirers surged toward the tracks, forming a line several feet deep. John A. and his party waded through the dense crowd toward a set of carriages waiting to transport them to Government House. As a hatless John A. passed, a couple of strands of his white hair spun wildly in the wind, prompting one onlooker to remark with surprise to a companion, "Seedy-looking old beggar, isn't he?" Shortly after their official reception concluded, the party spent a couple of days shopping at the city's "fine shops," in Agnes's words, and dined in "first-rate restaurants." Upon reboarding, they quickly sped toward Regina, where another crowd awaited the train's arrival. John A. again proceeded to Government House, where he greeted visitors, from English settlers to Indians. Two Sioux children, dressed in rigid broadcloth, sang hymns, and at the same time the North-West Mounted Police corps, returning from outpost duty at Prince Albert, galloped up to the building, dismounted, and saluted John A.

Early the next morning, at Gleichen, hundreds of Blackfoot gathered into a large square to the side of the train. They were wearing deerhides and moccasins, their thick, coarse hair flowing free or braided, faces painted with wavy lines of red and blue. Through an interpreter, the chief, Crowfoot, assured John A. of his tribe's loyalty, but he had two complaints. Fire-wagons, he claimed, were burning crops near the railway lines, causing crop devastation. He also asked John A. if the government intended to stop the Indians' rations, which the government had provided to them since decimating the buffalo herds during the building of the railway. As Crowfoot spoke, Agnes noted, "The minor chiefs kept up a low chorus of apparent approbation, as they sat smoking stolidly with half-shut eyes."

John A., who faced Crowfoot, calmly told him that, if it were possible to remove the problems caused by the fire-wagons, he would see to it, then explained that the Government Treaty entered into with the Blackfoot never promised food, but did provide the Indians with seeds. He informed him that, with these seeds, the Indians must learn to grow crops, as white settlers were doing, then sell some of the crops at a profit. "White men worked hard for their food and clothing, and expected Indians to do the same," he said.

With their conversation at an end, the two men exchanged gifts. John A.'s servants presented the Indians with rolls of cloth, sheeting, canvas for tents, pipes, hats, and tobacco.

Following their meeting, an Indian solemnly began pounding a large drum, as his fellow tribesmen shrilly cried out. As he beat the drums faster, the cries of his fellow Indians grew louder, rising "to a state of high excitement," in Agnes's words. The Indians held Winchester rifles and muskets in upraised hands as they galloped quickly alongside the train, whooping and shouting, their faces fierce and forbidding. With considerable trepidation Agnes watched the Indians surge toward the train, firing their weapons, reloading, and firing again, then suddenly halting, scowls on their faces. "It was hard to believe the whole proceeding was only a good sham, and not 'down-right earnest,' as the children say," she noted.

With the performance over, the relieved party relaxed on board the *Jamaica* as it raced through Banff toward Castle Mountain. During a brief stop at Laggan Station, thirty miles from the mountain's summit, Agnes spotted a monstrous engine, black and fiercely belching steam, standing on a siding waiting for her train to link up to it. Climbing down to the gravel below, she walked around the gigantic engine, her eyes resting on the "broad shining surface of its buffer-beam and cowcatcher," a six-foot-long, three-foot-deep, V-shaped iron beak attached to the train by bolts and used for shoving forward or tossing aside maimed or dead animals from the track. From that moment on, she decided that she would strap herself to that cowcatcher for the remaining six hundred miles of her journey.

John A., or "The Chief" as Agnes had come to call him, was sitting on a low chair on the rear platform of the car, with a rug over his knees and a magazine in his hands, as Agnes approached him to ask if she could ride on the cowcatcher. "That's rather ridiculous," he replied distractedly, barely looking up. Then, realizing Agnes was sincere, he added, "Are you sure you can hold on?" No sooner had the words escaped John A.'s mouth than Agnes was already confidently marching toward the "beak," where she had requested to sit on a candle box.

Assisted by an employee of the railroad, Agnes climbed onto the cowcatcher and sat on the candle box, a linen carriage cover tucked around her waist and feet and a linen hat drawn comically low over her eyebrows. "This is lovely," she smiled as the train whistle shrieked and the mighty engine chugged higher and higher. Soon, the train was speeding toward the summit of the Great Divide, fifty-three hundred feet above sea level. At the summit, the engine braked sharply, and the steam was cut off, causing an ominous silence. Then, like a rollercoaster car, the train sped at a sixty-degree angle down Kicking Horse Pass, blowing bugs into Agnes's open mouth and eyes. As the train streaked down the mountain, Agnes clung so hard to the railing in front of her that her fingers nearly bled. Out of the corner of her eye, rivers, trees, glaciers, gorges, and towering masses of rock all rushed by in a surrealistic smear of colours. Tiny, brightly coloured pebbles glittered beneath her feet. "There was not a yard of that descent in which I faltered for a moment," Agnes recalled. "There [was] glory of brightness and beauty everywhere, and I [laughed] aloud on the cowcatcher, just because it is all so delightful!"

Upon reaching British Columbia, the train stopped at the first station. Curious about how Agnes had fared in her perch, John A. walked up to the cowcatcher. When he saw Agnes's sooty face and windswept hair, he erupted in laughter. "Would the Chief step up and take a drive?" she beamed. As his nervous handlers looked on, John A. unsteadily climbed on board the buffer-beam. He and Agnes huddled together as their train neared Selkirk Mountain, the steepest mountain of all. Agnes and John A. may have successfully weathered the emotional storms that distinguished their almost twenty-year marriage, but they had less luck when it came to Selkirk Mountain. Before the train could creak its way up the mountainside, John A. asked the conductor to stop the engine, and he returned to his comfortable chair at the rear of the train's caboose. As the party passed through each town and village, spectators, some standing in groups of twenty and thirty on roofs or rock cliffs, some even perched on the branches of trees, applauded as they saw John A. bringing up the rear of what had become his wife's car. By the time they reached Selkirk Mountain, John A. had taken shelter in the train's cabin.

Agnes observed with political incorrectness that all along the track, camps of Chinese labourers "all ridiculously alike in form and feature, wearing queer little blue-and-white gowns, baggy trousers, wooden shoes, and thick flat straw hats," stood motionless, their shovels held at the same angle, ready to begin on the gravel the instant the train passed. "They had a curious effect, as of some mechanical apparatus with an awful semblance of humanity," she wrote.

The danger of striking cattle crossing the track was great. Luckily, this never happened; however, on the last day of the trip, as Joseph Pope sat on the cowcatcher beside her, the train struck a small black pig, its body flying with incredible speed past Pope's head and a pole he was holding on to for balance. Had the pig hit Pope full force, he almost certainly would have been seriously injured, even killed. Not surprisingly, the accident signalled Pope's last trip on the cowcatcher.

To Agnes's great disappointment, the *Jamaica*'s journey ended at Port Moody. She reluctantly alighted from the cowcatcher and joined John A. as he delivered a speech from the rear platform of the train. From Port Moody, they boarded the steamer *Princess Louise*, which took them to Victoria, where the party disembarked and remained for three weeks at the Driard House, known by experts as "the most prestigious hotel on the Pacific Coast." For entertainment, the Victoria Theatre, connected to the Driard House, had live theatrical performances, and the Ancient Order of United Workers (AOUW) Hall offered the only vaudeville shows in the Pacific Northwest. Before long, reporters with the *Port Moody Gazette* observed, "Sir John looks as happy as a lark," as they watched him arrive to cheers and applause from onlookers.

The trip home on board the *Jamaica* wasn't nearly as lively as the trip out west. By the time John A. boarded the train home, he was already worried about how many parliamentary seats the Conservatives would lose in Quebec's provincial election, scheduled for October 14.

As John A. predicted, the fallout from Riel's execution helped the Liberal Party gain several seats in Quebec that had previously been held by Conservatives. "The triumph of the Rouges over the corpse of Riel changes the aspect of affairs, *quoad* the Dominion government completely," he wrote to Charles Tupper. "It will encourage the Grits and opposition generally; will dispirit our friends, and will, I fear, carry the country against us at the general election."

On November 3, John A. returned to Toronto to fortify his Conservative support, which was dwindling among the Irish Catholics in Ontario. As an added obscenity, Oliver Mowat, his chubby schoolmate of youth, was poised to pull off a resounding victory as premier of Ontario and was planning to increase the province's northern borders exponentially. Forgetting that he was no longer a spry young ruffian on the political hustings, seventy-one-year-old John A. nevertheless plunged into a series of exhausting speaking engagements in Ontario, finally falling ill in December from a bronchial infection complicated by exhaustion. When the strain became too much for him, he rested on board the *Jamaica*.

In January, Governor General Lord Lansdowne dissolved Parliament. All told, among four provincial elections held in 1886, the Conservatives had lost two, drew one, and emerged bloody victors in the fourth. In the face of this dire situation, John A. agreed to schedule an election for February 22. The *Globe* newspaper ridiculed John A. as a tired old ploughhorse. To counteract this impression, John A. reminded audiences that this was the same *Globe* that had mistakenly reported his "suicide" in 1873 and had regularly anticipated his imminent demise from one malady or another ever since.

By the time the dust cleared in February, John A. had again triumphed. Contrary to predictions, the Conservatives took Nova Scotia, Ontario, and Manitoba, and though the party's majority had decreased, they remained in power.

John A. remained leader, however it was questionable whether he still wanted to lead or whether he was merely filling a vacuum nobody else wanted to fill. After all, he had been running his whole life, either from or to something.

He would return to Parliament, but one quite different from the one he had excitedly entered years before. Many of his friends and nemeses were now gone, including George-Étienne Cartier, Lord Dufferin, D'Arcy McGee, and even George Brown, whom a disgruntled *Globe* newspaper employee had shot to death in 1880. Meanwhile, many members of John A.'s family had either died or scattered in many directions.

And then there was Mary. Against all expectations, her mental capabilities seemed to increase as she matured, yet her dependency on her parents, or on caregivers, was absolute. Both John A. and Agnes had taken a firm-but-kindly hand with their daughter, but each seemed reluctant or unable to relate to her as an adult.

Hugh John was one of the first family members to notice the problem. After visiting with his father in Ottawa, he wrote a letter to James Williamson, noting that Mary's mind was developing and that she was becoming "more of a woman and less a child than she had heretofore been." What childishness remained in Mary, he thought, was due to his parents' insistence on treating her as a child, as well as because her companions were either women "well advanced in age" or "much younger than herself."

In the spring of 1887, Agnes approved the construction of a log cottage near the Banff Springs Hotel. There, Mary spent the late spring and summer, relaxing in the healing sulphur baths. Mrs. Dewdney, wife of the Lieutenant-Governor of the Northwest Territories, spent a few days with Mary and her nurses at Banff and came away amazed with Mary's acuity. Not only was Mary healthy and content, but she had even started to use her right hand to do her felt work. Pleased that Mary was enjoying the cottage, Agnes sent out a giant tent for her to sit under during the day, in case she wanted to work outside. However, Agnes's perspective of Mary's maturity differed markedly from Hugh John's. "I have tried to teach Mary [what] was best for her & for others & not grumble," she wrote, adding, "and she has perfect faith in our plans for her."

Agnes had probably done Mary a favour by sending her to Banff during the desultory parliamentary session of the spring and summer of 1887. She and John A. decided against going to Rivière-du-Loup and instead sweltered in the hot and muggy city. Agnes recorded all she saw inside the Parliament Buildings. She peered down from the gallery, recording bolder observations than she had dared to twenty years before under the lock and key of her private diary. This time, she was writing for publication, under the protection of anonymity.

In an article entitled "Men and Measures in Canada" written for Britain's *Murray's Magazine*, she observed that the "feeble and disorganized House," filled with "many elected for the first time and new to the business," chose to fall asleep. Early on in the proceedings, "the Leader of the Opposition gave up altogether, laid his arms on his desk, his head on his arms, and took no further interest in the proceedings! His lieutenants, valiant but disconcerted, did what they could to obstruct, but not even a Canadian Liberal can be energetic long when his leader is sound asleep, and grinning Tories fan their hot faces with the 'Orders of the day.'"

In case these observations weren't incriminating enough, Agnes listed a few more. "I counted four pages asleep at once round the steps of a chair in which the Speaker had gone to bed," she wrote. "Five members in one row lay back snoring peacefully; and in the next, one was making a sketch with ink on a reclining sleeper's bald and shiny crown; while another dropped iced water from a tumbler into his neighbour's left ear, as the unconscious victim, bowed in deepest slumber, presented a tempting opportunity."

In June, Governor General Lansdowne put the ministers out of their misery by proroguing Parliament. Agnes mused that Lansdowne's motives for this action were less than noble. "The Governor-General, after three hard months' labour at balls, parliamentary dinners, sliding parties, concerts and plays, varied by writing despatches about the pig-headedness of American politicians on the Fishery question, must have rejoiced when his Ministers asked him to prorogue," she wrote, adding, "Certain it is that His Excellency jumped out of the horrors of a tightly fitting uniform and into a homespun travelling suit and was off for his salmon waters up the Cascapedia almost before the last cannon's boom died away in the hot evening air."

Attacking Lansdowne's official actions was fair game, but disparaging his love of salmon fishing seemed hypocritical, since shortly after Parliament was prorogued, Agnes boarded the *Jamaica* and, along with some companions, travelled to the salmon streams of the Restigouche River in New Brunswick. "Fishing time is my holiday. It sets me up. I love the camping & the quiet of those green woods far away from everybody," she wrote to Louisa. With Agnes away for two weeks, John A. briefly considered returning to London, but decided that, due to a particularly high volume of paperwork, he would stay at Rivière-du-Loup. James Williamson, meanwhile, travelled to Winnipeg to visit with Hugh John, while Louisa stayed home in Kingston, resting. Hewitt Bernard was ensconced in comfortable lodgings in Ottawa, consisting of two large rooms. Now sick most of the time, he required around-the-clock nursing, plus quiet, and shunned the presence of most visitors beyond direct family members.

Shortly after her salmon-fishing excursion, a peripatetic Agnes invited a separate set of friends to accompany her by train to the Rockies, where she remained for three weeks. John A.'s sister Louisa disapproved of Agnes's frequent absences and worried that she was making John A. the same kind of bachelor husband he had been during his marriage to Isabella, but John A. wrote Louisa back, reassuring her that Agnes's chance of visiting the Rocky Mountains was simply "too good to lose."

The age difference between John A. and Agnes had never been more noticeable than now. He was proud of her fearlessness, but he was also intermittently lonely and tired. All his work seemed on the verge of being undone. Confederation had suddenly never seemed so fragile. The Liberals had started supporting the possibility of seeking commercial union with the United States, with French-speaking Canadians and the Maritime provinces in full support of unrestricted reciprocity. John A.'s National Policy, containing its promises of stiff tariffs against U.S. imports, was falling out of favour with five provinces, each provincial premier seeking to lessen federal authority while at the same time obtaining larger subsidies from the Dominion. John A. chose to ignore the rebellious provincial premiers, aware that he still possessed control of the House and Senate.

Meanwhile, the fisheries question continued to loom large. John A. had watched Charles Tupper leave for another Washington conference, and the two men burned up the telegraph lines drafting a proposal acceptable to both Canada and the United States. The unremitting work absorbed so much of John A.'s time that he was unable to visit Louisa in Kingston over Christmas 1887, despite her desperate entreaties. "I am chained by the leg here just now," he wrote her, "and cannot leave town for a moment, as the negotiations with Washington are going on and I am receiving cypher messages hourly which require immediate answer."

By the end of December, he was finally able to enjoy the peace of Earnscliffe for a few days, surrounded by most of the members of his family. Agnes, Mary, Daisy, Jack, Hugh John, Gertie, and Hewitt were all there, each attending to their own quiet hobbies or interests. Outside the windows, pine needles glistened with ice. Inside, the family members sat reading or playing board games near the living room's large fireplace. Two-year-old Jack, his hair a mass of golden curls, gaily placed wooden toys in Mary's lap.

As the ice thawed, John A. and Agnes stole away for a day to travel on board the *Jamaica* to Kingston to visit Louisa. When they arrived, John A. struggled to disguise his shock at Louisa's fragile appearance. James Williamson was happy to see John A. and particularly happy about the beneficial effect her brother's visit seemed to have on Louisa. "Louisa has I think been the better in health for your visit, and goes up this evening to take tea at Mrs John's. We hope to see you soon again," he wrote shortly after John A. and Agnes's departure.

In April, Williamson wrote John A. letters informing him that Louisa's ceaseless fight to resume her regular household duties often left her waxen with prostration. "Dr. Sullivan and I had a talk about you yesterday," John A. warned her by letter. "He says you are not strong, but on the whole pretty well. He speaks however in the strongest terms of your refusal to keep quiet.

Complete rest, he says, is your best medicine, and you won't take it. [The doctor] objects especially to your going up & down those stairs. Now my dear Louisa, you really *must* take better care of yourself or you & I will quarrel."

By May, John A. could inform Louisa that the Conservatives had enjoyed a "very successful session," in which they "didn't meet with a single reverse." This was more of a relief to John A. than even Louisa could have imagined. The uprising by the renegade provincial premiers had fizzled, and Confederation was again alive and well. He had stood against the Liberal onslaught of criticism without crumbling. Now it was time to rest.

On May 23, Governor General Lansdowne and his wife visited Earnscliffe to offer their farewells before they returned to England. Afterwards, John A., Agnes, and Mary travelled to Cape Breton Island and later hunkered down for the summer in Dalhousie, New Brunswick.

Even at his advanced age, John A. continued to attract acolytes and hangers-on of both sexes, and his maritime idyll was to be the occasion of a very disturbing incident. He began receiving what could only be called mash notes from Frank Muttart, the impressionable teenaged son of Dr. Ephraim Muttart, a Conservative MP from Halifax. From the contents of one of Muttart's notes, it appears he and John A. lunched on one occasion, after which Muttart virtually became John A.'s stalker, sending him cryptic instructions to enclose cards with the words *yes* or *no* written on them, signifying whether John A. wished to lunch with him again. Hoping to discourage Muttart's affections, John A. failed to respond. Instead of driving Muttart away, however, John A.'s indifference made his young admirer's effusions even more wildly ardent and indiscreet. "True and sweet lover, I have to have your touch," Muttart wrote John A. in desperation.

When John A. continued to ignore the delusional Muttart's purple prose, Muttart accused John A. of publicly speaking against him. In his final letter to John A., Muttart wrote, "I only <u>love</u> you very much & so cannot break up my love with you. [I] often express my great wish that I would honourably nail or sew your whole tongue, so that you may be unable to speak any of me in your life, I guess."

Muttart's letters to John A. ended as abruptly as they had begun when Ephraim Muttart committed his son to the care of a psychologist.

On September 3, John A. and Agnes returned to their rented house in Ottawa, as they awaited the completion of the extensive remodelling and redecorating on the Earnscliffe home.

John A. promised Louisa he would run up to Kingston on September 11, staying with a friend named Mrs. McIntyre so he could be as close as possible to Louisa's home. He never made it. On September 28, he sent Louisa a cheque for $150 in allowance, as well as to pay for a new carpet she wanted laid in her house.

In November, John A. and his family prepared to move back into Earnscliffe. On November 8, however, he received a shock. Louisa had taken a dramatic turn for the worse and hovered near death. John A. rushed to Kingston to see her. By the time he arrived at her bedside, she had revived enough to complain about the colour of the new carpeting she and James had laid in their home. Buoyed by the return of her signature crustiness, John A. returned to Ottawa. However, he had barely crossed Earnscliffe's threshold when he received a telegram informing him that Louisa was dead. "Lou," the terrible tomboy of John A.'s boyhood, the girl who had laughed as he aimed a loaded pistol at her head, the loyal sister whom he'd carried downstairs when the whole family suffered from the flu, and who'd told him how to cook dinner, Lou, one of Hugh John's surrogate mothers, was dead. The breakup of John A.'s nuclear family was complete. At her funeral at St. Andrew's Church, John A. wept, openly and copiously, clutching his top hat tightly in his hand.

John A. and Joseph Pope sat by a crackling fire in Williamson's home after the funeral. In an uncharacteristically backward-looking mood, John A. told Pope, "There is somewhere in Europe a monastery, a rule of which is, that, when any member of the Order dies, his portrait is painted and hung up in a place specially devoted to that purpose. In the course of time a picture gallery of very considerable proportions grew up, the care of which devolved on a member of the society. One day this old monk remarked to some visitors to whom he was showing the picture – 'Do you know that when I look upon the years I have spent gazing on these unchanging faces before me, and when I reflect upon the number of my companions who have died and taken their places upon these walls, I feel sometimes as if, after all, they (pointing at the pictures) were the realities, and we are the shadows!' "

Hugh John learned of Lou's death by telegram in Winnipeg. On November 20, he wrote to Williamson, "On Sunday I received news of my dear Aunt's death . . . [you] and she had lived together for so long that I don't think either of you realized how much you were to each other, and I daresay you will even be sur-prised to find what a change her death will make. [We] ought not to forget that death must have been a happy release for her, for during her last few years her life was full of suffering and she was able to enjoy but few pleasures."

Williamson *did* miss Louisa, even the petty fights that had dominated their discourse, and he turned to John A. for support. He made a rare visit to Earnscliffe during Christmas 1888 but broke down and became ill, retreating to bed for a couple of days. By January 5, he had returned to the home he and Louisa had shared, ceasing all correspondence with family members, a situa-tion that alarmed John A. On January 11, his seventy-fourth birthday, John A. wrote inquiring into James's health, adding that he, too, was feeling his age. "Today I am 74 years old – a fact which brings serious reflections. I am in fairly good health for my age, but can't expect that to last very long. As my work increases faster than my years, I must soon call a halt."

The fact was, John A. didn't know how to stop running. He had sacrificed everyone he knew to fulfill his desire for power, sometimes through charm, sometimes through chicanery, sometimes through bullying. All that remained now were the ghosts of fallen colleagues. Walking through the Senate lobby with Joseph Pope one evening, he pointed with his cane to various portraits of ex-Speakers and other government officials hanging from the walls. "Poor ___ was a good fellow; he was my colleagues for many a day; *dead, dead,* nearly all gone. Why whenever I come this way, I feel as if I were walking through a churchyard."

In his final years, John A. tried to make amends to his family for his frequent absences and lack of emotional closeness – with mixed results. To ensure Hugh John's daughter, Daisy, received a Catholic upbringing, as her mother, Jean, would have wished, he and Agnes enrolled her in the Convent of the Sacred Heart in Montreal, the same exclusive boarding school attended by famed singer Emma Albani. Albani was a frequent visitor to Earnscliffe, singing at Mary's birthday party in February 1889. In her memoirs, *Forty Years of Song,* Albani recalled that five hundred people filled the house, some lingering by the large roaring fireplace or drifting out onto the balcony for fresh air. Once the crowds departed, a core of guests remained for dinner, including Albani and her husband. Albani recalls, "Sir John was called out, and he asked my husband to go with him. It turned out that he had promised the people to open a new ice slide, and would not disappoint them. They drove two or three miles and were then put onto toboggans and shot across the Ottawa River in the dark, Sir John in the first one and my husband following in another. There was, of course, nothing to fear, but I was rather anxious until they returned."

In late April 1889, James Williamson wrote John A., begging him to come to Kingston to witness Louisa's interment beside Helen Macdonald at Cataraqui Cemetery. On April 29, John A. found an excuse to turn the invitation down. "The business of Parlt drags slowly and wearily on," he wrote. "There is I think no chance of its being prorogued on Wednesday. I think therefore you should not wait for me. I greatly regret not being able to join you in the melancholy duty."

On May 12, 1889, Williamson informed John A. by letter that he had laid Louisa's body to rest beside Helen Macdonald on May 3. Afterwards, he hinted that John A. should stop inventing excuses to avoid revisiting his past. "I would fain hope you will soon get rid of departmental work as much as possible," he told John A. "Surely you have enough else to do without it. Come up at all events and see your Kingston friends as soon as you conveniently can."

To keep his memories at bay, John A.'s mind had to remain in play. Whether he was afraid it would plunge him into a deep depression, or because he was genuinely distracted by work, John A. continued to evade Williamson's entreaties, though he invited Williamson to join the family at Rivière-du-Loup later in the summer.

At seventy-four years of age, he had largely given up alcohol but continued to suffer from gout, constipation, and a stomach ulcer whenever work became too stressful. There was no cure for a man who relentlessly drove himself until he risked self-destruction. He'd had presentiments of his demise. Upon meeting John Thompson, the Catholic he'd appointed as minister of justice, John A. told him, "I don't believe I shall trouble you long."

Nothing Agnes said could deter John A. from burying himself for hours at a time behind mounds of paperwork he brought home every night concerning the fisheries question and the Bering Sea seal hunts. Soon, she gave up trying. By now, she had developed a distressing physical ailment of her own: a severe case of neuralgia in one cheek. Sometime in the fall of 1890, she asked John A. if she might leave Ottawa to try to heal her physical symptoms. No doubt, she also hoped a journey would provide fodder for another one of her magazine articles. Rather than urge her to rest and recuperate, John A. heard the word *neuralgia* and immediately thought of Isabella doped to the gills and incapable of leaving her sickroom. With uncharacteristic testiness, he told Agnes that departing was "frivolous" and "unnecessary," adding "my grandmother had never complained of neuralgia, or asked for change and rest."

By now, however, Agnes knew the best way to win an argument was simply to wait her husband out. With a deep sigh and a downcast look, she informed him that routine aggravated her neuralgia, that calculating household accounts initiated severe spasms, and that the "sight of a butcher's boy was fatal." But, if her husband wished to condemn her to those terrible fates, she would just have to endure it.

At first John A. said nothing, then, with a half-smile crossing his lips, Agnes reports that he picked up "an awful-looking pile of blue-lined paper, ostentatiously labelled "Behring [sic] [Sea] Matter, pointed to the library door and, with a polite smile, asked if I would be good enough to leave the room?" As Agnes tried to subdue a smile of her own, he added, "You may go if you like," after which he picked up an article on the McKinley Bill and "with decision" ordered her out of the room.

To the surprise of no one, Agnes was already half-packed for a train trip to the Banff Springs Hotel, where she hiked around Lake Louise, took in the Hot Springs, and met up with Hugh, Gertie, and Jack. Mary remained in Ottawa with servants.

Agnes was still in Banff when John A., elderly, creaky, but still full of rhetorical fire, set off on the final election campaign of his life. In an attempt to belie his age, in the fall of 1890, he blazed through one small town after another on an extended speaking tour. Canadians had become afraid of annexation to the United States, and the issue became one of the focal points of the campaign. Once October arrived, he decided to move to the Queen's Hotel in Toronto, where he again set up his campaign headquarters. the CPR, known as "the Tory government on wheels," transporting him from one town to another. At each stop, supporters cried out, "You'll never die, John A.!"

They were almost right. As his tour picked up momentum, so, too, did John A. With Joseph Pope solicitously at his side, the two attended a reception at the Academy of Music in Toronto. The academy was founded in 1888 by Frederick Herbert Torrington, a British-born conductor, organist, violinist, and teacher. By 1890, it had four hundred students and more than fifty faculty members. That same year, it officially became affiliated with the University of Toronto. The academy granted its students certificates, medals, diplomas, and, in conjunction with the University of Toronto, Bachelor of Music and Doctor of Music degrees. Located on Pembroke Street, it included a concert hall that had a pipe organ. Upon entering the building, John A. and Joseph Pope noted that the hall was decorated with large banner that read, "Hail to Our Chieftain Ottawa, Not Washington / Our Capital / No United States Senators Need apply / No Tariff Discrimination Against Britain / Canadian Labour for Canadians."

John A.'s National Policy, with its protectionist message, was still popular among union members and those fiercely loyal to the British Crown. John A. played up those two principles. Dressed in his trademark flared coat, with cardinal-red tie and a cameo pin, and with Charles Tupper by his side, he sat on stage in a large Queen Anne chair, luxuriating in the waves of love emanating from the crowd.

So many acolytes had shown up for the event that the doors to the Academy of Music had to be shut, leaving hundreds to cool their heels outside. Meanwhile, the crowd of men and women inside waved their hats or handkerchiefs in the air, cheering, and singing, "For He's a Jolly Good Fellow." In response, John A. reminded them that he had been in power, almost without exception, for thirty years, and that his National Policy had enabled working men to prosper rather than be subsumed by American business.

But John A. wasn't finished. Toward the end of his oration, he produced a document written by *Globe* journalist Edward Farrer in which Farrer explained to Americans how they could force Canadians into accepting annexation by encouraging discontent in the Maritime provinces, fiddling with the fisheries industry, and cutting off the CPR connections by building roads on the other side of the border. The Farrer document unleased such animus in the crowd that they soon gathered around the *Globe* office building shouting insults at Farrer.

Within a week, John A. travelled from Toronto to Strathroy then to London, then to Stratford, St. Mary's, Guelph, Acton, and Brampton. It would have been a killing pace for a man half his age. Along the way, his voice became hoarse and he contracted a serious case of bronchitis. His next stop was Kingston, his hometown. By the time his train pulled in, the temperature outside was ten degrees above zero. He felt ill on the ride to the British American Hotel and spent a Sunday trying to rest in between accepting an interview with a reporter who sought him out.

Two days later, amid a thundering rainstorm, he spoke to a gigantic crowd gathered in Martin's Opera House in Kingston. Just as the applause died down, John A. darted through a door, and the room erupted in applause and cheers. He described his pleasure at being home and hoped that the realization of so many of his party's platforms would impress them enough to return him to office.

As soon as the meeting ended, John A. slumped in his carriage, telling his doctor, "I never have felt so wearied in all my life." Despite his doctor's orders to rest, however, he refused to miss one last stop: Napanee, the town where, at seventeen, he had opened a branch law office for George Mackenzie. John A. entered the town hall to thunderous applause and cheers. It was all a blur now, the years that had passed in this pursuit of power, this relentless search for approval. He sprinted up a small flight of stairs to the stage, his white hair half-stuck to his head from the humidity inside the hall. The sweat trickled down his neck, soaking his collar, but in spite of the discomfort, he managed to speak with his usual eloquence and flashes of humour. As soon as the event ended, he stumbled toward his open carriage and sighed deeply as the breeze cooled his cheeks on the ride to the train station.

When he and Joseph Pope reached his private train, John A. collapsed, ashen-faced, on his bed. Pope cancelled the remainder of the tour, and John A., now suffering a severe case of bronchitis, returned to Kingston to stay with James Williamson. On March 4, he felt strong enough to return to Ottawa but, upon arrival, took to his bed. Dr. Stewart noted that his heartbeats were weak and irregular, and said that he couldn't answer for the consequences if John A. didn't stay in bed.

By now Agnes had returned home from Banff and worried less about the results of the election than the health of her husband. In order to know the results of the election as quickly as possible, Pope had a special wire hooked up to Earnscliffe, where he sat waiting. For John A., however, it had all become too much. By ten o'clock, weary and beyond caring, he turned over and said, "I think that will do for tonight" and fell asleep.

By the morning, telegrams of congratulations arrived at Earnscliffe by the dozens. The Old Man had done it again. For the seventh time, he had been elected prime minister, though his majority was reduced by thirty-three seats. His support in Kingston, however, was the largest he had ever enjoyed in his entire career.

For most of March, John A. remained in bed. Even through April and the beginning of May, he found himself too tired to

John A. shortly before his death. *(Pittaway & Jarvis/LAC C000686)*

perform even the simplest shopping trips without half-collapsing with exhaustion. Agnes was nearly prostrate with worry. She had seen her husband sick, yes, exhausted certainly, but this time his symptoms were more than physical. He gave every indication he was done with the whole business altogether. She stayed by his side night and day, monitoring his colour, reading to him. Near the end of April, he began to rally enough to attend the opening of Parliament, mainly so he could revel in entering the House with Hugh John, who had successfully won election as an MP for Manitoba. Arms entwined, the two men walked toward their desks, to the thunderous applause of the members of the House.

It was the last ovation John A. would hear. Although he attempted to present a picture of jauntiness, those who knew him guessed the truth; he was failing, his life's work finished with the completion of the railway.

He had reason to worry, for the symptoms of paralysis he had seen in his mother were about to take their toll on him. On May 12, 1891, he entered Joseph Pope's private rooms in the

House of Commons and informed him that he was about to meet with the Governor General Lord Stanley and the minister of justice, John Thompson, at 4 p.m. With alarm, Pope noticed that there was "something wrong with his speech." "I felt sure this was a premonition of something serious," Pope noted. A few moments later, Pope entered John A.'s office to inform him that John Thompson was on his way. With uncharacteristic impatience, John A. replied, "He must come at once, because he must speak to the Governor for me, as I cannot talk. There is something the matter with my speech."

With the meeting at an end, both Thompson and Lord Stanley left John A.'s office wearing solemn expressions, Stanley telling Pope that John A.'s symptoms were alarming and similar to those he had seen in the case of a relative who had recently died of paralysis. Once they had gone, John A. wandered into Pope's office, attempting to look casual but unable to conceal the look of fear on his face. His left hand and fingers, he noted, were tingling slightly, and he had trouble holding a pen. "I am afraid of paralysis," John A. announced, pausing before continuing. "Both my parents died of it, and I seem to feel it creeping over me." Pope immediately rose to his feet to comfort John A., then reached for a telephone to call a cab, noting that, for the first time in his life he heard terror in John A.'s voice.

After calling for a cab, Pope escorted John A. down to the parliamentary grounds. The exercise seemed to revive John A. somewhat. He climbed into the carriage with little difficulty. His last words as the carriage pulled away were, "You must be careful not to mention this to Lady Macdonald."

Back at home, John A. headed toward his room as Agnes hosted her weekly Saturday-afternoon tea. The atmosphere in the house was casual and relaxed, the couple's black mastiff dog lying sprawled across the drawing-room rug. Occasionally, John A. would leave his work and drop in on Agnes's teatime guests to share an amusing anecdote.

He also attended Agnes's regular Saturday-night dinner party on May 16, and, though he appeared wan, successfully entertained visitors with stories and jokes. His speech was almost normal again, although his stamina dissipated easily. Throughout the week, he even performed well in Parliament. Although he didn't deliver any speeches, he did interject comments regularly, eliciting frequent laughter. All who witnessed him in action that week considered it a resurrection.

Agnes, who had guessed John A.'s problem, was always anxious now, though she tried to hide her fears for Mary's sake. Hugh John, too, held out little hope of his father's ability to recover after he heard of his first bout with paralysis. Everyone seemed braced for the worst but the victim himself.

On the evening of May 23, after a protracted Cabinet meeting, John A. took a cab home to join Agnes and their friends for dinner. As soon as she heard the horse's hooves clopping, Agnes flew out of the house and met her husband at Earnscliffe's front gate. She was alarmed by his pallor and the dark circles under his eyes, and immediately offered to cancel the dinner party scheduled for an hour's time. John A. refused to consider the idea. Nevertheless, he was tired, so tired that he did not resist when Agnes took his heavy briefcase from him and held his arm as they walked slowly up the path to the front door. That night, as he had done so many times throughout his life, John A. played the tragic clown. As soon as the final guest departed, he collapsed from strain into an easy chair, as Agnes flung open a window to allow the fresh, cool breeze to waft across his overheated face. His chest hurt him, and he was near collapse.

Agnes immediately called Dr. Powell, who ordered John A. to bed. By May 27, the rest seemed to be having a beneficial effect and, after a time, John A. went downstairs to his study to work with Pope on various pieces of business. At half past two the next morning, Agnes awoke with a start after hearing a yell. Was it a dream or the real thing? In the darkness of their bedroom, she could barely make out John A. lying on his back in their bed, his mouth open as if in silent amazement. She fumbled around to his side of the bed and leaned down to speak to him. In a barely audible voice, he told her that his left leg was almost totally paralyzed and the feeling in his left arm was completely gone. Trembling, Agnes picked up the phone and called Dr. Powell, who immediately recognized that John A. had suffered a "lesion" in the brain. It could have been worse. He still had his speech, and by the time afternoon arrived, he could lift his left leg and move his left arm above his head. Despite these encouraging signs, as soon as Agnes was out of the room, he summoned Joseph Pope and asked him to bring him his estate papers, "while there is still time."

While John A. lay in bed, bulletins concerning his health were distributed to the Privy Council room. Those ministers not stunned into silence openly wept.

By the morning of May 29, John A. was sitting up reviewing letters of the day with Joseph Pope. John Thompson called in and visited with John A., but, despite observing acuity in his thinking, and a general appearance of improved health, Thompson feared the worst, telling his wife, "The probability is that he will not be in the House again this session, if ever."

At three o'clock in the afternoon, Dr. Stewart, John A.'s Kingston physician, arrived. As he quietly asked John A. how he felt, John A. suddenly leaned his head back on his pillow, yawned twice, then went limp, dropping the reading material in his hand. He had suffered a third, and this time irreversible, stroke, lapsing into unconsciousness.

"Condition hopeless," read the message sent out to ministers of the House. Conservative Minister of Public Works Hector Langevin, first elected to the government in 1876, and the most senior minister next to John A., was shaken by grief. "My heart is full of tears," he announced to the ministers as he informed them that John A. was in the most critical condition, and had "only hours to live."

Members of the House milled around in stunned silence. By 10 p.m., the news was relayed by telegram to every newsroom across the country. In England, Queen Victoria learned the news, and sent Agnes a telegram of sympathy.

In the darkness of their bedroom, Agnes sat vigil at her husband's bedside, spoonfeeding him beef tea and champagne. Hugh John also sat vigil, helping doctors turn his father from one side to the other to prevent bedsores. Outside, the streets of Ottawa had fallen into an unearthly silence. Bells had been removed from the horse-drawn streetcars that passed Earnscliffe, steamboats and barges on the Ottawa River glided by without sounding their horns and whistles. Even raucous critics, such as the *Globe* newspaper, waxed elegiac, announcing that, "the birth of a young spirit who had arduously and valiantly won a wide fame and remained in later years in the front of battle, had at last reached the brink of eternity." Meanwhile, John Wilson Bengough of *Grip*, John A.'s most brilliant

A saddened Bengough drew this cover for *Grip*.

"Now let his errors be buried and forgotten." *Grip's* moving tribute to its favourite victim of ridicule. *(Metropolitan Toronto Reference Library)*

satirist, drew one last cover, depicting a woman in mourning, casting John A.'s sins into a deep pit, the caption reading, "Now Let His Errors Be Buried and Forgotten." Within a year, Bengough ceased *Grip's* publication, explaining that there was no politician as worthy of satirical lampooning as John A.

Other newspapermen gathered at a respectful distance down the walkway from John A.'s front door, pencils poised to write the final headline. They waited, and waited. For five days, John A. lingered, unable to allow his brain to sleep. On June 4, he rallied somewhat, and even doctors dared to hope that a miraculous recovery might be at hand. John A. was recognizing faces with ease now, and smiling. Agnes hadn't given up hope of her husband's ability to bounce back. She sat by the side of his bed, holding his hand, buoyed every time he squeezed her fingers in recognition. Even Hugh John's six-year-old-son, Jack, shyly approached his grandfather, who was lying with his eyes wide open and smiling brightly. Seeing the beneficial effect Jack had on John A., Agnes immediately summoned Mary into the room as well. Nevertheless, with Jack's hand in his, and Mary looking on, John A. slowly drifted into unconsciousness.

By 10 p.m. on June 6, most of the newspaper reporters had abandoned Earnscliffe for the comfort of their beds, believing there would be no story to file that night. For the few that remained, the first indication they had that the end had arrived was the sight of Joseph Pope, slowly making his way toward them down the path. It was 10:24, and John A. had been dead exactly nine minutes. "Gentlemen," Pope said, choking back tears, "Sir John Macdonald is dead. He died at a quarter past ten." After speaking, he posted the death notice on the gates of Earnscliffe and returned inside.

A Canadian telegraph operator sitting in a bell tent nearby tapped out a telegram containing the news. Within twenty minutes, steeple bells throughout Ottawa began to toll. After an hour, they tolled in most cities across the country.

The early summer air was so sticky, Agnes felt as if she'd been dipped in honey. Within an hour of her husband's death, telegrams of condolence arrived by the dozens at Earnscliffe. Opening them would only confirm that her love was gone and her status as the prime minister's wife would soon belong to someone else. Her head thick with weariness, she drifted off to sleep in one of the guest rooms, as John A.'s body remained lying in the marital bed. Slowly awakening two hours later, she travelled in her imagination to happier times, such as when she felt the wind whip her face as the *Jamaica* sped down Kicking Horse Pass or discovered she was pregnant with Mary, but reality soon returned like a sharp kick to the stomach.

Early Sunday morning, servants dressed John A.'s body in the uniform of an imperial Privy Councillor, the insignia of order by his side. Afterwards, they placed his body in a mahogany casket located in the house's spacious dining room, where he and Agnes had hosted so many festive events. In the afternoon, friends, associates, and fellow ministers paid their respects.

On the morning of Tuesday, June 9, Rev. J. J. Bogert of St. Alban's Church conducted a private funeral service for the family at Earnscliffe, at which Agnes said goodbye for the last time. Mary remained stoical in the face of her father's death. She told Hugh John that "she must try to be a comfort to her mother now, instead of a burden."

John A.'s funeral procession leaving Parliament Hill. *(LAC C007211)*

By the afternoon, John A.'s body left Agnes's presence forever. He lay in state in the Senate chamber of the Parliament Buildings as thousands of mourners from all parts of the country streamed by. For almost twenty-four continuous hours, people lined up to say goodbye for the last time. Before closing the casket, Queen Victoria's representative, Sir Casimir Gzowski, laid a wreath of roses on John A.'s chest, with the insignia "From Her Majesty Queen Victoria." Next, John A.'s casket was driven by carriage down Rideau Street, as citizens lined each side of the road to get a good view. Shortly after the procession departed for the train station, thunder and lightning filled the sky, while rain poured down on the heads of the mourners. John A. was going home to Kingston for the last time.

His body was placed in a draped hearse on a CPR funeral train, which sped by cities, towns, and hamlets as crowds of admirers lined the tracks. As the train chugged into Kingston station, thousands gathered to accompany the casket to the City Hall, where John A. again lay in state. Following the funeral service, the crowd followed the procession to Cataraqui Cemetery, where John A. was laid to rest beside Helen, Hugh, Margaret and Louisa, Isabella, John Alexander, and perhaps his brother James Shaw. There would be no more campaigns to take him away.

After seventy-six years, John Alexander Macdonald could finally stop running.

EPILOGUE

No longer referred to as Lady Macdonald, after John A.'s death, Agnes toured the party circuit as Baroness Macdonald, a title Queen Victoria bestowed upon her on July 2, 1891. Agnes's new title was as much a curse as a blessing. For one thing, she had to buy custom-made designs suitable for official occasions. After a lifetime worrying about money, Agnes constantly feared bankruptcy. Luckily, in his final years, John A., with the help of his private secretary, Joseph Pope, a trustee of the Macdonald estate, managed to invest wisely, amassing assets in excess of $45,000, not including a life-insurance policy worth $15,000.

Agnes struggled with more than mere grief. She missed the power she had wielded behind the scenes so effectively during her marriage to John A. She came to view herself as Ottawa's elder stateswoman, dispensing unsolicited advice to government ministers and officials. In this incarnation, she wrote Governor General Lord Stanley a sternly worded note, urging him to choose Sir Charles Tupper as the next prime minister, rather than John A.'s chosen successor, minister of justice, Sir John Thompson. She had good reason to prefer Tupper. It was Thompson, after all, who had characterized her as John A.'s "mole catcher of a wife," and over the years, he had never changed his mind. Agnes failed to sway Lord Stanley, however. He offered the position to Thompson.

Appearances notwithstanding, Agnes was lonely. As the weeks passed, the stream of visitors to Earnscliffe slowed to a trickle. As she had done so joyfully during her marriage to John A., Agnes now travelled out of restless desperation. Together with Hewitt and Mary, she journeyed in the winter of 1891 by train to Banff, staying at the Hotel Dallas. But with nothing but an open schedule yawning before them, the group soon got bored and returned to Earnscliffe. While Agnes was prone to cast her eyes backwards, she was satisfied that her husband's soul was at peace, and therefore she did not make pilgrimages to his grave. In a November 8 letter to James Williamson, she referred to Kingston as the place "where my Husband lies at rest."

In the summer of 1892, Agnes and Mary retreated to Rivière-du-Loup. For Agnes, the trip proved bittersweet. "We are the very last of the Mohicans!" she wrote to Williamson. "Every soul gone but ourselves, all the cottages barred & shuttered & hardly a figure to be seen in the woods. Today, no service, the clergyman gone on his holidays."

Hewitt, whose lung complaints confined him to a wheelchair, spent the winter of 1892 at a luxury hotel in Lakewood, New Jersey. Agnes decided to join him there, and readied Earnscliffe for rental, packing up boxes full of those valuables she wished to keep. Though she may not have been able to admit it to outsiders, she knew she would never again return to the house. Before leaving, she undoubtedly took one last look through the windows at the Parliament Buildings in the distance, once her second home.

In letters to Joseph Pope from New Jersey, Agnes admitted, "I live in my own rooms." Faced with a future devoid of hopefulness and excitement, she lapsed into lengthy reveries about her glory days in Ottawa. Himself a "sad sufferer," Hewitt was unable to rescue his sister from her melancholy reflections. Devoid of the close companionship of friends, Agnes drifted into a routine in which each day mirrored the last. In the early morning, she took brisk walks with a paid companion named Miss Peacock, then later in the day walked slowly alongside Hewitt and Mary, as servants pushed their wheelchairs down bumpy, pebble-strewn country roads. Even reading seemed laborious to Agnes.

In February 1893, Hewitt Bernard died at an apartment he rented in Montreal. He left his estate, totalling more than $16,000, to Agnes. Shortly after his death, Agnes travelled from Banff to Victoria to Ottawa, desperate now to gather as many stray threads of her past as she could. In most cases, it was too late. Most of the few personal friends she had made through her marriage to the powerful and charismatic John A. were either dead or conveniently otherwise engaged. Those who remembered her also remembered her disapproval of frivolous social occasions, including parties, so didn't invite her. Alone now, and lonely, Agnes was crushed. She hoped to be able to invite James Williamson, whom she referred to as "the one when *he* was gone who did not fail me as did others," to visit her at Earnscliffe some time in the summer, but her plans for moving back to the home fell through, and before the fall was out, James was also dead.

At last, in 1893, Agnes decided to leave Canada for good. She and Mary settled on England, specifically Sydenham Street near the Crystal Palace, where Mary liked to watch musical concerts. In the hot summers, Agnes moved with Mary to a summer villa in Italy that cost less money to maintain. All this time, Agnes fretted that her friends in Ottawa might forget her. She became haunted by visions of her late husband and imagined she heard the sound of his voice, or saw his vacant chair rocking in the corner of her bedroom.

On May 15, 1900, she reluctantly sold Earnscliffe, an event that occasioned one of the largest content sales in Ottawa's history. Anyone who was anyone was there, including a well-known gossip columnist of the day, who wrote under the pen name Amaryllis. In *Toronto Saturday Night*, Amaryllis took readers on a detailed tour of the sale, noting every "historical relic" on the block, including even the bed in which John A. had died. "Not to have made some purchase at the Earnscliffe sale is what few persons with aspirations after social distinction like to own up to, and not to have been there at all puts one quite outside the pale," she wrote. She noted that a perfectly modern kitchen range sold to a maid for a paltry $10, while items with little utilitarian function, such as "a desk made of many kinds of Canadian wood, a very hideous piece of furniture," went for three times its worth.

In total, the auction lasted three days. One after the other, photographs of Agnes and John A.'s illustrious peers fell to the auctioneer's hammer, bought mostly for their frames, not for the images contained within. One of the last items to be bought, for twenty-five cents, was a framed photograph of a young girl holding a violin, her identity unknown.

Agnes remained in England during the duration of the sale. She hired an assortment of servants to care for Mary, performed charity work, and corresponded at great length with her Canadian friends. The subject of many of her letters remained her enduring passion for her late husband. In a letter dated 1901, she wrote, "I don't think I shall ever be what I was before June 1891. The shock was so much returning that even now I quail before bare memory of it – in a sort of mute anguish and longing for just one moment as it was before he was struck down. But I would not call him back to this troublesome world. I know so well, he's well and at rest, but he is always very near us and my mind through all the world's din, is dwelling all the time on him. I don't know if you can understand that. It's like a sad note at regular intervals, sounding above all other sounds, yet I would not lose it altogether."

Hugh John, Gertie, and Jack visited Agnes during the Coronation celebrations of 1902, though Agnes noted Jack's weakness and persistent pallor. Less than three years later, Jack died in

Toronto, shortly before returning to his studies at the University of Toronto, cause unknown. For years after his son's death, Hugh John tried to drown his sorrows in alcohol, but faced with living the rest of his life as a single man, as well as being diagnosed with diabetes, he gave up drinking permanently. Eventually, he was appointed police magistrate of Winnipeg, a job he found less stressful than that of MP. A year after his appointment, he received the KCMG, the Order of Saint Michael and Saint George, for his services to the Commonwealth.

As the ultimate gesture of her devotion, Eliza Grimason arranged to be buried in a gravesite that lies contiguous to John A.'s in Cataraqui Cemetery. Each gravesite has a railing around its perimeter, and the tombstones, both tall and narrow columns rest on broad bases. Grimason's column reads, "Henry Grimason Died in Kingston, Ont. November 23, 1867 aged 56 years also his wife Eliza Grimason Died March 30, 1916 aged 95 years."

On September 5, 1920, Agnes died after having suffered a series of strokes. As requested, she was buried in Ocklynge Cemetery in Eastbourne, a city south of London, her tombstone reading "In Loving Memory of / Susan Agnes / Baroness Macdonald / of Earnscliffe / Widow of Sir John Macdonald / Late Prime Minister of Canada / Died at Eastbourne, 5th Sept. 1920. / Age 84 / 'Jesu, Lover of My Soul / Let Me to Thy Bosom Fly.'"

Shortly before her death, Agnes instructed her long-time servant, Sarah Coward, to tend to Mary's care. Incredibly, Mary's skills and comprehension levels had only increased with age. Doctors who examined her considered her constitution "extraordinarily strong" and predicted that she might indeed live to be "an old woman."

When Sarah Coward married, she, her husband, and Mary all moved to a luxurious flat in Hove in Brighton, where Mary spent the remainder of her life. She wrote home to Hugh John in Canada often, asking about news concerning people she'd known when she was a child. The two continued to correspond until Hugh John's death from complications from diabetes on March 29, 1929.

Life at Hove was "serenity itself" as Mary remarked, with the pace of life "calm and unhurried." As she aged, she still typed letters to friends, though it often took her two weeks to complete a one-page letter. She ate her food with a spoon, but with great difficulty. She enjoyed listening to the wireless over headphones and loved solving riddles. Ironically, of all the members of her family, she alone might have felt she'd lived a satisfying life. She died on February 7, 1933, and was buried in Hove Cemetery, though her grave to this day remains unmarked.

SOURCES

Biographers of Sir John A. Macdonald have an almost unlimited number of materials at their disposal, including books, magazines articles, and photographs. Most of these biographers have focused almost solely on the political side of John A.'s life, rather than on the personal side. In contrast, this book attempts to reveal John A. as less of a Canadian icon than a flesh-and-blood man, struggling to balance a sometimes tumultuous and tragic family life with his life as a politician.

A great deal of the contents of this book come from primary sources located in the Library and Archives Canada and in Queen's University Archives, including personal letters written by John A. to members of his family, and they to him. I have also included memorandum entries, diary excerpts, sales receipts, contracts; in short, bits and pieces of paper that helped me construct a chronological account of his life outside of the House of Commons. Newspaper articles from the *Globe* and the *Toronto Star* newspapers in particular also provided useful insights into historical events, including John A.'s alleged suicide attempt over the Pacific Scandal in 1873.

Other useful sites for information included the Toronto Reference Library (Baldwin Collection), North York Public

Library, Archives of Ontario, City of Toronto Archives, Kingston Historical Society, Manitoba Historical Archive, Manitoba Historical Society, Bellevue National Historical Park, and *Hansard*.

Issues of the Kingston Historical Society's publication, *Historic Kingston*, have also proved highly useful in providing background material.

In the following chapter-by-chapter breakdown of sources, I would also like to credit the authors of books I have found invaluable in obtaining insights into Macdonald's character.

CHAPTER I: ESCAPING THE PAST

The harrowing account of James Shaw Macdonald's murder at the hands of a drunken childminder named "Kennedy" appears in *Memoirs of the Right Honourable Sir John Alexander Macdonald* (Toronto: Oxford University Press, 1930) by John A.'s private secretary, Sir Joseph Pope. John A.'s written notation concerning the precise time and date of James Shaw's death appears as the final entry in Hugh Macdonald's Memorandum Book, located in Vol. 549 of the Sir John A. papers at the Queen's University Archives. (John A.'s birth was apparently officially registered in Glasgow as occurring on both January 10 and January 11. I have found no official records to indicate his official birthdate, so cannot validate the claim. More importantly for the purposes of this book, Hugh John listed his son's date of birth in his Memorandum Book as January 11. John A. also lists his birthday as occurring on the same date.) For information concerning the religious battles over the "Lower Burial Grounds," I consulted Queen's University Professor Brian Osborne's excellent book *The Rock and the Sword: A History of St. Andrew's Church, Kingston, Ontario* (Kingston: Heinrich Heine Press at Grass Creek, 2004). Dr. John Workman's "die somehow they must" letter to Dr. John Clarke, dated April 14, 1868, is located in F26 Charles Clarke fonds, microfilm reel MS 76 reel 1, in the Archives of Ontario. Excellent information concerning conditions on board the ship the *Earl of Buckinghamshire* appear in The Ship's List, which includes a plan of the layout between decks of the ship. Additional information appears in the essay "Immigrants to Canada. Voyage to Quebec on the *David* of London, 1821 with mention of the passengers of the *Earl of Buckinghamshire* and *Commerce*," excerpted from the book *Emigration to Canada: Narrative of a Voyage to Quebec, and Journey from Thence to Lanark, in Upper Canada by John M'Donald, 1826.* An excellent description of the voyage also appears in E. B. Biggar's *Anecdotal Life of Sir John Macdonald* (Montreal: John Lovell & Son, 1891). Alma Allison's admiration of John A., quoted in Lt. Col. J. Pennington Macpherson's book *Life of the Right Honourable Sir John A. Macdonald*, Vol. 1, (St. John, N.B.: Earle Publishing House, 1891), was shared by several of his female schoolmates. John A.'s theft of Guy Casey's black bass appears in Lena Newman's book *The John A. Macdonald Album* (Montreal: Tundra, 1974), as well as other books about John A. Macdonald.

CHAPTER II: THE APPRENTICE

Several books and essays address the difficulty John A. had in initially adapting to life apart from his family in Napanee. The best and most detailed account of John A.'s "standoffish" behaviour appears in Donald Creighton's *John A. Macdonald: The Young Politician, the Old Chieftain* (Toronto: University of Toronto Press, 1998). John A.'s fondness for "boon companions" was noted by Alexander Campbell, John A.'s one-time law partner, in the Campbell Papers, Archives of Ontario F23 MV479. Campbell was impressed with John A.'s skills before country court juries and documents his observations in an essay he wrote also located in the Campbell Papers – Memo re. parents of Sir John A. Macdonald. Books that were useful for background information on this chapter include a paper entitled "A New Perspective on Hugh Macdonald, Esq." (Sir John A.'s father) by self-described "amateur" historian David R. Taylor, 1999, the second entitled "Explore Sir John A.'s Napanee" by Jennifer Bunting (Kingston:

Cranberry Hill Enterprises, 1999). A description of John A.'s ability to study in the outdoors appears in E. B. Biggar's *An Anecdotal Life of Sir John Macdonald* (Montreal: John Lovell & Son, 1891). James Porter, a drinking buddy in Hallowell, recalls John A.'s miraculous ability to sober up in the E. B. Biggar book. George Mackenzie's letter concerning John A.'s dour demeanour in Napanee appears in several sources, including Donald Swainson's *Sir John A. Macdonald: The Man and the Politician* (Kingston: Quarry Press, 2nd rev. ed. 1989). Details about the terms of Alexander Campbell and John A.'s business relationship can be found in the Macdonald Papers, vol 194, Memorandum of the Terms of Co-partnership between Macdonald and Campbell (QA, MF 1121).

The best source I discovered describing the 1832 and 1833 cholera epidemics that swept through Kingston was in Margaret Angus's essay "Health, Emigration and Welfare in Kingston, 1820–1840," contained in the book *Oliver Mowat's Ontario*, edited by Donald Swainson (Toronto: Macmillan of Canada, 1970). Several books about John A. Macdonald's life describe Eliza Grimason, Kingston tavern keeper and his close friend. Eliza's tavern stands to this day, and documents relating to her still line the walls. The best description is found in Lena Newman's *The John A. Macdonald Album* (Montreal: Tundra, 1974). William Draper's opinion of John A.'s handling of the von Schoultz case appears in Sir Joseph Pope's *Memoirs of the Right Honourable Sir John Alexander Macdonald* (Toronto: Oxford University Press, 1930).

CHAPTER III: BACHELOR HUSBAND
Much of the material describing John A.'s trip to England as a bachelor appear in the Macdonald Papers, Family Correspondence, Vol. 569 (Queens Archive MR 1277). The best description of Isabella Macdonald's personality after she married John A. appears in J. Pennington Macpherson's *Life of the Right Honourable Sir John A. Macdonald*. (St. John, N.B: Earle Publishing House,

1891). Since the author's mother, Maria, was Isabella's sister, he had a particularly good opportunity to observe Isabella's behaviour. As a frequent visitor to John A. and Isabella's house, he could observe John A.'s library up close. John A.'s joke about having a "downfall so soon" appears in both Donald Creighton's *The Young Politician* and Lena Newman's *The Sir John A. Macdonald Album*. For background information on Montreal during the early 1850s, I consulted Edgar Andrew Collard's *Montreal Yesterdays* (Toronto: Longmans Canada, 1962). Oliver Goldsmith was not just one of John A.'s favourite poets, but one of Canada's most renowned poets. Goldsmith has been recognized as the first famous native-born Canadian poet by the Historic Sites and Monuments Board of Canada. Peter Waite in *Macdonald, His Life and World* (Toronto: McGraw-Hill Ryerson, 1975) notes that Montreal by gaslight was said to have been positively luxurious. Waite also notes John A.'s pledge to "protect the Canadian whores." Several books, including Creighton's *The Young Politician*, describe John A.'s odd way of walking and theatrical wardrobe. The bulk of the correspondence among family members during John A.'s marriage to Isabella is located in Vol. 545 of the Macdonald Papers of the Library and Archives Canada.

CHAPTER IV: ADDICTED TO LOVE
In order to understand the different ways opium could be applied in treating multiple ailments in the nineteenth century, I consulted *Opium: A History* by Martin Booth (New York: St. Martin's Press, 1996). The Memorandum of the Terms of Co-partnership between Macdonald and Campbell is located in the Queen's University Archives, MF 1121. John A. and Isabella's baby diary for Hugh John Macdonald appears in an article entitled "Sir Hugh John Macdonald," by George P. Macleod, Q.C., Manitoba Historical Society. A detailed discussion of Isabella's health appears in an essay entitled "The invisible lady: Sir John A.

Macdonald's first wife. Canadian Bulletin of Medical History," by James McSherry MB ChB, published in 1984.

CHAPTER V: JUMPING OFF THE TREADMILL

The two invoices answered by John A.'s law clerks were obtained from the Macdonald Papers, Vol. 551 (QA MF1264). The first is dated January 13, 1853, the second February 1, 1853. The letters between James Williamson, his father-in-law, Jo Gilchrest, and former sister-in-law Elizabeth are located in the James Williamson Fonds (QA 2259). To save money, both Jo and Elizabeth Gilchrest wrote both horizontally and vertically on the same page, making the pages almost illegible; nevertheless, once deciphered, the letters reveal how bitter the Gilchrests were about Williamson's affection for John A.'s son, Hugh John, over his own son, James. Several of John A.'s political colleagues, especially on the Opposition benches, considered him too glib to deserve the trust of the House. One, who labelled him too full of "boyish exuberance of animal spirits," was Sir Richard Cartwright in *Reminiscences* (Toronto: William Briggs, 1912).

CHAPTERS VI AND VII: PARTY ANIMAL AND PLAYING THE MARRIAGE CARD

John A. possessed a magnetic personality, especially with women, as Sir John Willison notes in *Reminiscences Political and Personal* (Toronto: McClelland & Stewart Publishers, 1919). The same quote also appears in Lena Newman's *The John A. Macdonald Album*. John A.'s habit of living a dissipated life just prior to Isabella's death in 1857 was noted by Sir Richard Cartwright in *Reminiscences*. John A. labelled "false as hell" any suggestion that he was a "dishonourable man." His denial appeared in the August 6, 1858 issue of the *Weekly Atlas* newspaper published in Toronto. Highlights of John A.'s trip down the Lachine Rapids with the Prince of Wales is captured in *Montreal Yesterdays*, in a chapter entitled "Shooting the Lachine Rapid." The anecdote concerning John A. rudely dismissing Lord Bury from his presence has been authenticated by Sir John Willison in *Reminiscences Political and Personal*. Willison reveals that, in the years after the tense meeting, Lord Bury often told the story with more affection than censure for John A. John A.'s quote that the government couldn't afford two drunkards appears in E. B. Biggar's *Anecdotal Life of Sir John A. Macdonald*. Agnes Macdonald's quote about the middle classes in England was written in the February 5, 1868, edition of her diary; however, her opinion concerning the importance of having a high financial status in order to enjoy England better was constant before and after this date. Quotes concerning Agnes's initial dislike of George-Étienne Cartier and his mistress, Luce Cuvillier, appear in Sandra Gwyn's *The Private Capital* (Toronto: McClelland & Stewart Ltd., 1984). Shortly after her marrying John A., Agnes began keeping a detailed diary of their life together and her struggles to adjust to her role as the wife of the prime minister of Canada. The red leather-bound diary can be found in the Library and Archives Canada Family Paper, Baroness Macdonald MG26-A. The diary also includes Agnes's detailed description of the evening of D'Arcy McGee's murder, as well as a description of the murder trial of Patrick Whelan. The incident of Sir Francis Monck's sister-in-law telling the story of John A. quoting Hamlet into a mirror while wearing a railway rug around him appears in Peter B. Waite's *John A. Macdonald* (Markham: Fitzhenry & Whiteside Ltd., 1999). An excellent account of John A.'s involvement in events following D'Arcy McGee's murder come from two sources: Agnes Macdonald's diary and a description contained in T. P. Slattery's *The Assassination of D'Arcy McGee* (Toronto: Doubleday Canada Ltd., 1966). Also useful was the Inquest into the murder of Thomas D'Arcy McGee papers, found in the Thomas D'Arcy McGee fonds, 1868 R430-0-6-E, LAC. The handwritten papers contain verbatim reports of the murder from witnesses, and a coroner's certificate pronouncing death.

CHAPTER VIII: FEELING THE SQUEEZE

Agnes writes movingly in her diary about the challenges of raising a hydrocephalic child. After examining photographs of Mary Macdonald, Dr. James Drake, a neurosurgeon at the Hospital for Sick Children, theorizes that Mary also suffered from cerebral palsy. Lord de Grey's quote regarding the "High Commission on joints" appears in Donald Creighton's *John A. Macdonald: The Young Politician, the Old Chieftain* (Toronto: University of Toronto Press, 1998). Hugh John's letters describing his trek to Manitoba to exact revenge on Louis Riel appear in an essay entitled "The Prime Minister's Son goes West," by Hugh A. Stevenson, appearing in *The Beaver: Magazine of the North, Winnipeg* (Hudson's Bay Company, Winter 1865). The letter in which Louisa asks John A. to mail her pills is located in the Macdonald Papers, vol. 539. For unknown reasons, Louisa never dated her letters to John A., so trying to estimate the exact time they were sent is often a challenge. Over his many administrations, John A. received several death threats. The death threat warning John A. that he could suffer D'Arcy McGee's fate, as well as a second anonymous threat, are located in the Macdonald Papers, Miscellaneous, Vol. 546–47 (QA MF 1262). Lord Dufferin's letters describing John A.'s health before and during the Pacific Scandal appear in the Pacific Scandal papers (QA MF 1082–83, 1098, 1150–51, 1289). Two newspapers reported on John A.'s purported suicide attempt over the Pacific Scandal. The first was the August 4, 1873, issue of *Montreal Witness*. The second article appeared in the August 5, 1873, issue of the *Globe*.

CHAPTER IX: A MATTER OF HONOUR

John A. and Agnes's visit to Thomas Charles Patteson of the *Toronto Mail* is described in detail in the essay on John A. Macdonald by J. K. Johnson and P. B. Waits in the *Dictionary of Canadian Biography*. Descriptions of the various homes lived in by John A. and James Williamson in the Kingston area are discussed in detail in the fine booklet entitled *John A. Lived Here*, by Margaret Angus, published by the Frontenac Historic Foundation, 1990. Detailed accounts of John A.'s illnesses and treatments over the years are described in an essay entitled "Sir John A. Macdonald and His Doctors," by A. A. Tavill, published in *Historic Kingston*, vol. 29, 1981. Eliza Grimason's impressions of her visit to Earnscliffe are described in Louise Reynolds's biography of Agnes Macdonald entitled *Agnes: The Biography of Lady Macdonald* (Ottawa: Carlton University Press, 1990).

CHAPTER X: HIS FINAL RACE

The best description of the Macdonalds' trip by rail across the country was written by Agnes Macdonald in a stirring essay entitled "By Car and by Cowcatcher" that appeared in the British publication *Murray's Magazine*, Vol. 1, John Murray, London, Jan.–June 1887. Information concerning the question of Louis Riel's sanity is located in the Augustus Jukes fonds – MG29-E66. The series consists of notes and letters by Louis Riel and Dr. Augustus Jukes, medical reports regarding Riel's sanity and execution, a narrative of Riel's vision, and letters from Jukes to Sir John A. Macdonald. The letter in which John A. expressed fear concerning Louisa's health was written on August 14, 1884. John A.'s quote concerning every dog barking upon Riel's death appears in Donald Creighton's *John A. Macdonald: The Young Politician, the Old Chieftain* (Toronto: University of Toronto Press, 1998). John A.'s letter to Charles Tupper in which he comments on the triumph of the Rouges over the corpse of Riel also appears in Creighton's book. John A.'s statement "I have felt so weary" is located in Joseph Pope's *Memoirs of the Right Honourable Sir John Alexander Macdonald* (Toronto: Oxford University Press, 1930). In fact, John A.'s final election campaign, 1890–91, is described in detail in this book.

Other books useful in locating anecdotes and the letters of John A. and his family members include J. K. Johnson's

Affectionately Yours: The Letters of Sir John A. Macdonald and His Family (Toronto: Macmillan of Canada, 1969); *The Papers of the Prime Ministers*, Vols. 1 and 2, edited by J. K. Johnson (Ottawa: Public Archives of Canada, 1968); *Sir John A.: An Anecdotal Life of John A. MacDonald*, edited by Cynthia M. Smith and Jack McLeod (Oxford University Press, 1989); and *Macdonald* by W. Stewart Wallace (Toronto: The Macmillan Company of Canada Limited, 1924).

ACKNOWLEDGEMENTS

Thanks to Dr. Brian Osborne, Donna Ivey, Norma Kelly, John Coleman, Heather Home, Clelia Scala, Patrick Blednick, Marie Gatley, Pat Kennedy, Elizabeth Kribs, Jennifer Bunting, David Taylor, Peter Waite, Hugh Gainsford, Gordon Goldsborough, Jennifer McKendry, Lorne Cheseborough. The author gratefully acknowledges the assistance of the Canada Council for the Arts in completing this book.

INDEX

Note: Page numbers in italics refer to illustrations.

strokes and death, 288-91, 293;
letter from Agnes, 297; travels
with Macdonalds, 267-68, 272
Pope, W. H., 166
Porter, James, 31
Powell (doctor), 290-91
Prince Edward Island: Confederation
campaign, 166, 186; fishing
grounds, 213

Quebec: 1887 elections, 273; formation, 169; support for Riel, 204,
262, 267
Queen's University, Kingston, 95-96

railway. *See* Canadian Pacific Railway
(CPR)
Ramsay, Tom, 27-28, 30, 36
Randolph (acquaintaince in
Philadelphia), 73
Rebellion Losses Bill (1848), 104
Rebellions of 1837-38, 42-44
Red River Colony, 202-4, 210, 258
Reform Party: 1849 Parliament and
Rebellion Losses Bill, 96-97;
1850 Parliament, 104; 1852–53
Parliament, 115-16; 1854 elec-
tions, 117; 1857 elections, 128-29;
1863–64 Parliament, 154-56
Reynolds, Thomas, 210, 216, 255
Richards, Albert, 154-56
Richards, William Buell, 191, 231-32
Richmond, Duke of (Charles
Gordon-Lennox), 250
Richot, Noël Joseph, 204
Riel, Louis: and public opinion of
John A., 218-19, 264-65, 273;
background, 202-3; battle at
Batoche, 260; condemns Scott to
death, 204; establishes govern-
ment in Rupert's Land, 203-4;
execution, 262, 273; flight to

United States, 208-9, 258; French
opposition to hanging, 264-65;
Hugh John's opinion, 207, 209-10;
negotiations with John A., 203-5;
portrait of, *208*; psychiatric exam-
ination, 261; return to Canada,
258; trial, 261
Robinson (friend of John A.), 73
Robinson, George (Lord de Grey),
214-15
Robinson, John Beverley, 67
Rodgers (doctor), 85
Rose, Charlotte, 184
Rose, John, 78, 123, 125, 184, 214

Sackville-West, Reginald (Lord de la
Warr), 54
Salt (Toronto landlord), 134
Sampson (doctor), 71-72, 77, 106
Schultz (military captain), 204
Scott, Alfred, 204
Scott, Louisa, 250
Scott, Thomas, 204-5, 209, 258, 265
Shallow, James, 32
Shannon, James, 232
Shaw, Anna (aunt), 5, 8
Shaw, Helen. *See* Macdonald, Helen
(mother)
Shaw, James (grandfather), 5
Shaw, John (no relation), 128-29
Shaw, Margaret (grandmother), 5
Shaw, Samuel (no relation), 12
Shaw, William (no relation), 5
Sioux people, 269
Smith, Alexander, 67
Smith, B. W., 160
Smith, Donald (Lord Strathcona),
203, 251, 262
Smith, H. (warden of Kingston
Penitentiary), 49
Smith, Henry (member of legislative
assembly for Frontenac), 67